A SHORT HISTORY

of the

jewish
people

From Legendary Times to Modern Statehood

RAYMOND P. SCHEINDLIN

Macmillan • USA

MACMILLAN
A Simon & Schuster Macmillan Company
1633 Broadway
New York, NY 10019-6785

Macmillan Publishing books may be purchased for business or sales promotional use. For information please write: Special Markets Department, Macmillan Publishing USA, 1633 Broadway, New York, NY 10019.

Library of Congress Cataloging-in-Publication Data

Scheindlin, Raymond P.
    A short history of the Jewish people / Raymond P. Scheindlin.
       p. cm.
    Includes bibliography and index.
    ISBN 0-02-862586-2
    1. Jews—History. I. Title.
    DS117.S45   1998   98-10824
    909'.04924—dc21   CIP

Printed in the United States of America

10 9 8 7 6 5 4 3 2 1

Book design by Nick Anderson
Maps created by Jeff Yesh

To Stanley and Phyllis Scheindlin

Contents

Acknowledgments

I wish to express my gratitude to friends and colleagues who have read and critiqued the portions of this book dealing with their areas of expertise: Professors Stephen Geller and David Fishman of the Jewish Theological Seminary of America, Mark Cohen of Princeton University, Arthur Goren of Columbia University, and Stefanie Siegmund of the University of Michigan. Professor Geller also drafted the sidebar on early Hebrew inscriptions that appears in chapter 1. Professor Siegmund drafted the sidebar on Jewish women engaged in business that appears in chapter 7. My daughter, Dahlia Scheindlin, did extensive preparatory work on chapter 11. My wife, Janice Meyerson, first put into my head the idea of writing a short history of the Jewish people and proceeded to follow the project from its inception down to the last comma with her customary zeal. Professor Mark Cohen also encouraged me from an early stage.

I take great pleasure in dedicating this book to two persons who have quietly devoted a shared lifetime to Jewish education.

Introduction

The very idea of a short history of the Jews seems paradoxical, since the Jewish people are fabled for their antiquity and the length of their history. Furthermore, the story of the Jews cannot be told in isolation, for they have always been a small nation whose history has been to a great extent a footnote to that of peoples more numerous and powerful. To grasp Jewish history, ideally, would be to grasp the entire theater of Jewish history, which embraces Asia from Iran to the Mediterranean, Europe and North Africa, and, across the Atlantic, North America. The shifts and changes within these many lands and cultures have shaped Jewish history as much as anything the Jews themselves have accomplished. To understand all of Western history and the Jews' role in it is obviously not a project for a short book. It is certainly too daunting a project for a reader who is just beginning his exploration of the Jews.

It is for just such a reader that this book is designed. It aims to make the long lines of Jewish history intelligible, to tell the story in such a way that its large narrative shape can be easily discerned. It also aims to enable the reader to begin to think systematically about some of the basic questions of Jewish history: Where did the Jews come from? Why did they leave their homeland? Where did they go? How did they retain their identity through centuries of dispersion? What are the large patterns that determined the character of their varied communities? How did they come to be so resented by others that much of their history is a tale of poverty, degradation, and expulsion? How were they affected by modernity? How have the Jews of the present, with their proud ethnic identity and their successful national homeland, emerged out of the downtrodden Jews of the past?

Jewish history is fascinating, but it is not miraculous or supernatural. The Jews' longevity may be unusual in world history, but it can be explained to the same extent as can other human institutions and endeavors. But because history plays such a huge part in defining Jewish identity, Jewish history is often told not as a narrative of real people with human problems and interests but as an idealized national myth. Jewish national heroes such as Judah the Maccabee, Rabbi Akiva, Maimonides, and David Ben-Gurion are lauded as paragons of all human values; their enemies are cursed as embodiments of cosmic evil; non-Jews who took the part of the Jews in some historical circumstance are described as "righteous Gentiles"; and Jews who pursued their own interests as opposed to those of the Jewish people at large are tarred as traitors. In such characterizations, hindsight causes distorted judgments; because, for example, rabbinic Judaism came to be the dominant form of Judaism in the course of the first centuries C.E., other contemporary forms of Judaism are branded as heretical.

National myth is essential to the formation of national identity, and there is no family, tribe, ethnic group, or nation in the world that does not have one. But amicable interaction among such groups is not possible on the basis of each group's official view of its own history because these myths are usually in conflict with one another. The present-day conflict in the Middle East is a perfect example of the irreconcilable confrontation of two national myths, and the world abounds in such examples. The history of the United States is told quite differently by American Indians, the American bourgeoisie, and American black nationalists. It is not possible for different peoples to coexist when each insists that its version of its history and national destiny is the only correct one. Hence, the vital importance to society of academic history, one of the purposes of which is to identify the interpretive distortions of national history and correct them by adopting as neutral an attitude toward the outcome as humanly possible.

The problem of untangling national myth from academic history particularly affects the earliest period of Jewish history. Much of our information on this period comes from the Bible, a national history par excellence, with its tales of miracles and its assumption of a divine hand controlling the destiny of Israel and the other nations. Furthermore, because the Bible is a sacred text, readers tend to approach it with one of two biases: Traditional believers tend to think that it is all literally true, and nonbelievers tend to assume that it is all false. When the Bible is read in conjunction with archaeological remains and other ancient sources, using the same tools as are used in reading other ancient religious texts, it can yield some useful historical data, but the Bible is the Jewish people's own story of their origins, and like any other story of national origins, it must be treated cautiously and critically.

A related kind of distortion that this book tries to avoid is what arises from superimposing on earlier periods geopolitical concepts taken for granted in our own time. We take for granted that there has always been a great cultural divide between what we call East and West, i.e., between the Muslim-dominated territories of North Africa, the Middle East, and western Asia on the one hand, and Europe on the other. This division has made sense for several centuries, but it only causes confusion when applied to the millennium and a half from Alexander the Great to the Crusades. In the earlier part of this period, what we call the East was more Hellenized than most of what we call the West—Iraq in the first century B.C.E. was far more "Western" than what is now France; in the latter part of this period, the lands of the Mediterranean, whether Christian or Islamic, were more closely linked by culture and commerce than one might expect, given the differences of religion and language. Finally, during much of this period, regions that today lag behind Europe and America in economic, technological, political, and cultural development were far more advanced—were, in fact, the "developed countries" of their age. This book tries to give full weight to the Jews of the Middle East, a community often treated as marginal or exotic, but that for many centuries was actually the strongest and most successful Jewish community in the world.

An analogous distortion that this book attempts to correct is the overlooking of the role of Middle Eastern and Sephardic Jews in modern Jewish history. These two communities (often confused in contemporary discussions), though diminished with the decline of their host countries in modern times, remained important communities both in numbers and in cultural activity until the founding of the State of Israel, and their descendants are a large and newly powerful force in the State of Israel itself, yet they are often passed over in even sophisticated treatments of Jewish history. This book tries to give them, too, their due.

Since the Jewish people have been scattered among many different nations and cultures, the Jewish communities of one region have had somewhat different experiences from those of other regions, and their cultures have taken different forms. For much of Jewish history, a rigidly chronological scheme is therefore somewhat artificial and even confusing. For some periods, the narrative line becomes clearer when we separate the larger Jewish communities and tell their story in chronologically parallel units. This approach also lays a better groundwork for understanding the different character of the various Jewish communities of modern times, showing why, for example, the Jews of prewar Poland were so different from those of prewar Turkey, Morocco, or the United States.

This book is not a history of the Jewish religion. Like all human institutions, like the Jewish people themselves, the Jewish religion has changed over centuries, and the fascinating story of this evolution deserves to be told for its own sake. But it is important to make clear that the Jewish people and the Jewish religion are not at all the same thing, certainly not in modern times. On the threshold of the twenty-first century, relatively few Jews in the world are defined as Jews primarily by religious belief or behavior, and the vast majority of Jews in the world—even many of those who are actively Jewish—would be hard-pressed to give a coherent account of Jewish religious doctrine and practice. Although most Jews would probably not put it this way, it is reasonable to maintain that the Jews are a people who share not a religion, but a history. Accordingly, though religion is touched on in this book, it is treated as only one of several components of Jewish identity, alongside the Jews' languages, their books (both secular and religious), their institutions, and their history itself, for our subject is not Judaism but the Jewish people.

The short compass of this book did not permit me to mention every Jewish community. I ache for the interesting Jewish communities I have had to omit or could only mention briefly, including the Jews of India, Ethiopia, Georgia, Bukhara, Yemen, and China. To make this book twice as long would not only have been easy, it would have been easier than making it this short. I have tried to stick to the principle of treating systematically only the dominant communities in each period, those that afford a view of the large picture; by way of compensation, I have provided enough bibliographic references to enable the reader to follow up whatever aspects of Jewish history interest him the most.

Since I have emphasized above the importance of doing whatever is humanly possible to achieve a global perspective on whatever history one studies, I had better confess that my own relationship with the subject of this book is hardly a neutral one. I see myself as an active participant in Jewish history, a fervent Hebraist, a selective participant in Jewish religious traditions, and a professional scholar of medieval Hebrew literature. Despite my personal engagement in the subject, I have endeavored to maintain the global perspective advocated here. I find everything about the Jews interesting and engaging, but especially how they have interacted with the nations and cultures among whom they have lived, adapting to their environment while retaining a variety of continuities. I hope that some of this enthusiasm will cling to the reader of this short account of Jewish history.

Early Aramaic inscription found in Tel Dan, dating from the ninth century B.C.E. and mentioning "the house of David" in line 9. Photo © Zev Radovan. Used by permission.

ONE

Israelite Origins and Kingdom

(Before 1220 B.C.E. to 587 B.C.E.)

The first act in the long drama of Jewish history is the age of the Israelites. Around 1000 B.C.E., the Israelites established a kingdom in the land then known as Canaan, at the eastern end of the Mediterranean Sea, a kingdom that lasted over four hundred years, until it was liquidated in 587 B.C.E. The history of the Israelite kingdom is not a legend; the narrative of its kings and wars, some information about its social and economic conditions, and a good deal of information about its religion are preserved in the historical books of the Bible (mainly Kings and Chronicles), and some of the information found there can be corroborated or corrected by archaeological remains and the surviving records of other nations in the region. For although the kingdom of the Israelites (which for part of its history was divided into two kingdoms, as we shall soon see) was small, its geographical position made it important to the great powers that were its neighbors.

Southwest of the land of Canaan was Egypt, a great and powerful kingdom with a continuous history known to us from about 3200 B.C.E. To the northeast and, behind a desert, to the east was

TIMELINE

JEWISH HISTORY		GENERAL HISTORY
	c. 3200 B.C.E.	Establishment of Egyptian kingdom
Patriarchal period	c. 1900	
	c. 1728–1686	Hammurabi king of Babylonia
	c. 1720–c. 1550	Hyksos in Egypt
	c. 1370–c. 1353	Akhenaten pharaoh in Egypt
	c. 1290–1224	Ramses II pharaoh in Egypt
Exodus from Egypt	c. 1280	
	c. 1224–1216	Marniptah pharaoh in Egypt
Conquest of Canaan under Joshua	c. 1250–1200	Philistines settle in Palestine
Period of the Judges	c. 1220–1200	
Samuel	c. 1050	
Saul	c. 1020–1000	
David	c. 1000–961	
Solomon	961–922	
Divided Kingdom: Rehoboam in Judah, Jeroboam I in Israel	922	
Jehosaphat in Judah	873–849	
Ahab and Jezebel in Israel	869–850	
Athaliah in Judah	842–837	
Jehu in Israel	842–815	
Jeroboam II in Israel	786–746	
Uzziah in Judah	783–742	
	745–727	Tiglath-pileser III king of Assyria
Ahaz in Judah	735–715	
Hoshea in Israel	732–724	
	727–722	Shalmaneser V
	722–705	Sargon II
Fall of Israel; exile of ten northern tribes	721	
Hezekiah in Judah	715–687	
	705–681	Sennacherib
Sennacherib besieges Jerusalem	701	
Josiah	640–609	
	612	Nineveh falls to Babylonians
Battle of Megiddo	609	
	605–562	Nebuchadnezzar king of Babylonia
Jehoiachin exiled to Babylonia	597	
Zedekiah	597–587	
Fall of Jerusalem; beginning of Babylonian exile	587	

Mesopotamia, the home of an age-old civilization also known to us from the fourth millennium B.C.E., which produced several powerful states. The dominant ones contemporaneous with the Israelite kingdom were first the Assyrian and then the neo-Babylonian empires. These Mesopotamian states and Egypt were the great contenders for power in the region during the Israelite period, with the Israelite territory being a kind of geographical bridge between them. Much of the political history of the Israelite kingdom is the history of the rivalry between Egypt and Mesopotamia. The kingdom (or kingdoms) of the Israelites had its greatest successes when its important neighbors were weak or preoccupied; when they were strong and their rivalry was intense, the Israelite kingdom could enjoy a modest prosperity under the patronage of one or the other of its neighbors, but it could also become caught up in their rivalry. It was finally destroyed when it chose the wrong one as its protector.

But where did the people of the Israelite kingdom come from? On this question, sources are vague. The earliest definite reference to the Israelites outside the Bible is an Egyptian inscription dating from about 1220 B.C.E., commemorating the victory of the Egyptian pharaoh Marniptah over them and several other peoples in the land of Canaan. But the Israelites' origins and subsequent history down to the establishment of the monarchy are obscure. Like most peoples, the Israelites developed a story of their origins that is based partly on fact, partly on a particularistic reading of much larger events, and partly on folklore.

From nonbiblical records, we know that the early second millennium B.C.E. saw waves of migration into Mesopotamia (the region of the Tigris and Euphrates Rivers, corresponding to present-day Iraq and eastern Syria) and Canaan by a seminomadic people known as the West Semites or Amorites. These people were probably the ancestors of both the Arameans, who settled in the northern parts of Canaan (corresponding approximately to present-day eastern Syria), and the Israelites, who settled in the southern part (corresponding approximately to present-day Israel). The immigrants were ethnically

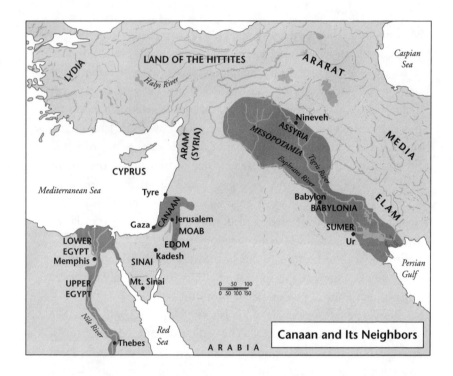

Canaan and Its Neighbors

related to the native Canaanites, whose language and culture they adopted. Some of these migratory peoples lived a seminomadic existence, mostly in the central hill country and the arid southern region, raising cattle, sheep, and goats and occasionally farming; sometimes they came into conflict with the sedentary population, but for the most part they kept to themselves. Such marginal people were found also in Mesopotamia and Egypt; they were known as Habiru or Apiru. These names, which designate not an ethnic group or clan but a social class, may be at the origin of the term "Hebrew," which the Bible attaches to Abraham.

Some Canaanites and Amorites made their way to Egypt, taking advantage of the weakness of the Egyptian Middle Kingdom to establish themselves in the Delta area around 1720 B.C.E. Around 1650, they took control of the country and established their own Egyptian dynasty, known as the Hyksos dynasty, which lasted approximately 100 years.

The Israelites' own story as recounted in Genesis and Exodus fits neatly into these large movements. Genesis names Abraham the Hebrew as a Mesopotamian who migrated to Canaan in obedience to a command from God. He and his son Isaac lived there, but his grandson Jacob migrated to Egypt on account of famine. There, Jacob's son Joseph became a powerful courtier. He and Jacob's eleven other sons, the ancestors of the twelve tribes of Israel, became prosperous, but their children were enslaved by the Egyptians. The biblical account of the migration to Egypt could very well reflect the appearance of the Apiru in Egypt in the fifteenth century B.C.E.; Joseph's rise to power is paralleled by occasional documented cases of non-Egyptian courtiers in the Eighteenth and Nineteenth Dynasties. The Bible's description of the enslaved Israelites being forced to build the cities of Pithom and Ramses may be related to the construction of the temple of Seth at Avaris during the reign of Sethos I (ruled c. 1305–1290 B.C.E.) and the foundation of a new capital at Pi-Ramses under Ramses II (ruled c. 1290–1224 B.C.E.). Contrary to a very common impression, the Israelites could not have been involved in the building of the famous pyramids at Giza, for these were completed nearly a thousand years before they could have arrived in Egypt.

The Israelites' flight from Egypt, known as the Exodus and described in the biblical book of that name, would thus have occurred in the reign of Ramses II. That would fit nicely with the Marniptah inscription's reference to the Israelites in Canaan around 1220, as mentioned earlier. But were the Israelites mentioned in the inscription identical to the people who had come to Canaan from Egypt? The main account in the Bible implies that they were identical, for that account assumes that the entire people were in Egypt. But other accounts in the Bible strongly imply that when those who fled Egypt entered Canaan, they joined up with other ethnically related tribes who were not descended from Abraham, Isaac, and Jacob and who had not been in Egypt. If this is true, it was the unification of these different groups that created the people who came to be known as Israelites. This is the version accepted by most historians today.

The biblical account attributes all the events of early Israelite history to divine providence. According to the Bible, God commanded Abraham to leave Mesopotamia and take up residence in the land of Canaan. Once Abraham reached Canaan, God informed him that his descendants would become slaves in Egypt, but that they would eventually be rescued and return to the land of Canaan, where they would live forever as His people. Abraham's son and grandson, Isaac and Jacob, lived in Canaan, but Jacob's sons sold their brother Joseph to a band of Ishmaelite merchants who brought him to Egypt; these events were part of the divine plan, unknown to the participants, to provide for the family during a period of famine. After many adventures, Joseph rose to a high administrative position and was able to provide for his father and brothers when they did eventually arrive in search of food, settling them in a part of the Nile delta that the Bible calls the land of Goshen.

The Bible goes on to relate that after both Joseph and the pharaoh who had elevated him died, the descendants of Jacob became so numerous that the new ruler turned against them and made them into slaves. They were saved by Moses, an Israelite born in Egypt. The new pharaoh had decreed that all Israelite children should be drowned in the Nile, but Moses had been rescued by Pharaoh's own daughter and raised in the palace. Moses performed many miracles in a vain effort to induce Pharaoh to release the Israelites; at last, he led them to a body of water that the Bible calls the "Sea of Reeds" (usually translated "Red Sea," but not to be identified with the body of water known by that name today). He prayed to God, whereupon the sea miraculously parted to let them cross, then closed over the troops of the Egyptians. The Israelites then marched to Mount Sinai, in the southern part of the Sinai peninsula, and encamped at the foot of the mountain now known as Jebel Musa (Moses' Mountain). There, they miraculously beheld God and received His law. It was this event that, according to Israelite tradition, consecrated the Israelites to be God's chosen people and imposed upon them the duty of obeying His special commands.

On leaving Egypt, the Israelites prudently avoided the coastal road, with its string of Egyptian fortresses, that enters the land of Canaan at the southwest. But when they attempted to enter the land from the south, they found that route blocked. After encamping for a long time at Kadesh, an oasis just south of Beersheba, and wandering for some time in the wilderness, they made a large detour to the east, skirting the newly formed kingdoms of Edom and Moab (southeast and east of the Dead Sea, in the present-day Kingdom of Jordan), to conquer the Amorite kingdom of Heshbon, which lay on the east bank of the Jordan. The way was now clear for them to cross the Jordan opposite Jericho. Moses died and was succeeded by Joshua.

The Bible gives two different versions of what happened next. According to one version, the Israelites conquered Jericho, swept through the land, subdued it in three swift campaigns, and divided it among the twelve Israelite tribes. But other parts of the Bible describe the conquest as slow, uncoordinated, and incomplete at Joshua's death. Archaeological evidence is not conclusive, but it does confirm the destruction of a number of Canaanite cities in the last part of the thirteenth century B.C.E., and it suggests that some were destroyed, rebuilt, and redestroyed in the same period. It seems certain that the Israelites were at first more successful in the central mountain region than on the coastal plain or the plain of Jezreel.

From the end of the thirteenth century to the end of the eleventh century B.C.E., the Israelites were organized in Canaan as a confederation of twelve tribes. Two tribes (Reuben and Gad) were completely settled in the Transjordan; one tribe (Manasseh) controlled territory on both sides of the Jordan. Judah controlled the southern part of the territory west of the Jordan; the central part was occupied by

Benjamin, Ephraim, and Manasseh; smaller tribes occupied the territory north of the plain of Jezreel. But there were enclaves of Canaanites here and there, and the coastal plain was partly in the hands of hostile invaders from the Aegean, known collectively as the Sea Peoples; of these, the Philistines were to become the most troubling to the Israelites. It was these people whose name much later became attached to the entire land, when it came to be called "Palestine," the name by which it is often known today.

The Israelite confederation had no formal central government or capital city, but the tribes were bound in responsibility to one another by a covenant and a common deity, known as Yahweh. The covenant was embodied in a shrine, the Ark of the Covenant, that came to be situated in Shiloh, in the central hill country. The council of the tribes could be convened for common activity in time of need, but ordinarily the tribes governed themselves and pursued their own activities, either separately or in temporary alliance. From time to time, a charismatic leader would emerge to lead groups of the tribes—or all of them—into battle. Such leaders, known as "judges" in the Bible, were the heroes of colorful stories of cunning and valor; the most famous of them were Ehud, Deborah, Gideon, and Samson.

The Israelites gradually developed from a seminomadic to an agricultural people; they established towns, cleared forests, improved their technology, and dealt as required with the hostility of such Canaanite groups as remained unconquered and unabsorbed. But their confederation was not strong enough to deal with the Philistines, an aggressive military aristocracy that was not content with raiding its neighbors, but was also bent on exploiting the weakness of Egypt to take control of all Canaan. The Philistines had a major technological advantage in knowing how to work iron and in being skilled in the use of chariots. Around 1050 B.C.E. they won a major battle at Aphek, seizing the Ark of the Covenant (which had been brought into the battle), destroying Shiloh, and occupying much of the land. The Israelites responded by creating a monarchy to enable them to fight in a more coordinated fashion, electing as their first king a man named Saul.

Not all were content to see the charismatic form of government replaced by a monarchy; Saul owed his elevation not only to the support of a respected seer named Samuel (who at first had resisted the change), but also to his own charismatic personality, which made his rule seem like a continuation of the old regime. But though he was at first effective in fighting the Philistines, he proved unstable, being subject to fits of depression and rage as well as lapses of judgment. Samuel shifted his support to David, a youthful officer of Saul's who had distinguished himself in single combat against Goliath, a renowned Philistine hero. David's popularity as a warrior eclipsed that of Saul; inflamed with jealousy, Saul flung his spear at the youth, who fled and took refuge among the Philistines. Among them, David played a dangerous double game; he pretended to harass the tribe of Judah with his own militia on behalf of the Philistine king of Gath, but he actually used his freedom to harass the Amalekites and other Canaanite tribes hostile to the Judeans, thereby winning a reputation among the Judeans as their protector.

About 1000 B.C.E., the Philistines inflicted a crushing defeat on the Israelites in the Jezreel Plain. Three of Saul's sons were killed, and Saul himself committed suicide; Eshbaal, a surviving son of Saul, was not able to assert his succession. David now reaped his reward from the Judeans, for they elected him as their king in Hebron, probably with the consent of the Philistines. When the weak Eshbaal was murdered, David easily won the loyalty of the northern tribes as well. Within a few years he succeeded in conquering an important Canaanite enclave on the border between Judah and Benjamin, and took its main city, Jerusalem, as his own personal holding, transferring to it the Ark of the Covenant (which had earlier been recovered from the Philistines). In this way, Jerusalem became the capital of a monarchy, consisting of two distinct parts—the southern tribe of

Judah and the northern tribes, collectively known as Israel—as well as the center of the shrine that united them.

The Israelites worshiped a deity named Yahweh. But although Yahweh had a proper name, as did the gods of the pagan nations, He was unlike the gods of the Israelites' neighbors. Unique among the peoples of their time, the Israelites were monotheists; that is, they recognized only Yahweh as a true god, creator of heaven and earth, master of the world, controller of all peoples' destinies. Pagan nations recognized many gods; most had the idea that there was a chief god who dominated the others and was their own particular patron, but they accepted the fact that other peoples would be loyal to their own gods. But the ancient Israelites did not concede the legitimacy of any other deity. Yahweh was sometimes represented in forms similar to those employed by the Israelites' pagan neighbors in their worship, and He was often described in terms inherited from the pagan religions of the region, but fully developed Israelite monotheism did not allow Yahweh to be represented in any form and did not permit the use of idols in worship. Yahweh's worship consisted mainly of sacrifices of animals and produce offered at His shrine by members of a hereditary priesthood. Such worship was performed throughout Israelite territory, but when the monarchy was strong, attempts were made to restrict it to the royal shrine at Jerusalem.

David's accession marks the true beginning of the mature Israelite monarchy and the emergence of the Israelites into clear historical view. The (approximately) eighty years of his reign and that of his son Solomon, combined, figured in the Jewish imagination throughout the centuries as the golden age of Jewish history. David expanded his state to the east and southeast, defeating the Transjordanian kingdoms of Ammon, Moab, and Edom; in the north, he defeated the recently established Aramean states in what is now Syria; and on the Mediterranean coast, he compelled the Philistines to pay him tribute. Controlling most of the territory from the Mediterranean to the

David

The biblical account of the life and reign of King David, making up the Books of 1 and 2 Samuel, is one of the longest and liveliest stories in the Bible and may be the earliest preserved narrative in Hebrew. It combines folklore and historical facts.

The Book of 1 Samuel tells how David became king of Israel. According to this account, David started out as a Judean shepherd boy, a typically folkloristic way of depicting a person as suited for the role of "shepherd of his people." The prophet Samuel, who had decided to replace King Saul with a more effective leader, anointed him in secret (in ancient Israel, anointing with oil, rather than crowning, was the ceremony by which kings were consecrated). Young David came to King Saul's attention by defeating and killing the Philistine champion Goliath in single combat, using only his shepherd's sling. This feat made him a popular hero, but it also aroused Saul's jealousy and hostility.

Saul, who was subject to bouts of depression, invited David to join his court to soothe him by playing the harp when his dark moods overcame him. One night, in a fit, he threw a javelin at David. David fled to the land of the Philistines, and joined the court of the King of Gath, Saul's enemy. He organized raids, ostensibly against Judea, but actually against the Canaanites, while awaiting the opportunity to return. When Saul and his son Jonathan were killed in a battle with the Philistines, David, by now an experienced military leader, became king of Judea, with his capital at Hebron. A few years later, he became king over the northern tribes, uniting Judea and Israel into a single kingdom. He captured the Canaanite city Jebus, on the border between Judea and the northern tribes, and made it his capital, under the name Jerusalem.

The Book of 2 Samuel tells a series of stories about David's reign, depicting him as a gallant, but not always righteous, leader. He had to face several rebellions against his rule. Of these, the most painful was that of his own

continues

son, Absalom, which so seriously threatened David that he had to flee temporarily with his court across the Jordan. When Absalom was killed by one of David's soldiers as he fled his father's counterattack, David mourned him bitterly.

The books of Samuel do not hesitate to report on David's weaknesses. In his lust for Bathsheba, the wife of one of his captains, David had her husband sent to the front to meet his death, then married her. Forcefully rebuked by the prophet Nathan, David repented and was forgiven. The son who was later born to him and Bathsheba was Solomon, who succeeded David as king.

The later Jewish tradition remembers David not only as a warrior and king but also as a poet. He is said to have written many or all of the poems that were collected in the biblical Book of Psalms.

eastern desert, and from the Sinai desert northward toward Tyre (the capital of a Phoenician state along the northern part of Canaan's Mediterranean coast) and northeast to the Euphrates, he had in effect fulfilled the ambition of the Philistines of controlling the entire region and had made himself the center of a tiny empire.

A number of rebellions showed that not all the Israelites were content with this state of affairs. The rebellion of David's own son, Absalom, may simply have reflected generalized discontent and Absalom's personal ambition, but the rebellion of Sheba ben Bichri was a sign of the restiveness of the northern tribes under Judean dominance. In David's old age, his son Adonijah attempted to subvert his plan to hand the succession to Solomon, but David had Solomon crowned in his own lifetime.

Having inherited a stable kingdom, Solomon (ruled c. 961–922) devoted less attention to warfare than to the commercial development of the state. He established alliances with Egypt and Tyre and exploited his geographical position between two seas and

The Kingdom of
David and Solomon

CYPRUS

Mediterranean Sea

Daphne

SYRIA

HITTITES

ASSYRIA

Tiphsah

Rezeph

Arvad

HAMATH

Hamoth

Gebal

Emesa

Tadmor

PHOENICIA

ARAM

Baalbek

ZOBAH

Rehob

Sidon

Damascus

Tyre

ARGOB

Dan

Acco

Hazor

ISRAELITES

JEZREEL
PLAIN

Dor

Bozrah

Shiloh

Aphek

Joppa

PHILISTINES

Rabboth-ammon

Jerusalem

AMMON

Gaza

Beersheba

MOAB

EGYPT

EDOM

Sela

Eilat

Ezion-geber

Euphrates

Orontes

Jordan

– – the Kingdom of David,
strengthened by Solomon

athwart major trade routes to develop trade in the Red Sea and
Arabia. He mined copper in the southern desert and traded in
horses and chariots with the Egyptians, Cilicians, and Hittites. The
result of all this activity was unprecedented prosperity, with concomitant urban expansion, technological advances, population

growth, and the emergence of a cosmopolitan culture. Prosperity permitted Solomon to engage in numerous building projects, including the palace complex and Temple in Jerusalem, for which an architect was brought in from Tyre. Prosperity also encouraged the development of a literary culture, for in this period were written the court history of David (the nucleus of the biblical Book of Samuel), and the story of Israel's origins. This work is no longer extant in its entirety, but the author of the Pentateuch (the part of the Bible that the Jews call the Torah, consisting of Genesis, Exodus, Leviticus, Numbers, and Deuteronomy) used it as one of his main sources and quoted it extensively. Scholars, who refer to the Pentateuch's sources by letters of the alphabet, call this lost work the J source.

But Solomon's projects and the administration of the empire were a burden on the population. They necessitated the introduction of a complex administrative system and bureaucracy, heavy taxation, and the despised practice of compulsory labor on behalf of the state. A trade deficit developed with Tyre that forced Solomon to cede certain northern towns. Many resented Solomon's favoritism to his own tribe of Judah. Local priests resented the ascendancy of the Jerusalem Temple and the diminution of their own status. Two generations of monarchy had transformed the state from a loose tribal confederation of simple farmers and shepherds into a socially stratified economic machine in which the masses were exploited by a small aristocracy and subjected to the needs of a court that was becoming ever more foreign in tone and style.

Solomon himself did not have to face the consequences of the resulting discontent, but upon his death, the kingdom fractured into two states. His son Rehoboam was able to hold on to Judah and Benjamin, but the northern tribes repudiated the union with Judah that had been effected by David and elected as their king Jeroboam, a former official of Solomon's court. This northern kingdom, with its capital first at Shechem, then at Tirzah, and finally at Samaria, survived for 200 years under several short-lived dynasties, until its destruction by the Assyrians in 721 B.C.E. Meanwhile, Judah continued under the rule of the Davidic dynasty until its destruction by the Babylonians in 587 B.C.E. It is a confusing fact of Israelite history that the northern kingdom was known as Israel; therefore, during this period, the word "Israelite" normally refers not to members of the people as a whole but only to the inhabitants of the northern kingdom.

Neither Judah nor Israel was strong enough to hold on to David's and Solomon's acquisitions. Ammon, Moab, and the Philistine cities became independent again; the Aramean holdings also were lost; and Damascus became an important rival power. Judah and Israel were reduced to the status of second-rate rival states: Judah was often under pressure from Egypt, Israel was often under pressure from Damascus, and both states were continually pressuring each other, both by direct intervention and by political maneuvering with neighbor states. The rivalry between Judah and Israel found religious expression when Jeroboam established his own official cult, building temples at Dan and Bethel, so that his subjects would no longer look to the Jerusalem Temple, the official shrine of the Davidic monarchy, as their cultic center. But Jeroboam did not repudiate the national religion or introduce idolatry, as claimed by prophets who remained loyal to the Davidic dynasty.

Judah remained stable for several generations, but Israel was relatively unstable, with frequent changes of ruler, until the accession of Omri in 876. He established a dynasty that lasted until 842 and restored Israel to a position of strength based on peace with Judah and the Phoenicians. These relations were sealed by marriages: Omri's son Ahab was married to Jezebel, the daughter of the king of Tyre, and Omri's daughter (or granddaughter) Athaliah was married to the son of the king of Judah. (Both these strong women were to play important parts in the events of their times.) Thus strengthened,

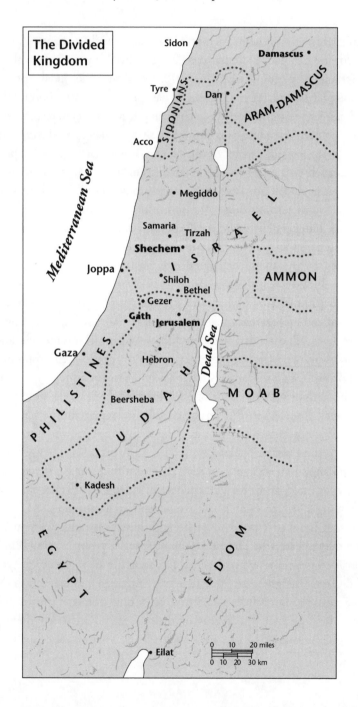

The Divided Kingdom

Sidon

Damascus

Tyre

Dan

ARAM-DAMASCUS

Acco

SIDONIANS

Mediterranean Sea

Megiddo

Samaria

Tirzah

Shechem

I S R A E L

Joppa

Shiloh

Bethel

AMMON

Gezer

Gath

Jerusalem

Gaza

Dead Sea

Hebron

PHILISTINES

J U D A H

MOAB

Beersheba

Kadesh

E G Y P T

E D O M

0   10   20 miles
0   10   20   30 km

Eilat

Israel was now able to reconquer Moab, and Judah was again able to control Edom. Ahab also went to war against Aram-Damascus, but dropped the hostilities in order to cooperate with Aram and other northern states in repelling a much greater threat from Assyria. Later, he did go to war against Aram and was killed. The deterioration of his dynasty is marked by the loss of Moab by his son Jehoram; this event is described in a lengthy inscription known as the Mesha stele, which is now in the Louvre.

Severe opposition to the Omrid dynasty came from religiously conservative elements, especially from prophets such as Elijah and his disciple Elisha. Such men objected to the foreign cults that had become popular in Israel as a result of Israel's close cooperation with Tyre. Jezebel was a particular object of their wrath because she systematically propagated her own pagan religion and persecuted the worshipers of Yahweh. In 842, Elisha engineered a coup in which a general named Jehu seized control of the state, threw Jezebel—literally—out the window, and massacred the entire family of Ahab as well as the adherents of Jezebel's Tyrian cult.

Meanwhile, Judah was undergoing a similar development under the influence of Athaliah. After the successive deaths of her husband, Jehoram, and her son, she seized power for herself, killed all of Jehoram's relatives who might oppose her, and fostered the cult of Baal. But Athaliah had no real following. One infant prince had been saved from her purge by the wife of the chief priest; in 837, when he reached the age of seven, he was crowned in the Temple by the priest, and Athaliah was executed.

Both Israel and Judah remained weak until the 780s, when the reduced power of Assyria and the presence of able kings in both states permitted them a temporary resurgence. Under kings whose reigns were nearly exactly contemporaneous, Jeroboam II (ruled 786–746) in Israel and Uzziah (ruled 783–742) in Judah, the two states expanded, together reaching almost the extent of Solomon's kingdom. But soon after the death of Jeroboam II, Assyria had a resurgence under a powerful new ruler, Tiglath-pileser III. The remainder of the history of the northern kingdom and much of the remaining history of Judah were determined by Assyria's terrifying military machine.

Tiglath-pileser III embarked on a campaign of conquest, subduing Babylon and then turning his attention toward the west. By 738 he was taking tribute from all the states of Syria and northern Canaan, including Israel, which fell into near anarchy. Israel and Damascus tried to pressure Judah into joining a regional coalition against the Assyrians, but the Judean kings Jotham and Ahaz refused. During the reign of Ahaz, the members of the coalition invaded Judah with the intention of replacing him with a more cooperative ruler. Faced with this invasion and the attacks from several other quarters, Ahaz appealed to Tiglath-pileser III for help. The Assyrian swept into the region with his invincible army and simply wiped out the coalition. Overrunning Israel, he deported part of its population, reduced its territory, and established a puppet king named Hoshea to rule over the remains. But Hoshea withheld his tribute and appealed to Egypt for help. By defying the great empire, he destroyed his own kingdom. In 724, the Assyrian king Shalmaneser V attacked, took Hoshea prisoner, and occupied most of the land. Samaria, the capital, fell to Sargon II in 721, ending the history of the northern kingdom.

The conquering Assyrians followed their usual practice of deporting the native population and replacing them with deportees from some other conquered territory. Much of the population of the northern kingdom was transferred to upper Mesopotamia, where they merged with the local population; the territory of the northern kingdom was filled up with people from Syria and Babylonia, who mingled with the remaining Israelite population. This event is known in traditional Jewish history as the exile of the ten northern tribes. But the newcomers adopted the worship of Yahweh that they learned from those Israelites who remained, and the two populations merged.

Though they continued to regard themselves as closely related to the people of Judah, this relationship would sour in the fifth century B.C.E. and would turn to active hostility after the conquests of Alexander the Great in the fourth century B.C.E.

Assyria had but little more than a century left before its own disappearance from world history. In 703, an uprising in Babylon provided an opportunity for Tyre, the Philistine cities, Judea, and others to form an anti-Assyrian coalition, in which the Judean king Hezekiah (ruled 715–687) played a central role. In preparation for Assyrian retaliation, Hezekiah strengthened the fortifications of Jerusalem and dug the famous Siloam tunnel (which can still be visited) to guarantee the city's water supply. When the Assyrian king Sennacherib marched into the region in 701, terrible slaughter and extensive deportations ensued, and Hezekiah had to cede some of his territories and increase his tribute. But Sennacherib abruptly departed from the scene without taking Jerusalem, the result, according to the biblical account, of the miraculous sudden death of his troops. Nevertheless, Judah remained under tribute to Assyria until the time of Josiah (ruled 640–609), whose reign coincided with the decline and collapse of Assyria in the face of the rising power of Babylonia.

Josiah's reign was the last period in which Judah was able to assert some degree of independence. He recovered some of the territories of northern Israel that had been taken by the Assyrians and instituted a sweeping religious reform, purging the state of the foreign cults that had been imposed by the Assyrians. He reasserted Judah's independence and his own religious authority by rigorously restricting sacrificial rites to Jerusalem. The Bible describes this event as resulting from the discovery in the Temple of an ancient scroll (presumably, the Book of Deuteronomy) ordaining that sacrifices could be offered in no other place. The promulgation of the new law was celebrated by the renewal of the covenant between Yahweh and the people and the celebration of the hitherto neglected festival of Passover.

In 609, the Egyptians marched through the Jezreel valley to assist the nearly defunct Assyrian empire in its struggle against the Babylonians. Josiah was killed when he attempted to use his troops to stop the Egyptians and thereby forestall an Egyptian-Assyrian victory. With Babylonia now in control of Mesopotamia, Egypt set out to take control of Palestine and Syria. Jehoahaz, the new king of Judah, was deposed and replaced by Jehoiakim and the land placed under tribute to Egypt.

The westward expansion of Babylonia at the expense of Egypt set in motion the developments that ended in the destruction of the kingdom of Judah. The Babylonian general (soon to become king) Nebuchadnezzar defeated the Egyptians in Syria and pressed southward toward Judah, making Jehoiakim his vassal in 603–602. Jehoiakim attempted to rebel, turning to Egypt for help. During the ensuing war with Babylonia, he died and was succeeded by his eighteen-year-old son, Jehoiachin, who held out against Nebuchadnezzar for three months and then surrendered. Together with the court, leading officials, and much Judean treasure, he was deported to Babylonia, and his uncle Zedekiah, a son of Josiah, was established as puppet king.

Zedekiah, in turn, attempted to revolt, apparently expecting help from Egypt. What help did arrive was inadequate, and in 587, after a long siege, Nebuchadnezzar's troops broke through the walls of Jerusalem. Zedekiah's sons were killed before his eyes and he was then blinded and taken to Babylon. Jerusalem was burned to the ground and its walls leveled. Many of the leading officers were killed, others deported, and the state of Judah was liquidated. A Judean nobleman, Gedaliah, was appointed governor over this new Babylonian territory, but he was soon assassinated as a collaborationist by a conspiracy of Judean officials.

The Judean monarchy had lasted over 400 years, a respectable duration for a small nation occupying a highly contested strip of

Inscriptions

The written record that has survived from biblical times is not huge, but it affords insight into the social and economic situation of ancient Israel. The oldest datable Hebrew inscription is the Gezer calendar, dating from the period of Solomon. It is a small tablet of soft limestone inscribed by a child, probably as a school exercise, and lists the agricultural activities appropriate to the various months of the year.

From the time of the Judean and Israelite kingdoms, many pottery shards (called *ostraca*) with ink inscriptions in old Hebrew script have survived. One group of ostraca contains lists of goods, such as wine and oil, delivered to the royal palace at the capital of the northern kingdom in Samaria in the eighth century B.C.E. From the end of the seventh century B.C.E. comes an ostracon containing an agricultural worker's protest against his treatment by an overseer. From the Negev comes a group of ostraca constituting the archive of a commissar named Elyashiv, who was in charge of the stores of Arad. These documents record the distribution of supplies to the Judean troops and the mercenaries attached to them. Another group of ostraca consists of letters to Yaush, the military governor of Lachish (a town near Jerusalem), written shortly before the siege of the capital by the Babylonians in 587 B.C.E.

From the end of the eighth century comes a monumental inscription commemorating the completion of the Siloam tunnel. According to the biblical Books of Kings and Chronicles, King Hezekiah undertook this operation in order to convey water from Gihon creek to Siloam pool, inside the walls of Jerusalem, and thereby guarantee the city's water supply in anticipation of an Assyrian siege. Another monumental inscription, the largest one yet discovered in the region, is written in Moabite, a Canaanite language that closely resembles Hebrew. It commemorates the rebellion of the Moabite king Mesha against the Israelite kingdom after the death of King Ahab, as described in 2 Kings. The style of the inscription is remarkably similar to the

continues

style of the biblical Book of Kings, but it describes the political events from the Moabite perspective. Mesha claims to have destroyed Israelite cities, taken Israelite captives as slaves, and seized sacred implements from a temple of Yahweh at Nebo. The biblical version of the outcome is quite different, and the conflict has not yet been resolved.

Very controversial are the inscriptions on large storage jars from a traveler's way station in the northern Negev. Written in the ninth century B.C.E., these inscriptions refer to the god "Yahweh of Samaria" and his "Ashera." The word *ashera* appears frequently in the Bible as the name of a Canaanite religious cult, and in Canaanite inscriptions as the name of a goddess. Some scholars interpret the word in these inscriptions as being an attribute of Yahweh, but others explain it as the name of the Canaanite goddess, who may have been considered to be the wife of Yahweh. If this theory is true, it would reflect a stage of Israelite history, before the advent of monotheism, in which Yahweh was a pagan deity like the deities of the other nations of the region.

Finally, engraved on two little silver tablets is a prayer almost identical with the blessing of the priests, recorded in Num. 6:24–26 and still recited every day in traditional synagogues. The silver tablets were amulets, written in the second half of the seventh century B.C.E. and worn for protection. This is the only biblical text that has come down to us from biblical times outside the Bible itself. It reads, "May the Lord bless you and keep you; may the Lord cause His face to shine upon you; may the Lord lift His face up to you and grant you peace."

territory. But its people would not allow it to be forgotten. They took their memory of the kingdom with them into exile, and there they nourished themselves on the dream that it would ultimately be restored to the glory of its early days. This idealized restoration later came to be known as the messianic age. In Babylonia, the exiles created religious institutions that would enable them to keep the memory of their kingdom and the dream of its restoration alive for centuries. Along with the principle of monotheism, the messianic dream was to become one of the defining features of Judaism.

Ezra reading the law; a wall painting from the ancient synagogue of Dura Europos (in present-day Syria), c. 245 C.E. Photo of painting © Zev Radovan. Used by permission.

TWO

Judea and the Origins of the Diaspora

(587 B.C.E. to 70 C.E.)

Though mighty, the Babylonian Empire was of short duration; by 539 B.C.E., it had been conquered by Cyrus the Persian, who went on to establish an empire stretching from India to Ethiopia, the most extensive empire known until then. Cyrus's treatment of his conquests was more lenient than that meted out by his predecessors, the Assyrians and the Babylonians; he generally permitted his subject peoples a degree of autonomy, granted their princes political responsibility, and respected their religious cults. Thus, it came about that in 538, soon after conquering Babylon, Cyrus ordered the restoration of the Judean community and cult in the newly established Persian province of Judea. The exiles were permitted to return under the leadership of Prince Sheshbazzar, the son of Jehoiachin, the next-to-last king of Judah.

Jehoiachin, who had been exiled to Babylonia in 598, had been released from imprisonment by Nebuchadnezzar's successor and granted certain dignities even before the collapse of the Babylonian Empire; in Babylon, he must have become the central figure of a circle of exiled Judean aristocrats. With the rise of the Persian Empire,

TIMELINE

TIMELINE

JEWISH HISTORY		GENERAL HISTORY
Judah killed, replaced by Jonathan	160	
Jonathan high priest	152	
Onias IV, a former high priest, builds temple in Leontopolis, Egypt	c. 145	
Jonathan killed, replaced by Simeon	142	
Simeon named ethnarch and high priest	140	
John Hyrcanus high priest	134–104	
Aristobulus I	104–103	
Alexander Jannaeus	103–76	
Salome Alexandra	76–67	
Pompey intervenes in civil war; Rome takes control of Judea	63	
	44	Assassination of Julius Caesar
Herod	37–4 B.C.E.	
	27 B.C.E.–4 C.E.	Augustus Roman emperor
Rebuilding of Temple	19 C.E.	
Judea, Samaria, and Idumea a Roman province	6–41 C.E.	
Pontius Pilate	26–36	
Jesus crucified	c. 30	
Crisis because of Caligula's demand that he be worshiped	37–41	Caligula emperor
Anti-Jewish riots in Alexandria	38	
Herod Agrippa	41–44	
	41–54	Claudius emperor
	54–68	Nero emperor
	62	Death of the apostle Paul
Massacre of Jews of Alexandria	66	
Beginning of Judean revolt; Vespasian conquers Galilee	66	
	69–70	Vespasian emperor
Titus conquers Jerusalem; Temple destroyed	70	
Fall of Masada; Temple in Leontopolis closed	73	

many of the Judeans of Babylonia prospered, and some of the members of this upper echelon rose to positions of dignity in the Persian court. Such Judeans had little incentive to return to the new Persian province of Judea. The Judeans of Babylonia continued to feel connected to the people of Judea by history, family ties, culture, and religion, and they remained organized as a distinctive ethnic and religious group; but they ceased to be truly exiles, for they remained abroad by choice. A parallel development occurred in Egypt. Here, a garrison of Judean mercenaries had been established on Elephantine (an island in the Nile near Aswan) perhaps as early as the mid-seventh century B.C.E.; this colony remained in existence—and in contact with the Persian province of Judea—for over 200 years. The Jews of Elephantine had a temple at which they offered sacrifices, as was done in Jerusalem, and continued to do so long after the first Jerusalem Temple was destroyed. Nor were they the only Judeans in Egypt, for after the destruction of the kingdom of Judah in 587 B.C., some Judeans fled to the northern part of the country.

The communities of Judeans in Babylonia and Egypt may be considered the first and longest-lived Diaspora communities, that is, communities of Jews outside the Land of Israel. The Jewish community of Iraq lasted continuously until 1951; that of Egypt, though several times reduced to near-extinction, sprang back to life several times, but it now seems to have petered out for good.

It is from this period that it becomes appropriate to begin speaking of the Jewish people, meaning all those who, throughout history and around the globe, have regarded themselves as linked to one another and to the people of the ancient Israelite kingdom, either by ethnicity, culture, intellectual heritage, or religion.

How could such identity be maintained in the absence of a common political framework, a common language, or national institutions? The solution devised by the leaders of the Babylonian Jewish community took the form of a book. The Jewish religious tradition maintains that this book, the Torah (consisting of the first five books

The Bible

The Bible is a collection of ancient Hebrew books. Despite all efforts, we do not yet know exactly how or when these books were selected and made into an authoritative canon. We do know that by the first century C.E., all the books that are today considered to belong to the Bible were already considered to be sacred Scripture. In Hebrew, the Bible is called *Miqra* (Reading) or *Kitve haqodesh* (Sacred Scriptures); sometimes it is called *Tanakh*, an acronym for the three parts into which it is divided in the Jewish tradition. These three parts are the Torah (also called the Five Books of Moses), the Prophets, and the Hagiographa (or Sacred Writings).

The Torah tells the story of the Israelites, from Abraham's migration to the land of Canaan to the death of Moses. In between, it tells how the Israelites descended to Egypt, were enslaved, escaped, and wandered for forty years in the desert until they reached the point from which they would cross the Jordan and reenter the land. The narrative also serves as the framework for the laws that were to govern the lives of the Israelites in their land—the Ten Commandments, as well as myriad civil and religious regulations that later became the basis of Jewish religious law. It also devotes a great deal of attention to the sacrificial rites that, during the period of the Israelite kingdom, constituted the people's main religious observance.

The section of the Bible called Prophets contains two different kinds of books. The first four books continue the narrative of the Torah, from the time the Israelites entered the land of Canaan under the leadership of Joshua, through the age of the Judges, the establishment of the monarchy by Saul, the reigns of David and Solomon, and the divided kingdom, down to the destruction of the First Temple and the end of Israelite sovereignty in 587 B.C.E. The remaining prophetic books contain the speeches of the prophets of Israel, religious leaders outside the Temple hierarchy, who, beginning in the seventh century B.C.E., preached to the people and admonished the kings about their religious duties and about the religious meaning

continues

of political events. The most famous of these orator-prophets were Isaiah, Jeremiah, Hosea, Amos, and Ezekiel. The latest of these prophets (Haggai, Zechariah, and Malachi) preached during the early years of the return to Judea after the Babylonian Exile.

The third part of the Bible contains miscellaneous books, mostly from the Persian period. It begins with the Book of Psalms, 150 religious poems that may have been sung as part of the Temple service. Proverbs is a collection of maxims on religious and moral conduct. Job is a poem on the problem of suffering, framed by a folktale about a man who bore his suffering with patience and was rewarded. Then come five short books known as the "scrolls": a love poem (Song of Songs); a lament on the destruction of Jerusalem (Lamentations); a meditation on the meaning of life (Ecclesiastes); a story about one of King David's ancestors (Ruth); and a story about a Persian court intrigue that nearly led to the destruction of the Jews of Persia (Esther). Daniel contains the visions of a Jewish courtier in Persia concerning the exile and restoration of the Judean kingdom; Ezra and Nehemiah tell the story of the restoration (Nehemiah is actually the personal memoir of one of the governors of Judea in the fifth century B.C.E.), and Chronicles recapitulates the story of the Judean kings.

of the Bible; the word means "instruction"), had been given to Moses at Mount Sinai, but that it had fallen into neglect, and that at this time, the Judean elders in Babylonia promulgated it anew and made its study and the observance of its laws the people's chief religious duty. The process is described somewhat differently by historians. According to them, the Torah actually came into existence at this time. Using ancient documents preserved from the period of the monarchy, the Judean elders in Babylonia compiled an official national history and codification of laws, customs, and religious practices, enabling them to reorganize the national identity around religious behavior and to some extent to turn the national identity itself into a religion. These changes have left their stamp on Jewish identity and on the Jewish religion to this very day.

Judea itself was merely a tiny strip of land around Jerusalem. Here, efforts were made to rebuild the ruined Temple under Sheshbazzar and Zerubbabel, another descendant of the Judean royal house, who led a group of returnees under the emperor's authorization. These early attempts at restoration had only modest success, for the Judeans had to contend with poverty and a succession of poor agricultural seasons. Politically, Judea remained subordinate to the larger Persian province of Samaria, out of which it had been carved, and its efforts at independent action met with the hostility of the Samarian authorities. When the Temple was finally completed in 515, it could not compare with the magnificent old Temple of Solomon (which a few old-timers could still remember), and it did not win the loyalty of the Yahweh-worshiping inhabitants of Samaria. Jerusalem's fortifications remained in ruins.

Attempts were made to reconstruct Jerusalem's walls, but this project was not accomplished until taken in hand, under imperial authority, by Nehemiah, a Jewish courtier of Artaxerxes I who governed Judea from 445 to sometime after 433 B.C.E., and then for another, shorter period. Nehemiah was an effective and strong-willed leader who wrote his own memoirs—which have survived, as a book of the Bible—describing the opposition he had to face from Sanballat, the governor of Samaria (who even tried to have him assassinated), and Tobiah, the governor of Transjordan. In his second tour of duty, he devoted his attention to strengthening the province's religious institutions.

Some time during the last half of the fifth century B.C.E., probably overlapping with the governorship of Nehemiah, another Jewish official, Ezra, arrived from Babylonia with a commission from the Persian emperor to institute the Torah as the law of the land. The biblical Books of Ezra and Nehemiah preserve the Aramaic document containing Ezra's commission as well as a description of the moving

The Persian Province of Judea and Its Neighbors

Sidon
• Damascus
DAMASCUS
Tyre
Acco
KARNAIM
GALILEE
HAURAN
Dor
GILEAD
• Samaria
Joppa
SAMARIA
TOBIADS
Modein
Mizpeh • Jericho
Ashdod
Jerusalem
Ashkelon
JUDEA
Lachish
MOAB
Gaza   IDUMEA
(EDOMITES)
Beersheba

Mediterranean Sea

ARABIA

Eilat

0   0   40 miles
0   30   60 km

ceremony at which the Torah was first officially read in public and promulgated as the law of the province of Judea on the authority of the Persian emperor. This was a key moment in Jewish history, and one that is ceremonially reenacted in synagogues at every service at which the Torah is read.

Judean authorities attempted to regulate the religious practices of Elephantine, but they do not seem to have attempted to shut down the Elephantine temple itself, despite the fact that its existence was contrary to the law of Deuteronomy (as described in chapter 1). It continued to function until 410, when some Egyptian regiments rebelled against the Persian regime, while the Jewish garrison remained loyal. The priests of the neighboring temple of the Egyptian ram-god Khnum took the opportunity to destroy the Jewish temple, which offended their own cult through its animal sacrifices. On suppressing the rebellion, the Persian authorities permitted the rebuilding of the Elephantine temple, in consideration of its great antiquity; but in a bow to the sensibilities of both the Jerusalem authorities and the Egyptian priests, they restricted its sacrifices to vegetable offerings. The temple was rebuilt, but the Jewish colony in Elephantine disappears from view early in the fourth century B.C.E.

The remainder of the Persian period of Judea's history is a dark age for the historian. We can say little more than that Judea was a kind of theocracy ruled by the high priest and a Persian-appointed governor. The story line resumes only with the arrival of Alexander the Great, about a century after Nehemiah. This event precipitated drastic changes in the fortunes of the Jews.

Alexander first attacked the Persian Empire in 334 B.C.E. When he died, eleven years later, at the age of thirty-three, he had conquered it all, including Judea (333 B.C.E.) and Egypt. All these territories, which included virtually the entire Jewish Diaspora, became strongly marked by Greek culture. Jews would be both fascinated and repelled by this culture for centuries to come; even those who resisted it most bitterly could hardly escape its influence. On a broader scale, the interplay between Jewish and Hellenic ideals was to become one of the characteristic themes of all Western civilization.

Under Alexander, the city of Samaria revolted, and in punishment, it was settled with Macedonian colonists. Asserting their religious difference from the pagan Macedonian settlers, the native inhabitants (who were descended from the inhabitants of the old northern Israelite kingdom and the settlers who had been imported by the Assyrians in the eighth century B.C.E.) established their own Yahwist sanctuary at Shechem (now known as Nablus). This religious community, from then on known as the Samaritans, has remained in

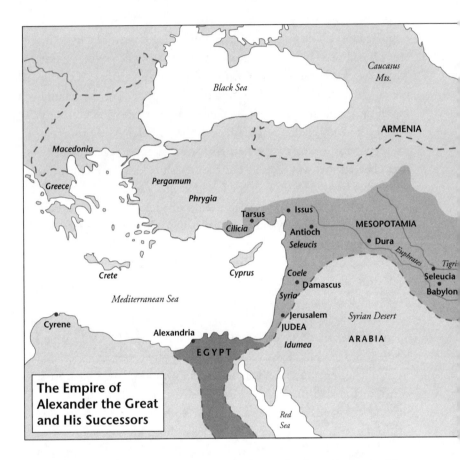

The Empire of Alexander the Great and His Successors

existence ever since, though in greatly diminished numbers; the New Testament story of the "good Samaritan" reflects the contempt in which they were held by the average Judean three centuries later.

When Alexander died, his empire was divided among his generals, with the result that the Jews fell under two different jurisdictions. Seleucus, who acquired the eastern territories of Iran, Mesopotamia, and Syria, founded the Seleucid dynasty, which included the Jews of the Babylonian Diaspora community. Ptolemy founded the Ptolemid dynasty, which was to rule Egypt, with its own Jewish Diaspora community, until 30 B.C.E. As in the period of the Israelite monarchy, the

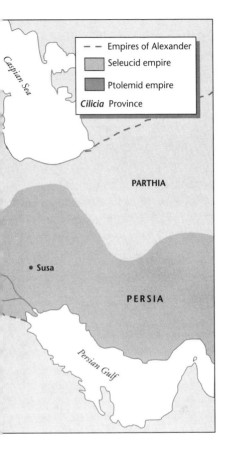

territory on the eastern coast of the Mediterranean, now known as Coele-Syria, and including the province of Judea, was an object of contention between a great Mesopotamian power and a great Egyptian power. Egypt at first had the upper hand, winning control over it in 301 B.C.E. For the century of their domination, the Egyptians did not interfere in Jewish affairs, but allowed the administration of the Judean theocracy to continue under the rule of a high priest and a council of elders. This century also saw the rapid growth of the Jewish community of Egypt, especially in the recently founded city of Alexandria, which soon became a major center of Jewish life. Particularly noteworthy is the prominent role of Jews as soldiers, continuing the military tradition of the old Elephantine garrison. They were so Hellenized that they were regarded legally as Hellenes, that is, as belonging to the same social class as the rulers, rather than to the social class of the subject Egyptian population. It was for the use of these Hellenized Egyptian Jews that the Torah was translated into Greek in this period. By the end of the third century B.C.E., there were probably more Jews living in the Diaspora than in Palestine.

Palestine came under Seleucid control in 198 B.C.E., when the Seleucid ruler Antiochus III (the Great) drove the Ptolemids out of

Asia. Antiochus III allowed Judea to continue as a semiautonomous state. But under his second successor, Antiochus IV Epiphanes (175–163), relations between Judea and the Greek rulers disintegrated. The great problem of the Seleucid state was the expansion of Rome, which had already inflicted a humiliating defeat on Antiochus III. Pressed for cash, the Seleucid rulers took to plundering the temples of their subject peoples. Temples were always good sources of money because of the precious metals used in their ritual equipment and decorations and because, being regarded as inviolable, they often served as depositories for public, and even private, funds. In this way, the Judean temple came to the attention of the Seleucids as a possible source of treasure.

But the conflict between Antiochus IV and the Jews went beyond Antiochus's coveting of the treasures of the Jerusalem Temple. Antiochus IV was eager to unify his subject peoples by imposing upon them the new international Hellenistic culture of the Middle East, consisting of the Greek language, fashion, religious practices, and educational curriculum, including philosophy and physical training. The Judeans themselves were divided in their attitude toward the Hellenic culture made available to them by Alexander's conquest. Many Judean aristocrats, including members of the priesthood—which, in the theocracy, formed the ruling class—adopted it in their personal lives. Some were eager to modernize the national religion and culture, even to the extent of reorganizing the Temple ritual along Greek lines and abrogating the laws of the Torah that seemed strange and primitive to Greek taste. Such Judean aristocrats had a common interest with Antiochus against those Judeans who resisted the changes.

A Judean priest named Joshua or Jason (it is typical of the period that upper-class Judeans had both Hebrew and Greek names, just as many American Jews today have both Hebrew and English names) bribed Antiochus IV to make him high priest, offering both money and the promise to Hellenize the state. The legitimate high priest fled, but was assassinated; his son fled to Egypt, where he established a temple at Leontopolis, and this temple remained an important site of Jewish sacrificial worship for centuries to come.

Jason introduced the gymnasium into Jerusalem. In this typically Greek institution, games in honor of pagan deities were conducted in the nude (the word "gymnasium" itself derives from the Greek word for nudity). The religious character of the games was profoundly offensive to Yahwist sensibilities. Furthermore, the nudity of the gymnasium called attention to the traditional practice of circumcision. To avoid appearing provincial or backward, many Judeans gave up the practice, or, at the cost of painful surgery, had their own circumcision undone. Thus, the introduction of the gymnasium was seen as the first step in turning Jerusalem into a Greek city.

Jason was succeeded as high priest by Menelaus, who outdid Jason's bribe by selling the Temple vessels and helping Antiochus IV plunder the Temple in 169, even stripping the gold leaf from its façade. By now, the populace was fiercely opposed to the Hellenizers and to Seleucid rule. To quell this opposition, Antiochus IV partially destroyed the city, killing some of the people and pulling down the city walls. He built a citadel, known as the Akra, near the Temple and there installed a Seleucid garrison, which became the main focus of Judean hatred for Greek rule for twenty-five years. He also embarked on a policy of enforced Hellenization. The Torah, instituted as the law of the Judeans by the Persian emperor Artaxerxes I, was now abrogated by the Seleucid king Antiochus IV. Copies of the text were destroyed, and typical Jewish religious institutions, such as circumcision, the Sabbath, and the festivals, were outlawed. Pagan altars were built throughout the land, and people were compelled to eat pork to demonstrate their obedience to the new law and cult. In December 167, the Temple itself was formally converted into a pagan shrine and a sacrifice of pork offered on the altar. Antiochus IV also demanded that he himself be worshiped as a god. The practice of king worship had been introduced by Alexander and was not considered odd among the pagan subjects of the Hellenistic rulers of the Near East, but to the monotheistic Judeans it seemed madness itself, and it was not long before they were lampooning his title, Epiphanes (meaning, "the God manifest"), by distorting it into Epimanes (meaning, "the madman").

Antiochus's measures mark the beginning of one of the dominant themes of Jewish history—the notion of Judaism as a persecuted religion. Until this point, whatever misfortunes had befallen the Jews had been purely political consequences of the fact that they were a small nation living in a territory that was contested by the great powers to the south and to the east. Their religion, so different from the religions of their pagan neighbors, was merely a feature of their national culture, and had never been attacked as such. By contrast, Antiochus's measures were directed not so much against the Judean state, which he already controlled at the beginning of his reign, but against the Judean religion and culture, which he—like many Judeans—was determined to harmonize with the religion and culture of the rest of his kingdom. The result of his efforts was to create the first Jewish martyrs and to incite a rebellion that contributed to the undermining of his control of the region.

The rebellion was begun by an obscure family of conservative country priests, headed by a certain Mattathias in the village of Modein. He and his five sons began a campaign of guerrilla warfare, harassing the Seleucid troops and destroying pagan altars. Mattathias was succeeded by his third son, Judah, known as Judah the Maccabee ("the hammer"). His successive victories attracted rebels in ever greater numbers until, in December 164 B.C.E., he was able to enter Jerusalem, besiege the garrison in the hated Akra, and restore the profaned Temple to its ancient rites and the worship of Yahweh. In commemoration of this event, the festival of Hanukkah was introduced and is still celebrated throughout the Jewish world. But Judea remained a Seleucid province.

In 162, Antiochus's successors formally abrogated his policies, restored the Torah as the law of Judea, and appointed a new high

priest named Alcimus. This step put an end to the party of Judean
Hellenizers and should have put an end to Judah's rebellion. But
Judah objected to the appointment of Alcimus, considering him religiously compromised by his behavior during the Antiochene persecutions. Accordingly, he marched again, this time not against pagans
but against Alcimus's Judean supporters, many of whom had once
fought at Judah's own side against Antiochus's troops. The new
Seleucid king, Demetrius I, sent a general named Nicanor against
Judah, but Judah conquered him and again entered Jerusalem in triumph in 161. This victory made Judah master of the country. Like
other heads of smaller states subject to the deteriorating Seleucid
kingdom, he turned to Rome for support, and the Senate confirmed
the freedom of the nation of the Judeans. For the first time since the
Babylonian conquest of the kingdom of Judah in 587 B.C.E., the
Judeans were recognized as an independent power. This moment,
however, also marks the fateful entrance of Rome into Judean affairs.

Judah was killed in 160 and was succeeded as head of the family
by his brother Jonathan, who, eight years later, was appointed high
priest by the pretender to the Seleucid kingdom in return for his military support against Demetrius I. This appointment changed the
character of Maccabean rule; their uprising had begun in opposition
to the Seleucids and the Hellenization of Judea's ruling class, but
Jonathan came to power by Seleucid appointment and behaved like
any other minor Hellenistic despot, fighting according to his own
political interests—now for one, now for another pretender to power
in the Seleucid kingdom. His brother Simeon, who succeeded him,
obtained freedom from tribute to the Seleucids and conquered the
Akra; in 140, Simeon was proclaimed high priest by a national assembly, taking the additional title of ethnarch and establishing a dynasty
that would last until 37 B.C.E. This dynasty was known as the
Hasmonean dynasty.

The Hasmonean state flourished during the long decline of the
Seleucids, as long as its existence was convenient for Rome. Its greatest

achievements were under the rule of John Hyrcanus (ruled 134–104 B.C.E.), Aristobulus I (ruled 104–103 B.C.E.), and Alexander Jannaeus (ruled 103–76 B.C.E.). Hyrcanus extended the realm northward over the Galilee, destroying the Samaritan temple, and southward over Idumea (roughly equivalent to the present Negev), forcibly Judaizing its population. Aristobulus took the title of king, in addition to the traditional title of high priest; and Jannaeus completed the conquest of the coastal strip and extended the realm to the Transjordan. In the process, the whole character of the ruling family changed, from priestly rebels dedicated to the overthrow of a Hellenized ruling class to a succession of Hellenized despots.

In reaction to these developments, some of the population withdrew from society at large and renounced the Temple cult, seeing it as desecrated by the behavior of the Hasmonean high priests. Religious communities of this type sprang up in several parts of the country; the best-known is that of the Essenes, a semimonastic organization in the wilderness by the Dead Sea that originated in the second century B.C.E. Most scholars agree that the Dead Sea Scrolls, which were discovered in 1947 and are still not completely published and deciphered, come from the library of this community.

Another group that was sometimes in opposition to the Hasmoneans was the Pharisees. They seem originally to have been nonpriests who were eager to observe a strict rule of ritual purity and religious probity, and who therefore sometimes came into conflict with the authorities. Their leadership did not claim a cultic function, like the priests, but rather expertise in religious law and lore based on a body of religious traditions supplementary to the Torah, which they called "the oral Torah." They laid stress on the obligation of each individual to observe religious practices of ever-increasing complexity and detail, rather than simply relying on the priesthood to accomplish the nation's religious duties vicariously by offering sacrifices on their behalf. By the first century C.E., their numbers included some priests and aristocrats as well. John Hyrcanus and Alexander Jannaeus sometimes resorted to

The Dead Sea Scrolls

Beginning in 1947, a large number of manuscripts and manuscript fragments were discovered in the wilderness west of the Dead Sea. Some of these fragments consist of parts of books of the Bible and other known ancient books; others contain fragments of works that were formerly unknown. Most of the fragments are written in Hebrew on parchment or papyrus, and a few are in Aramaic and Greek. Most of them appear to have been written before the war against Rome (66–70 C.E.). Because no other Hebrew manuscripts of such antiquity exist, and because of the hitherto unknown material they contain, the Dead Sea Scrolls have proved of immense importance for our understanding of Judaism in the late Second Temple period.

The greatest number of the Dead Sea Scrolls were found in a group of caves in Qumran, on the northwest corner of the Dead Sea. Though some scholars dissent, most agree that the Qumran scrolls were placed there by members of a religious community that inhabited the region in the century or two preceding the fall of Judea, either as an archive or for safekeeping during the war against Rome. Many believe that this community was an Essene settlement. The community's regulations and beliefs are expounded in such documents as *The Manual of Discipline*, the *Damascus Document*, the *Thanksgiving Psalms*, and the *War Scroll*. From these works, we learn that the members of this community considered the priestly leaders of Jerusalem as usurpers and that they reviled the Hasmonean kings of Judea, revering instead an earlier high-priest family, especially the mysterious, martyred Teacher of Righteousness. They claimed to have their own revelation, informing them of the true interpretation of the Torah, and their own religious calendar. They believed that they were living on the brink of a cataclysmic war between themselves, the Sons of Light, and their opponents, the Sons of Darkness, a war that would lead to the End of Days and their own restoration to power. If indeed they were Essenes, they lived in a community that was closed to outsiders, held property in common, and were so strict

continues

about the laws of purity that they regarded outsiders as impure; some did not marry. Some of their doctrines seem related to those of early Christianity.

The fragmentary nature of the Dead Sea Scrolls, compounded by problems of professional competition among the scholars involved, has made their publication and interpretation a very difficult and drawn-out task. The recent controversy over this delay has obscured the fact that a good number of the scrolls were published and translated into English and have been widely available since the 1950s. Most of the remaining scrolls have now been published in provisional form.

violence in order to suppress them, but Jannaeus's widow and successor, Queen Salome Alexandra (ruled 76–67 B.C.E.), seems to have been under their influence, and in her reign they may even have had considerable power. Some scholars believe that the teachings of the Pharisees were the core from which rabbinic Judaism, the dominant form of religious Judaism today, eventually developed.

We also hear of a group in this period known as the Sadducees, but little is known about them. They seem to have included mostly the cosmopolitan, aristocratic priesthood, the object of the opposition of the first-mentioned two groups.

The Romans had been players behind the scenes of Judean politics ever since the days of Judah the Maccabee; during the dynastic confusion that followed the death of Salome, they intervened directly. In the course of his great march throughout the Near East, Pompey occupied Jerusalem and turned Judea into a vassal of Rome, stripping Hyrcanus II (ruled 63–40 B.C.E.) of his title of king (though leaving him as high priest, the titular head of the nation) and reducing his territories. In 37 B.C.E., the Romans simply put an end to the Hasmonean dynasty and reorganized the province, establishing Herod (37–4 B.C.E.) as king of Judea.

Herod's rule marked an interesting turn in Judean history because he was not even of Judean descent. His ancestors were Idumeans, inhabitants of the territory just south of Judea that had been conquered and absorbed by John Hyrcanus; Herod's father had held governorships under the Hasmoneans and had actually been appointed regent of Judea by Julius Caesar. Herod could not serve as high priest because of his foreign origin and was never accepted as the legitimate ruler by many of the Pharisees, with whom he was in constant tension. He was completely loyal to Roman interests and devoted to Hellenistic culture, though he made gestures toward Judean culture and religion out of a desire to win the support of his subjects. He was able to rule because a succession of Roman generals and emperors found use for his qualities as a ruthless manipulator, brilliant diplomat, and large-scale personality.

Herod's career intersects with one of the determining events of Roman history, the conflict between Marc Antony and Octavian. Herod supported Antony. But Cleopatra, the Ptolemaic queen of Egypt and Antony's lover, intrigued to discredit him with Antony, hoping to wrest Palestine away from Herod and restore it to her own realm. When Octavian beat Antony and Cleopatra at Actium (31 B.C.E.) and became the emperor Augustus, Herod was therefore in a position to gain his trust despite his former allegiance to Augustus's rival, and managed to convince him of his potential usefulness. As the emperor Augustus (27 B.C.E. to 14 C.E.), Octavian allowed him to become the most powerful of the petty Roman rulers of the East. Herod's territories became nearly as extensive as had been those of John Hyrcanus and Jannaeus, including many non-Jewish populations. He took a free hand in reorganizing the administration of the state to his own advantage, reducing the power of the Sanhedrin (the highest Judean deliberative body), limiting the terms of office of the high priests, and hiring a mercenary army of foreigners who were personally loyal to him.

Herod and the kingdom both prospered. Herod introduced measures to better the living conditions of the peasantry, expanding irrigation and suppressing banditry. As a sophisticated and cosmopolitan ruler, he welcomed Greek writers and scholars into Judea. He enhanced the state by means of impressive building projects, constructing aqueducts, theaters, and other public buildings. He built new cities—notably, Sebaste on the site of ancient Samaria and Caesarea on the Mediterranean; new fortresses, including the Antonia in Jerusalem, Herodion just south of Jerusalem, and Masada, on a cliff overlooking the Dead Sea; and a luxurious palace for himself. His most famous project was the rebuilding of the Temple, replacing the modest structure, now over four centuries old, with a magnificent cultic complex on a greatly expanded site. Even Herod's detractors were impressed with this act of homage to the national religion, and indeed, Herod may have undertaken this project partly for the sake of winning the loyalty of his conservative Jewish subjects. The present-day Wailing Wall in Jerusalem (known also as the Western Wall) is a remnant of the retaining wall of Herod's temple.

But all this achievement came at a cost. Pathologically mistrustful, Herod killed any members of the Hasmonean family who could possibly threaten his claim to power, including his wife, Mariamne, and three of his own sons—and in some of these cases, his suspicions were completely justified. But he also suffered from guilt and depression over some of his more vicious actions. His court was a decadent center of cruelty, intrigue, and treachery. Yet Herod was one of the most accomplished and colorful characters in all of Jewish history, and fully deserves his customary title, Herod the Great.

This title is also necessary to distinguish him from the other members of his family who bore the name Herod and who ruled parts of his kingdom when it was divided by the Romans after his death. One of these, Herod Antipas, also known as Herod the Tetrarch, ruled the Galilee and part of the Transjordan (4 B.C.E. to 39 C.E.); he is the Herod who killed John the Baptist, supposedly at the request of his wife, Herodias, and his stepdaughter, Salome.

Relations between Judea and the Roman Empire now entered into the long deterioration that would lead to the explosion of the Jewish revolt in 66 C.E. The first step was the reorganization of Judea, in 6 C.E., as a Roman province under a series of foreign-born governors, known as procurators. Most of these were corrupt incompetents who exacerbated the tensions between the Jewish population and the Roman administration. The best-known was Pontius Pilate, during whose procuratorship (26–36 C.E.) the execution of Jesus took place. As fateful as this event was for the future history of the world, not to mention for later Jewish history, it was, when it happened, only one of many incidents reflecting the brutal Roman administration of Judea during this period; Pilate's decision to put the Roman imperial eagle on the legion's standards caused greater unrest. Resentment accumulated over many years against the Roman provincial administration, heavy taxation, and the ubiquitous presence of hostile Roman troops with their pagan ritual observances. This resentment nearly boiled over into rebellion when the emperor Caligula (37–41 C.E.) demanded that he be worshiped as a deity and ordered the erection of his statue, in gold, in the Temple of Jerusalem for this purpose. Only the death of the mad emperor stemmed the unrest.

Conditions improved briefly under Caligula's successor, Claudius, who made Herod Agrippa, a grandson of Herod the Great, ruler of the northern part of the country and then king of Judea (41–44 C.E.). Herod Agrippa was personally close to the emperor, who granted him some flexibility in managing the troublesome state; at the same time, he was more sympathetic to the Judean way of life and religion than Herod had been, and therefore he was more trusted by his subjects. The Pharisees considered him their ally, but he was disliked by his non-Jewish subjects, especially by the still-tiny band of Jesus' followers.

But Judea proper continued to be governed by a succession of procurators who progressively discredited Roman rule, and tensions mounted. *Sicarii* ("dagger-men") appeared in the streets of cities, knifing persons suspected of collaborating with Roman rule. Jews clashed with Greeks in Caesarea (the procuratorial seat), and conflicts between citizens and soldiers were constant. When Florus, the last procurator, attempted to raise a large sum of money by appropriating some of the Temple's treasures, the revolt that had been brewing could no longer be contained. In 66 C.E., the priests stopped offering the sacrifice on behalf of Rome and a popular uprising occurred, which quickly turned into the conflict known to Roman history as the Jewish War.

The war that ensued lasted four years, partly because the Romans were not prepared for it and partly because the Roman general Vespasian left the scene on the death of the emperor Nero in 68 C.E. in order to contend for the succession. During the lull, the Jewish factions in Judea battled among themselves, contributing to the eventual debacle. Particularly troublesome were the Zealots, violent revolutionaries who attacked the aristocracy and other groups that they considered insufficiently committed to the war. Once secure as emperor, in 69 C.E., Vespasian sent his son Titus to complete the conquest of Judea. When Jerusalem fell in 70, the troops destroyed Herod's temple. Some fortresses held out a few years longer; the *Sicarii*, besieged in Masada, committed suicide in 73 or 74, rather than fall into the hands of the Romans.

Vespasian celebrated the fall of Jerusalem, his first great military victory as emperor, as a major triumph. He issued a commemorative coin and had the Judean captives and ritual objects taken from the Temple paraded through the streets as trophies of war. A victory arch was erected in the Forum of Rome to commemorate the occasion; its friezes depict the seven-branched candelabrum from the Temple. The arch can still be visited among the Forum's ruins.

The Hellenized Jews of Egypt continued to multiply and prosper after the Roman conquest of Egypt (30 B.C.E.); they were recognized as an autonomous community under the authority of a leader known as the ethnarch, later replaced by a council of elders. But their status was less favorable than it had been under the Ptolemids, for the Romans did not recognize them as Hellenes, classifying them instead with the Egyptian subject population. The Romans saw as presumptuous the demand of the Egyptian Jews to be recognized as an autonomous communal organization and at the same time to enjoy the full rights of citizenship.

Accordingly, the position of the Egyptian Jews deteriorated under Roman rule. In 38 C.E., Flaccus, the Roman governor of Egypt, incited the mobs to riot against them. The riots subsided when Flaccus was removed and executed (for other reasons) by the emperor Caligula, but the Jews did not get satisfaction until after Caligula's assassination (41 C.E.), by means of a riot of their own. They rioted again in 66, and one final time, in 115–17, as part of a Jewish uprising that occurred simultaneously in Cyrene (in present-day Libya) and Cyprus during the reign of Trajan. This rebellion led to the violent suppression of the Jewish community of Alexandria and the destruction of their famous synagogue. The community went into a decline that lasted until well after the Muslim conquests.

The Jewish community of Babylonia, however, flourished under the Parthian Empire, which had taken control of Iran and Mesopotamia from the Seleucids in the mid-second century B.C.E. After the Romans took over Palestine, and as Roman rule there became ever more oppressive, the eastern Jews came to be more and more confirmed in their loyalty to Parthia, Rome's great rival and enemy in this period. The Parthians responded by granting them favorable treatment, and a measure of autonomy, like the Persians before them. Parthian Jewry prospered, gradually shifting from agriculture to urban mercantile life.

Jewish self-government in Parthia may already have been administered by an official known as an exilarch, though this office is much better known from later times. According to tradition, it was always

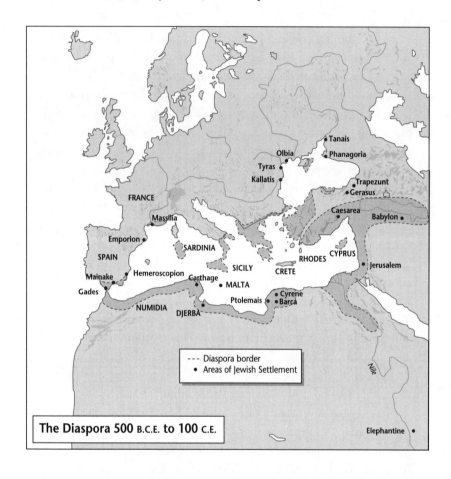

The Diaspora 500 B.C.E. to 100 C.E.

held by a descendant of the Judean dynasty that had begun with David. It will be remembered that Judean king Jehoiachin (exiled in 597 B.C.E.) had ended his days in Babylonia, where he had been first imprisoned, then released and accorded royal honors. The Diaspora community of Babylonia took comfort and pride in being governed by a scion of the house of David. The office was to survive Parthian, Sassanid, and several centuries of Islamic rule, disappearing only in the eleventh century C.E.

By 70 C.E., the Jews were no longer simply the inhabitants of a small state in the Middle East. Even in the early sixth century B.C.E., there were important Diaspora communities in Babylonia and Egypt, as we have seen, and by 70 C.E., there were important Jewish communities throughout the Middle East, as well as in the city of Rome and in the western Roman provinces, including Spain. Jews continued to see themselves as descendants of the inhabitants of the ancient Judean kingdom, and they continued to be identified by the Romans as Judeans. From all over the world, they sent the annual Temple tax of half a shekel to Jerusalem, and when the Jews of Judea revolted, they had to suffer anti-Judean riots in reprisal. Thus, in many respects, Palestine remained the center of Jewish identity, but at the same time, Judaism was well on the way to redefining itself as a religion that could be carried anywhere in the world.

A seven-branched menorah with other temple objects, found in late Roman Beth Sheean. Photo © Zev Radovan. Used by permission.

THREE

Roman Palestine and Sassanid Babylonia

(70 C.E. to 632)

When the Romans destroyed the Temple in 70 C.E., they did not devastate Judea or expel the Jews from Jerusalem, but the measures they took were sufficiently harsh. Many Jews were captured, others fled the country, and large numbers were impoverished through the confiscation of their lands. The territory officially became a Roman province. A punitive tax was imposed on the Judeans, the *fiscus Judaicus*, consisting of two drachmas that had to be paid annually to the temple of Jupiter Capitolinus in Rome in lieu of the half-shekel annual contribution formerly given to the Temple. But there was no mass expulsion as there had been in 587 B.C.E., and it was mostly the aristocracy that suffered. Daily life went on as before.

The national religion, on the other hand, was deeply affected and permanently changed by the destruction. The loss of Judea's cultic center entailed the ruin of the priesthood, which, besides being Judea's ruling class, had also been its religious leadership. The collapse of the priesthood provided the opening for a new popular religious leadership, the nonpriestly specialists in religious traditions and laws described in chapter 2, who were now called "rabbis" (the word

TIMELINE

JEWISH HISTORY		GENERAL HISTORY
Jewish revolt in Egypt	115–117	
	117–138	Hadrian emperor
Bar Kokhba revolt	132–135	
Hadrianic persecutions	135–138	
Judah the Patriarch compiles the Mishnah	c. 200	
Jews become Roman citizens	212	
Rav arrives in Babylonia	219	
	226	Beginning of Sassanid dynasty in Persia
	306–337	Constantine I
	313	Edict of Milan extends religious toleration to Christianity
	354–430	Saint Augustine
	360–363	Julian the Apostate attempts to reverse Christianization of Roman Empire
Palestinian Talmud completed	c. 380	
Patriarchate abolished	429	
	476	End of western Roman empire
Babylonian Talmud completed	c. 499	
Emperor Justinian interferes in Jewish worship	553	
	590–604	Pope Gregory I
Persians briefly conquer Palestine	614–617	

"rabbi" signifies "master" or "teacher"). It was they who now took charge of the reorganization of the nation's religious life.

Legend accounts for the transfer of religious leadership from the priesthood to the rabbis. One of the leading rabbis, Johanan ben Zakkai, had opposed the war against Rome. When Jerusalem was besieged by the Romans, he succeeded in escaping the city by letting it be understood that he was dead and then having his disciples carry him out in a coffin (the Romans courteously permitted the besieged to bury their dead outside the city). He then came before Vespasian, who, impressed with his audacity, wisdom, and opposition to the war, granted him the right to establish a school in Jamnia (*Yavne* in Hebrew). The rabbi's priorities were clear: The city, the Temple cult, and political sovereignty were all dispensable. What had to be guaranteed was the religious tradition embodied in the Torah and in the ever-proliferating body of religious law. Johanan ben Zakkai and his colleagues thus took an important step in reorganizing Judaism into rabbinic Judaism, the form of the religion most widespread until the present. Rabbinic Judaism centers on the constant study of the Torah and the oral traditions associated with it and involves the meticulous observance of religious regulations, which are understood as constituting a legal system. By placing the study of the Torah at the center of Jewish religious life, the rabbis incidentally laid the foundation for the preoccupation of later Jewish culture with intellectual activities of all kinds.

The synagogue also emerged at this time as a characteristic institution of Jewish life. The word "synagogue" comes from Greek and means "assembly"; as places of assembly, synagogues existed everywhere, and they may have been used for some ritual purposes, including prayer (especially outside of Palestine), even before the destruction of the Temple. But after the destruction, they became the main public religious institution, as communal prayer services came to be held regularly and as the reading and explication of the Torah came more and more to be thought of as an important public religious function. By decentralizing public worship, the destruction of the Temple thus contributed to the rabbis' program of putting the responsibility for religious life in the hands of each individual. The destruction of the central religious institution was a traumatic event, but recovery was possible because a basis for religious continuity was found.

The Judeans were not affected by the Diaspora Jewish uprisings of 115–17 mentioned in chapter 2, but tensions caused by the harshness of the Roman occupation and the impoverishment of the peasantry mounted until they boiled over in a second major Judean war. The immediate cause was the plan of Emperor Hadrian (ruled 117–38) to rebuild Jerusalem, as he had rebuilt temples and cities all over the empire (including temples in Tiberias and Sepphoris); it was to become a Roman city dedicated to Jupiter, under the name of Aelia Capitolina. Such desecration of the ancient capital was intolerable to the Jewish population.

This revolt, which broke out in 132, was much better organized than the war of 66–70 had been, and unlike the previous war, it was supported even by rabbis, such as the revered Akiba. The leader of the revolt was Simon bar Kosiba, who may well have been viewed as the messiah, for he styled himself "Prince of Israel" and issued coins bearing legends such as YEAR ONE OF THE REDEMPTION OF ISRAEL. He was popularly known as Bar Kokhba, meaning "son of the star" (referring to the traditional messianic interpretation of a phrase in the Torah), and he behaved like an ancient Judean king and military leader. But Bar Kokhba's undoubtedly commanding personality, his popularity, and the support of famous rabbis were not enough to accord him a victory. He was killed in 135, and the remnants of his troops were wiped out after being besieged in Bethar and Ein Gedi.

The Romans, who had reacted to the first revolt with restraint, now brought down the full weight of their revenge upon the hapless province. They deported the entire Jewish population of Judea and replaced them with non-Jews. Many were sent to the Galilee, in the north, but others were sold as slaves; the number of Judean captives exported from Judea for this purpose was said to have been so great as to depress the price of a slave to that of a horse. Jerusalem was definitively turned into a pagan city, with a statue of Hadrian and perhaps a temple to Jupiter Capitolinus in its center; Jews were prohibited from even entering it. Circumcision was outlawed, as were, according to tradition, the teaching of the Torah in public and the ordination of rabbis. The name of the province was changed from Judea to Syria-Palestina, replacing the name derived from the ancestral tribe of Judah with one derived from that of Judah's ancient enemies, the Philistines, who had long since vanished. Thus, everything possible was done to efface the Judean nation and its religion from the region.

The result of these measures was disaster. Many fled the region, swelling the Jewish populations of Syria, Asia Minor, and Rome (where their catacombs, or underground burial places, can still be visited) and even increasing the small Jewish populations of Spain, Gaul, and the Rhineland; others abandoned Roman territory altogether and joined the untroubled Jewish community of Parthian Babylonia. The prohibition of rabbinical activities resulted in a wave of martyrdom, when rabbis such as Akiba went on teaching anyway and were caught, imprisoned, and gruesomely executed; Jewish tradition speaks of the Ten Martyrs of the Hadrianic period, which it regards as one of Judaism's darkest times. In Jewish lore, Hadrian is a figure of nearly satanic evil, on a par with Antiochus IV and Titus.

With the province pacified, the religious restrictions were gradually relaxed under Hadrian's successors, and a kind of compromise emerged between Rome and the Jews of Palestine in the course of the second century. The Jews were expected to keep their extremists under control and to prevent outbreaks of violence. In turn, their religion was granted the status of a "permitted religion," and they were exempted from emperor worship and other civic duties involving pagan observances. The prohibition on circumcision was relaxed by later emperors, but only for Jews; it remained prohibited for non-Jews, and therefore amounted to a prohibition against conversion to Judaism. (Conversion was explicitly outlawed later in the century; it was then that Judaism acquired what would later come to appear a traditional reluctance to acquire converts.) The burden of the two-drachma Jewish tax was significantly reduced through the effects of inflation. Most important, the Romans permitted Jews to create institutions of self-government.

Soon after the failure of the Bar Kokhba revolt, a rabbinic assembly was convened in Galilee, now the center of Jewish life in Palestine, and here a central deliberative and legislative authority was established. This body was named "Sanhedrin," like the similar body that had existed before the destruction of the Temple, and was placed under the leadership of an official called the patriarch, also continuing a title that had existed before the destruction. The patriarch was a descendant of Hillel, an influential figure a century before the destruction of the Temple, who, like the Babylonian exilarch, was reputed to be descended from King David. Wealthy and distinguished descendants of Hillel had exercised authority in the generation before the destruction of the Temple and later at the academy in Jamnia. In the course of the second century, the patriarchate won the recognition of the Jews and then of the Romans as the Jews' central political institution. The patriarchs and their administrative bodies developed legislation, raised taxes, appointed judges and other communal officials, and regulated religious practice—especially the religious calendar. As these institutions became rooted, the Romans gradually accorded the Jews a greater measure of autonomy, and the rabbis gradually came to cooperate with the hated Roman authorities. In time, the office of patriarch acquired great prestige, so that in the fourth century, patriarchs were granted senatorial rank and collected taxes from Jews all over the empire.

For the first time, a body of rabbis had acquired government recognition as the central organization of Jewish life; this development was an important step toward making rabbinic Judaism the dominant form of the Jewish religion for all time. A landmark in this process was reached toward the end of the second century, when Rabbi Judah the Patriarch composed and promulgated the Mishnah, a book that quickly became and still remains the core textbook of rabbinic Judaism. The Mishnah is a collection of laws covering every field in which the rabbis had legal competence in that period—not only ritual law, but also commercial transactions, property, inheritance, legal procedure, and torts—as well as areas that had lapsed, such as the laws pertaining to the Temple. Ever since its composition, the Mishnah has served as the fundamental text and organizing principle of rabbinic scholarship, though rabbinic jurisdiction over most of these areas has lapsed in modern times.

The Jews and the Romans had worked out a modus vivendi. The Jews of Palestine were now treated much like the other small nations that formed part of the great empire, except for being freed from pagan observances, and, like the other subject nations, they were granted Roman citizenship by Emperor Caracalla in 212. Whatever troubles the Jews of Palestine endured in the third century were less the result of the old hostility between Judea and Rome than of the general economic and political weakness of the empire during this period. Palestine was impoverished, and its population continued to decline.

Babylonian Jews, on the other hand, did fairly well during this period. They suffered some persecution and loss of autonomy when the culturally diverse and politically decentralized Parthian Empire was replaced by the Sassanid Empire in 226; the new regime began by instituting measures designed to propagate Zoroastrianism and to suppress the cultural and religious diversity of its subject peoples. For a time, the Jews imagined that even Roman rule might be preferable to that of the Persians. But by the time of Shapur I (241–72), the religious measures were relaxed, and the original relationships were restored: The Persian rulers permitted the Jews considerable autonomy under their exilarch, and the Jews could be counted on to support the Sassanids against Rome, by now their traditional enemy. Though the Babylonian Jews had never been suppressed by Roman legions, they retained their loyalty to the Jews of Judea and a strong sense of their historical identity.

Until the beginning of the third century, the Jews of Babylonia continued to look to the rabbis of Palestine for religious guidance, and the patriarch in Palestine was regarded as the final religious authority, even in the areas controlled by the exilarch. One way in which the patriarch's authority was exercised was through his control of the religious calendar, which was determined for each year annually and announced to the Diaspora communities. The status of the Babylonian schools was enhanced when many Palestinian scholars fled

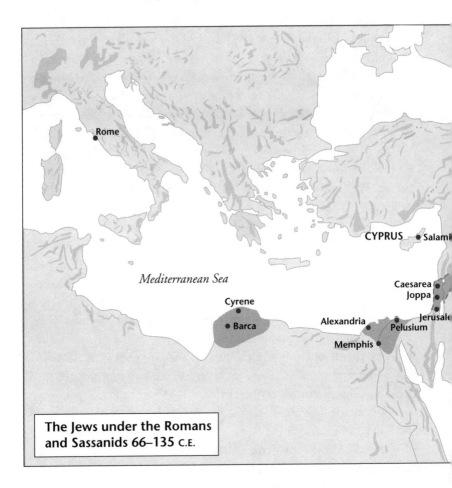

CYPRUS • Salami

Mediterranean Sea

Caesarea
Joppa

Cyrene

Alexandria   Jerusale
• Barca   Pelusium

Memphis •

**The Jews under the Romans
and Sassanids 66–135 c.e.**

Palestine in the time of the Hadrianic persecutions, but Babylonia
came into its own as a center of religious studies only as a result of
the activities of two third-century rabbis: Samuel, a Babylonian
scholar, a wealthy man who had good connections with Emperor
Shapur I; and Rav, a Palestinian rabbi and disciple of Rabbi Judah
the Patriarch, who arrived in Babylonian in 219. It was Rav who introduced the Babylonian Jews to the Mishnah. Rav established his academy at Sura; Samuel established one at Nehardea, but when that town

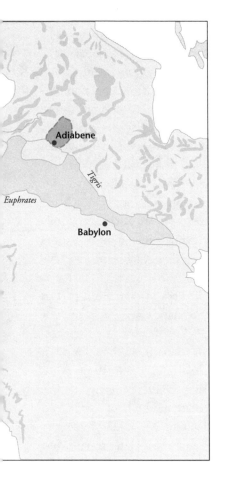

was destroyed, the school relocated to Pumbeditha, and has been known ever since by that name. These schools soon became important rivals to the declining Palestinian schools and to each other, and would survive until the eleventh century as major centers of Jewish intellectual and religious activity.

The equilibrium that had been achieved between the Jews and the Roman Empire during the third century lasted until the reign of Constantine I (306–37), who altered the course of Western history and with it the course of Jewish history by personally adopting Christianity and starting the process that made it the religion of the Roman Empire. As a Jewish sect—that is, as a religious movement within Judaism and directed at Jews—early Christianity had had only modest success, given the implacable hostility to it of the rabbis and given the rabbis' authority to regulate Jewish affairs under the Roman government. But as a proselytizing movement aimed at pagans in Roman Palestine, Syria, Asia Minor, and elsewhere in the empire, Christianity had great success.

In the process of adapting itself so as to appeal to non-Judean pagans, Christianity underwent a radical change. Judaism remained the religion of a particular nation with a particular history that we have been tracing until this point (monarchy, Babylonian exile, restoration, Roman occupation, destruction) and a particular set of national aspirations (restoration of the monarchy and status as an independent nation). Christianity created a supranational community focused on a common faith rather than on a common history and on a legislated way of life. Thus, it transformed the Jewish idea of national restoration by a king into a conception of individual redemption through a personal savior, and it discarded nearly all the rituals and practices that had come to be the most obvious distinguishing features of Judaism. Yet Christianity retained the exclusivity of Jewish monotheism, so puzzling to enlightened pagans, rejecting the legitimacy of all other religions—including that of its parent in monotheism, Judaism. The fascinating story of how Christianity managed, in the course of three centuries, to emerge as the religion of the greatest empire of Western history is not part of Jewish history, but that outcome was to shape Jewish history until our own time.

The roots of future Jewish-Christian relations are to be found in the period between the rise of Christianity and the age of Constantine. The Roman Empire, during the first century C.E., was full of people who no longer believed in the gods of Greek and Roman paganism and who sought enlightenment among the exotic religions of the East. Such people did not cease being pagans, but they incorporated into their religious lives some of the gods and rituals associated, for example, with the Persian deity Mithra, the Egyptian Isis, or the Phrygian Cybele. Likewise, Judaism, in both its traditional and its Christian varieties, found adherents among some members of the upper class in the eastern provinces and even in Rome itself. Few Romans went so far as to become full-fledged converts to Judaism, with its painful initiatory rite of circumcision and its seemingly arbitrary prohibitions, but many adopted Jewish practices such as lighting lamps in honor of the Sabbath, attending the synagogue, and observing some of the Jewish festivals, as they might observe those of other religions as well. Such people, who came to be known as "God fearers," were sometimes mocked by Roman sophisticates. But Judaism had some successes as a proselytizing religion. The most notable case was that of the little kingdom of Adiabene, in upper Mesopotamia, whose ruler from 36 to 60 C.E. was a convert to Judaism and a great donor to the Jerusalem Temple.

Already under the apostle Paul (d. 62 C.E.), Christianity had broken down the great barrier to conversion posed by the Jewish rituals by simply declaring them abrogated, giving Christianity an advantage in its competition with traditional Judaism for converts. Paul justified the abrogation of the rituals with the claim that the Jews of Palestine and the Diaspora were not the authentic heirs to the religion of Israel. Rather, he claimed, "true Israel" was the spiritual community of the adherents of Jesus. In this way, Paul appropriated the authority that Judaism possessed by virtue of its antiquity, while undoing its association with a particular national history and way of life. "True Israel" was not the provincial people of Judea with their particularistic rituals and hopeless national aspirations, but rather the international community of Christians.

Christianity used two polemical techniques in support of its claims. One was the Christological interpretation of Scripture, the use of the Hebrew Bible to demonstrate the authenticity of Christian doctrine. This approach was designed particularly for arguing with Jews, but it could be useful in appealing to pagans who were already attracted to Judaism. The other approach was the denunciation of Judaism, making use of and expanding an already existing body of anti-Jewish ideas that had originated in Hellenistic times and that had been further developed by pagan Romans.

While some aspects of Judaism were widely admired in antiquity, as we have seen, others had aroused hostility. Enlightened pagans could not understand the Jews' inability to share their own respect for other peoples' gods and rites; to pagans, who accepted all gods, the Jews, who denied all gods but their own, seemed like blasphemers

Talmud, Midrash, and Piyyut

The Talmud, Midrash, and Piyyut were the chief literary creations of the Jewish intellectual centers of Palestine and Babylonia in Byzantine and Sassanid times.

The Talmud has been the main object of study and devotion by traditional Jews since the Middle Ages. It is a huge compilation of legal argumentation, folklore, anecdotes, and proverbs. In premodern times, when rabbis served as judges not only in matters of ritual but also in all areas of business and social organization, the Talmud's legal discussions were the basis on which they made legal decisions. To this day, the Talmud is the main subject of rabbinical training in Orthodox seminaries and is widely studied as a ritual act of devotion to God's word by strictly traditional Jews.

The Talmud is organized as a commentary on the Mishnah, the legal code composed by Rabbi Judah the Patriarch around 200 C.E. There are actually two Talmuds—the Palestinian Talmud, compiled around 380 C.E. in Tiberias, and the Babylonian Talmud, compiled around 499 C.E. in what is now Iraq. The Babylonian Talmud became authoritative in the course of the Middle Ages and is much more widely known today. It is written in Aramaic, the language used by the people of Iraq before the Muslim conquests, in a concise and allusive style that takes years of study to master. The ability to "learn a page of Talmud" is a skill that confers prestige on a layperson in the traditional Jewish community. In order to facilitate study of this all-important work, commentaries were composed in the Middle Ages, of which the most famous is that of R. Solomon b. Isaac, known as Rashi (1040–1105), who lived in Troyes (present-day France). In modern editions of the Talmud, this commentary is always printed in a narrow column parallel to the text of the Talmud itself, and the student works through the page with one finger pointing to the text and another finger of the same hand pointing to the commentary. Other commentaries composed in medieval and modern times accompany the printed editions.

Midrash (plural, *midrashim*) was originally a manner of formulating religious ideas by quoting a passage from the Bible and developing it either by expounding its contents or by extending it in a new and unexpected direction. As a technique, midrash was used to develop religious ideas and to find the solution to problems of religious law. But midrash also became the name of a literary genre, since particular midrashim were compiled into books. These were sometimes arranged in the order of the biblical verses they treated, and volumes of midrash were produced for the books of the Torah and other books of the Bible. Much of the legal discussion in the Talmud consists of examining midrashim that are the source of particular laws to determine which midrash is authoritative and under what circumstances. Other midrashim deal with religious ideas and attitudes, and these often serve as the basis of sermons.

Piyyut (plural, *piyyutim*) is the poetry that was written for use in the synagogue service. In many ancient congregations, it was customary to use poetic versions of the prayers instead of the standard prose versions that developed into the modern traditional prayer book. The cantor was expected not just to sing the service, but to compose a different poetic version of the service for every Sabbath and festival, so that the congregation would not hear exactly the same service twice. Later, when the text of the prayer book became fixed, piyyutim were recited alongside the standard prayers. The composition of piyyutim was the most important artistic activity of the Jews throughout the Middle Ages (in some Middle Eastern communities, until modern times). Some piyyutim are still recited in synagogues today, though the composition of piyyutim has ceased.

and atheists! Furthermore, the Jews' religious objections to emperor worship, a corollary of their strict monotheism, made them suspect of disloyalty to the state, especially given the Judeans' rebellious history. There was a more clearly political reason as well. In Greek cities, Jews liked to live among themselves and to function as much as possible as a separate corporate entity; at the same time, they wanted the rights of citizenship. We have seen that this contradiction in their aspirations was one of the issues behind the hostility of the Alexandrian governor Flaccus and the riots of 38 C.E., discussed in chapter 2. Finally, there was an element of pure propaganda. Antiochus IV attempted to justify his attack on the Temple in the second century B.C.E. by attacking Judaism as a religion; an Alexandrian writer named Apion wrote a more elaborate anti-Jewish propaganda piece to justify the events of 38 C.E.; and the famous and influential Roman historian Tacitus continued the tradition of disparaging Judaism in his discussion of the destruction of the Temple in 70 C.E.. Thus, by the second century, there was already in existence a body of anti-Jewish literature that could be exploited by Christian leaders and amplified with the far more emotional and specifically Christian charge of deicide.

Until the early fourth century, Christianity had more problems with Rome than had the Jews. The Jews' ambitions to statehood had been completely crushed; their numbers in their homeland had been greatly reduced, and they simply no longer posed a threat to the Roman Empire. But Christianity was perceived as a threat, and it was actively persecuted by Rome for over two centuries. Persecution lent Christianity rage, and the moment it acquired power as the official religion of the Roman Empire, it vented this rage on the parent religion. Accordingly, the situation of the Jews in Palestine deteriorated drastically.

In the course of the fourth century, the Roman Empire split into an eastern empire, centered on Byzantium (Constantinople), and a western empire, centered on Rome. The western empire sputtered on, sometimes united with the eastern empire, sometimes separate, and ever more subject to barbarian invasions until it finally collapsed and fragmented in the course of the fifth century; Romulus Augustulus, the last Roman emperor of the West, was deposed in 476. Meanwhile, Palestine was controlled by the Greek-speaking Christian Byzantine Empire.

During the period of Byzantine rule over Palestine, from the fourth to the seventh centuries, laws were gradually introduced limiting the Jews' religious and commercial activities. Marriages between Jews and Christians were forbidden, and Jews were barred from holding public office and from building new synagogues. The patriarch Hillel II was stripped of his authority to declare the dates of the festivals to the Diaspora. (He responded, as he had to, by circulating the principles by which the religious calendar was determined, freeing the Diaspora communities from an important sphere of Palestinian control.) A serious economic blow was dealt the Jews when they were prohibited from owning Christian slaves. As repugnant as slavery is to us today, in the Roman Empire it was the basis of agriculture; the prohibition made it impossible for Jews to compete with Christian slaveholders, effectively excluding them from anything but subsistence farming. Although this restriction could have had direct effect only on a few large-scale landholders, it was a first step in the alienation of the Jews from the land, a process that ended with their becoming a nearly completely urban people in the Middle Ages.

Some leaders of the Church argued in favor of outlawing Judaism altogether and giving the Jews the same choice between conversion and death that the Christians themselves had been given by the Romans in the third century. In Spain, this approach actually became policy, when the Visigothic king Sisebut (ruled 612–21) made the Jews choose between conversion, death, and exile. But the attitude toward the Jews that became authoritative for many centuries to come, as formulated by Saint Augustine (354–430) and confirmed as Church policy by Pope Gregory I (ruled 590–604), was a milder, though sufficiently intolerant one: For their obstinacy in rejecting Jesus as their messiah, the Jews fully deserved to be crushed and humiliated. Yet they should not be completely destroyed; instead, they should be permitted to survive in a state of humiliating poverty and social exclusion so that they might be punished for their stubborn refusal to acknowledge the message of their own Scriptures (now called the

"Old" Testament by Christians, who believed that the Jewish Scripture encoded a message authenticating the new religion) and might serve as an everlasting testimony to the superiority of Christianity and the fate of the nonbeliever. To validate his recommendation for the treatment of the Jews, Augustine quoted Scripture: "Do not destroy them, lest my people forget," words originally spoken by an ancient king of Judah as he cursed the enemies of his people, now applied by Augustine to the Jews themselves. Augustine's principle was harsh, but it was upheld repeatedly during the Middle Ages by the popes, and it sometimes served the Jews as a frail theological lifeline.

There were two moments in the fourth century when it seemed as if the Jews might get some relief from Byzantine oppression. When the Persian emperor Shapur II threatened the Roman Empire in Mesopotamia, some Palestinian Jews sought to take advantage of the situation by rebelling in 351, under the leadership of a certain Patricius, but the rebellion was quickly suppressed. Better-founded hopes were stirred under the reign of Emperor Julian (known as Julian the Apostate, ruled 360–63), because he undertook to reverse the Christianization of the empire and reinstate an enlightened paganism as the official religion. Not only did Julian rescind the anti-Jewish legislation of the preceding reigns, but he promised to rebuild the Temple and resettle the Jews in Jerusalem. His early death, however, prevented any of these plans from being put into effect, and his successors, who were all Christians, went even further than his predecessors in restricting the Jews' livelihoods, reducing their status, and pressuring them to become Christians. The patriarchate, the last vestige of Jewish autonomy, was abolished in 429, around the time that Christians became the majority of the population of Palestine. In the reign of Justinian I (527–65), Roman control finally intruded on the inner life of the Jews, for in addition to tightening the existing anti-Jewish social legislation, Justinian intervened in a dispute on a liturgical practice. He used the opportunity to make certain stipulations about the conduct of synagogue services, even, apparently, prohibiting the rabbinic interpretation of Scripture from being part of the service.

But the Palestinian rabbinical academies continued their activities and reached an important landmark with the compilation, in the fourth century, of the Palestinian Talmud (sometimes incorrectly called the "Jerusalem Talmud"). This work is a massive compendium of rabbinic discussion and commentary on the Mishnah, including many ancient legal and religious traditions. This period also saw the compilation of midrash, collections of sermons in abbreviated form and homiletical interpretations of Scripture. Another area of intense literary activity in this period was the composition of liturgical poetry, which remained the main Jewish artistic activity throughout the Middle Ages. Babylonian rabbis were also active, for in the fifth century they composed the collective work known as the Babylonian Talmud. Like the Palestinian Talmud, it is a collection of rabbinic lore surrounding the Mishnah; unlike the Palestinian Talmud, it would, in the course of the Middle Ages, become the authoritative sourcebook of rabbinic Judaism for Jews worldwide. It is still the chief focus of rabbinic training and devotional study for Orthodox Jews. (How the Babylonian Talmud achieved this degree of authority will be discussed in chapter 4.) Thus, despite the pressures under which the Jews of Byzantine Palestine lived, they did produce some literary works that, together with the Babylonian Talmud, constitute the basic library of rabbinic Judaism up to our own time.

The closest the Jews of Palestine came to release from the dark period of Byzantine domination occurred near the end of that period, during the final war in the centuries-old conflict between Rome and Persia. The Persian king Chosroes II began his attack on the eastern provinces of Rome in 603, and by 614 was able to conquer Jerusalem, thanks partly to the cooperation of the Jews, who had long looked to Persia as their potential liberator. Chosroes killed and deported large numbers of Christians, then handed the city over to the Jews, who now, nearly 300 years after officially being prohibited from setting

Greek and Roman Anti-Semitism

The conquests of Alexander the Great carried the Greek language and literature to large parts of Asia. Greek expansion exposed Greek scholars and writers to new—and to them, exotic—Asian cultures, including that of the Jews. Early Hellenistic writers admiringly described the Jews as a nation of philosophers, like the Brahmins of India, probably because the Jews' dietary restrictions reminded them of Pythagorean asceticism and because the laws of the Torah struck them as an attempt to create a political and religious utopia. Later, a Roman writer praised the Jews for worshiping Yahweh, who he thought was the same as the Roman Jupiter, and for prohibiting images. Many first- and second-century Romans were attracted to Judaism, and some (including even a cousin of the emperor Domitian) went so far as to convert. But even the Greek ethnographers mention with distaste such Jewish practices as circumcision and ridicule their refusal to eat pork.

Slanders against the Jews arose among political propagandists. As early as 200 B.C.E., a pro-Idumean (and therefore, anti-Judean) Greek writer informs us that the Jews worship a golden ass's head in the Jerusalem Temple. (Among later writers, the ass supposedly worshiped in the Jerusalem Temple is replaced with a pig.) In the context of the tensions in Egypt described in the text, Egyptian writers circulated distorted and insulting accounts of Jewish history. The Jews, they claimed, originally came to Egypt as alien conquerors, set fire to Egyptian towns, destroyed their temples, and mistreated the inhabitants until they were expelled. Others said that the Jews who came to Egypt in the time of the pharaohs were expelled from Egypt when the pharaoh decided to purge the country of lepers and other polluted persons. He set them to work in quarries and, later, settled them at Avaris. There, their leader Moses decreed that they should not worship the Egyptian gods or eat the meat of animals revered by the Egyptians and that they should keep strictly to themselves. Similarly political in motivation was the accusation circulated after the desecration of the Jerusalem Temple by

Antiochus IV that Antiochus discovered there a Greek man being fattened in preparation for an annual human sacrifice.

Anti-Jewish propaganda is a frequent theme among first- and second-century Roman writers who resented Jews because of the Judean revolts against Rome and Jewish success in proselytizing among the Roman upper class, which conservative Romans saw as an incursion of foreigners and foreign customs. Roman writers especially mocked the Jewish prohibition against eating the meat of the pig—an animal particularly valued by Romans both for food and sacrifice—and they speak of circumcision as mutilation and of the observance of the Sabbath as laziness. The influential Roman historian Tacitus spoke for conservative Romans in decrying Judaism as "foreign superstition." At the same time, however, many important Roman writers, especially the philosophers, carried on the early Hellenistic tradition of admiring the Jews, especially Moses, whom they portrayed as a philosopher and lawgiver.

foot there, were again its masters. But their satisfaction did not endure, for it soon became clear to the Persians that the Jews were no longer sufficiently strong or numerous enough to guarantee the Persian foothold in Palestine. In 617, Chosroes reversed course and restored Jerusalem to Christian domination. A few years later, the Roman emperor Heraclius began his counteroffensive, and in 629 was able to enter Jerusalem and formally restore it to Byzantine control.

Heraclius's victory was a bitter disappointment for the Jews, but their consolation was not long delayed. Only a few years later, the age-old rivalry of Rome and Persia ended forever, as Byzantium lost its hold on Palestine and Egypt and the Persian Empire simply vanished. The course of the region's and the Western world's history would now be determined by a new force that appeared in the seventh century: Islam.

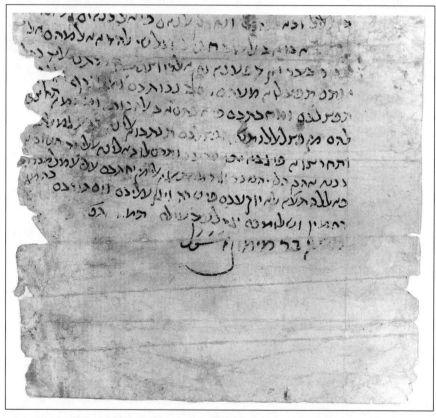

An autograph letter by Maimonides, written in Judeo-Arabic, and discovered in the geniza. Maimonides' signature occupies the last line of the document. Photo of letter © Suzanne Kaufman. Courtesy of the Library of the Jewish Theological Seminary of America, New York.

FOUR

The Jews in the Islamic World

From the Rise of Islam to the End of the Middle Ages (632 to 1500)

By the seventh century, the Byzantine Empire and the Sassanid Empire and their subject peoples were exhausted by centuries of warfare. Into the vacuum stepped a new power that had arisen in Arabia.

The inhabitants of the Arabian peninsula included both desert nomads and town dwellers. They were quite familiar with both the Roman and the Persian worlds, having for centuries lived on the margin of the two great empires, trading with them, serving as mercenaries in their armies, raiding their caravans, and sometimes establishing miniature kingdoms under the protection of one or the other. They were mostly pagans, but some of them were Christians and Jews. It seems to have been through conversations with them that Muhammad (c. 570–632), a businessman from Mecca, came to believe in the principles of monotheism: one incorporeal God who reveals himself through sacred scriptures and who will come to judge all humanity in a final day of judgment. He experienced visions in which he was commissioned to disseminate this message among his own people in the Arabic language.

TIMELINE

JEWISH HISTORY		GENERAL HISTORY
	622	The Hijra: Muhammad enters Medina
	638	Jerusalem conquered by Arabs
	642	Egypt conquered by Arabs
Judaism outlawed in Spain	694	
	711	Spain conquered by Arabs
	762	Baghdad founded
Anan begins Karaite movement	c. 765	
Saadia gaon	882–942	
Aaron ben Asher in Tiberias establishes authoritative text of Hebrew Bible	930	
Hasdai Ibn Shaprut becomes courtier to Muslim ruler of Spain	940	
	969	Cairo founded next to Fustat
End of Khazar kingdom	early 1000s	
Death of Hai, the last influential gaon	1038	
Death of Samuel the Nagid	1056	
Massacre in Granada	1066	
	1071	Seljuk Turks conquer Jerusalem
	1099	Jerusalem conquered by crusaders
Death of Judah Halevi	1141	
	c. 1146	Almohads in Spain
	1171	Saladin takes control of Egypt
	1187	Saladin conquers Jerusalem from crusaders
Death of Maimonides	1204	
	1248	Christian conquest of Spain complete except for Granada
	1258	Baghdad conquered by Mongols
Nahmanides in Palestine	1267–70	
	1269	Merinid dynasty takes control of Morocco
	1291	Crusader domination of Palestine ends with fall of Acre

In 622, Muhammad, together with his adherents, emigrated to Medina, where he established a community based on the principles of his religion—which was called Islam—and this community soon became a small but successful state. After his death, Muhammad's revelations were compiled into a book, the sacred scriptures of Islam, known as the Quran. His followers raided and conquered the adjacent territories, disseminating the new religion. Inside a few decades, they took Palestine and Egypt from the Byzantine Empire and Iraq and Persia from the Persian Empire. By the mid-eighth century, the Persian Empire, created by Cyrus more than 1,200 years previously (see chapter 1), was gone, and the Byzantine Empire was reduced to the Balkans, Asia Minor, and parts of southern Italy.

Most of the Jews in the world were now inhabitants of a single Islamic empire stretching from the Indus River in the east to the Atlantic Ocean in the west, including Spain. This development brought the Jews of Palestine, Egypt, and Spain nearly instant relief from the persecutions, harassment, and humiliation that they endured under hostile Christian rule. It also brought them, for the first time since the beginning of the Diaspora, into a single cultural, economic, and political system. Both these new conditions would enable them to flourish and to create the most successful Jewish Diaspora community of premodern times.

The Arabs did not embark on their conquests with the intention of converting the world to Islam. There was some religious compulsion, but on the whole, people converted to Islam because conditions under Islamic rule were favorable to Muslims; likewise, they adopted the Arabic language simply because it was the language of government and public life. Islam, like Christianity and Judaism, was implacably hostile to paganism, but it respected both Christianity and Judaism for possessing a divinely revealed book and viewed them as its sisters in monotheism. Therefore, the Muslims permitted Jews and Christians to retain their ancestral religions, provided they adhered to certain conditions.

Jews and Christians living under Islam were considered *dhimmis*— protected subjects—and their status was defined by a set of rules known as the Pact of Umar. Under these rules, the lives and property of *dhimmis* were guaranteed and the practice of their religion tolerated in exchange for payment of special taxes and on condition that they behaved in a manner considered appropriate to a subject population. They were not to build new churches or synagogues or repair old ones, hold public religious processions, or proselytize. They were not permitted to strike a Muslim, carry arms, or ride horses, and they had to wear distinguishing clothing. In time, other restrictions were added: They were forbidden from building their homes higher than Muslim homes, adopting Arabic names, studying the Quran, or selling fermented beverages, and they were excluded from government service.

Putting up with such degrading restrictions—and having to pay for the privilege—was humiliating and burdensome for Christians and Zoroastrians who fell under Islamic rule, so that for them the Pact of Umar was an incentive to convert to Islam. But for the Jews who had lived under Christendom, the Pact of Umar, severe as it may sound, actually brought relief, because it meant that the Islamic religion and state recognized their status and guaranteed their right to live and to practice their religion—not grudgingly, as under the humiliating logic of Saint Augustine, but freely, as enjoined by the prophet Muhammad himself. Although Muhammad had denounced the Jews in his later career and had persecuted the Jews in Medina, Islam had not, like Christianity, come into being in direct competition with Judaism, and had little historical reason for animus against it. Thus, the discriminatory regulations of the Pact of Umar were often disregarded in the first centuries of Islam or only loosely applied. In general, whenever Islam was in a state of strength, as it was until about the tenth century, and as it would again be in the Ottoman Empire (as we shall see in chapter 6) in the fifteenth and sixteenth centuries, Jews built impressive houses and adopted Arabic names, and some studied the Quran; Christians owned inns where they sold fermented beverages (often even to Muslims); and nobody minded wearing distinguishing clothing, as that was already customary anyway.

Another reason that the early rule of Islam fell lightly on the Jews was that, unlike their situation under Christian rule, they were not the only group subject to discriminatory regulations and certainly not the largest of those groups. That distinction fell to the Christians themselves, whose religious status under Islam was rather more problematic than that of the Jews. Although the Quran put Christians and Jews into the same category of "people of the book," the doctrine of the Trinity made the Christian religion theologically suspect to the rigorously monotheistic Muslims, and the prominence of crucifixes and icons in Christian worship made its adherents appear to Muslims, who rigorously excluded all images in worship, as idolaters. The Jews, a far smaller group, as rigorously monotheistic and nearly as averse to images as the Muslims themselves, attracted far less attention and suspicion during this period. Finally, unlike the Christians, the Jews did not have a political identity, for their statehood had long since lapsed; but facing the Muslim world across the Mediterranean (and adjacent to it in parts of western Asia) was the Byzantine Empire, a Christian theocracy constantly at war with Islamdom, whose Christian *dhimmis* were naturally suspected of being in league with the enemy, or at least of wishing the enemy well. For all these reasons, the lot of Christians was less favorable at first than that of the Jews.

With the establishment of the Islamic Empire, the focus of Western history shifted from the Greek- and Latin-speaking world to an Arabic-speaking empire greater in extension than either had been at its height. This is a reality that twentieth-century American and European readers have to work hard to internalize, because, as cultural heirs of Europe, we quite naturally tend to think of the mainstream of history as being European history. But from the seventh to the thirteenth century, Europe was far from the mainstream. After the barbarian invasions of the fifth century, the western Roman Empire had decayed politically, economically, and technologically, and European civilization entered a decline (often known as the Dark Ages) from which it took centuries to recover. The Byzantine Empire, which had succeeded Rome in the East, was drastically reduced in scale and on the defensive against Islam. But Islam forged a vast, powerful, and prosperous empire, unified by the Arabic language and the Islamic religion, much of it in territories formerly belonging to the Roman and Byzantine Empires, in addition to the territories of the Persian Empire and much more. With great scale came great wealth and great culture, as the skills and scholarship of the conquered peoples were incorporated into a new international Islamic culture. Thus, Europe's Dark Age corresponds to the golden age of Islam, and most of world Jewry were inhabitants of that great empire and beneficiaries of its greatness.

The Jewish community of Palestine recovered somewhat under Islamic domination, but it did not regain its position as the dominant Jewish community that it had held before the Christianization of the Roman Empire. The Arabs had conquered Jerusalem from the Byzantine Empire in 638 and revoked the prohibition that had officially been in effect since the time of Hadrian against Jews inhabiting the city. But when the Abbasid dynasty took control in 750 and built Baghdad as its capital (762), Palestine was left what it had generally been in the past—a passage between Mesopotamia and Egypt. Baghdad, on the other hand, became a world metropolis, and therefore the Jewish community of Iraq (still known as the Babylonian community, though the Babylonian Empire was long extinct) thrived in the capital of great caliphs like Harun al-Rashid as the most prominent Diaspora community. The Muslims confirmed the semiautonomous status that the Jews had enjoyed under Persian rule. The exilarch, at least in theory, became a courtier and the head not just of a local Diaspora community but of all Jewish communities under the caliph's sway, raising taxes and appointing judges for Jewish courts throughout the empire. We are told that when he would come to the caliph's court, a herald would run before him in the streets crying, in Arabic, "Make way for our master, the son of David!" for the exilarchs continued to claim descent from Jehoiachin, king of Judah (see the preceding chapters) and were to some extent treated as royalty.

Conditions under Islamic rule favored urban life and trade, and Jews were affected by this empire-wide trend, becoming ever more urbanized and drawn away from agriculture and toward commerce. By the end of the eighth century, it was far more common for Jews in the Muslim world to be town-dwelling craftsmen or businessmen than for them to be farmers. The unification of the Mediterranean and the Red Seas under a single political, cultural, and linguistic

sphere facilitated international trade, and as individual Jews accumulated wealth, some of them became active in trade between the
Mediterranean and India (where a Jewish community first comes into
view near Cochin around 1000 C.E.).

For both the Muslim majority and the Jewish minority, prosperity fostered cultural growth. The centralization of Muslim power in
Baghdad lent worldwide authority to the Jewish institutions of Iraq.
The academies of Sura and Pumbeditha moved to Baghdad; they
raised funds and attracted students from all over the Muslim world,
and their leaders came to be considered the chief expositors of the
Jewish religious tradition and the highest authorities in matters of
religious law and practice. They came to be known by the title *gaon*
(plural, *geonim*); the term derives from a Hebrew word meaning
"splendor" and is short for the flowery title "head of the academy of
the splendor of Jacob."

In most of the Islamic world, the Jews enjoyed some measure of
autonomy; rabbis functioned as judges and communal authorities,
not just as experts in ritual and family law. From all over the Islamic
world, local rabbis would direct difficult cases to the geonim for adju-
dication, cases that might involve matters of communal organization,
business, inheritance, and divorce (then, as today, often more a matter of the division of property than a purely religious one). The
answers to such questions are called *responsa* (they are the Jewish
equivalent to the Islamic *fatwa*).

The main subject taught in the academies of Iraq was religious
law. The chief textbook was, quite naturally, the Babylonian Talmud,
the great codification of the religious tradition that had been made by
the predecessors of the geonim, the heads of the academies of Sura
and Pumbeditha during the Sassanid period (see chapter 3). It was
the worldwide authority of the Babylonian geonim that gave the
Babylonian Talmud primacy over the Palestinian Talmud, so that the
former became much more widely disseminated and studied
throughout the Jewish world, and remains so to this day. Likewise,
the prayer books compiled by the geonim became the standard for

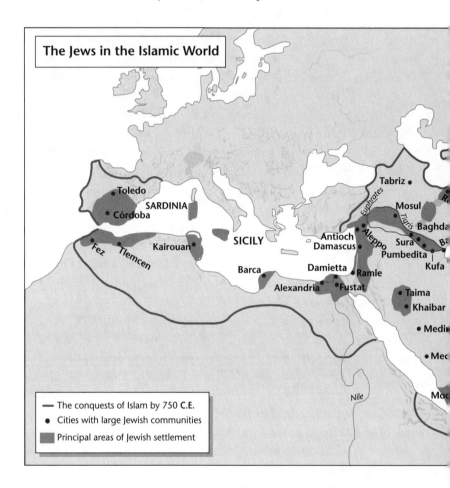

The Jews in the Islamic World

— The conquests of Islam by 750 C.E.
• Cities with large Jewish communities
▇ Principal areas of Jewish settlement

Jews worldwide, so that the old Palestinian prayer rituals have now completely fallen out of use. The geonim put a permanent stamp on many aspects of Jewish religious life; it is only appropriate that the period from the seventh to the eleventh century is known to Jewish history as the geonic period.

One of the most energetic and influential of the geonim was Saadia ben Joseph (882–942), gaon of Sura, whose career may be considered a milestone in Jewish intellectual life. Saadia was the first important rabbinic authority to write books in Arabic on Jewish law and religion,

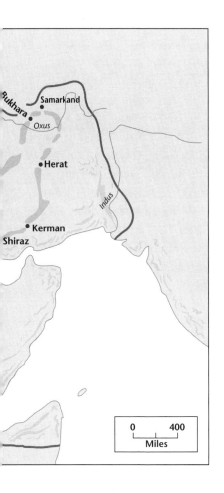

a bare linguistic fact that symbolizes the extent to which he revolutionized Jewish intellectual life. Saadia actually represented a new type of rabbi, since he did not cultivate only the Jewish legal and homiletical traditions, but dealt with a wider range of intellectual concerns than had been traditional.

The Jews generally spoke the language of their environment, so that when Iraq was conquered by the Muslims, they, together with the other inhabitants of the region, gradually shifted from Aramaic to Arabic. During the period of Islamic expansion, Arabic, once the language of a marginal tribal people, became the language of a great and cosmopolitan culture. Muslim scholars absorbed the wisdom of the ancient civilizations with which they came into contact—India, Persia, Greece—blending them with the old literary traditions native to the Arabian peninsula; they translated books from the ancient languages, particularly from Greek, into Arabic, pondered them, and developed their ideas in new ways, trying to harmonize them with Islam and with the Arabic literary tradition. This intellectual ferment created a class of cosmopolitan intellectuals, consisting mostly of Muslims, but also Christians, Zoroastrians, and Jews, who had a common heritage of philosophy and science, and that common heritage provided a broad basis for mutual understanding, permitting members of different and sometimes hostile religious sects and communities to work together. Broadly speaking, we may say that the common intellectual ground was Greek science and philosophy, and the common language was Arabic.

Thoroughly versed in Arabic language and literature, Saadia had access to this wide range of the new, broad intellectual life, and he was the first important rabbinic authority to attempt systematically to rethink the Jewish tradition in its light. His only predecessor in this attempt was Philo of Alexandria, who, in the first century, had tried to rethink the Jewish tradition in light of Hellenistic philosophy. Like Philo (who wrote in Greek), Saadia wrote in the language of his environment; unlike Philo, Saadia lived long after rabbinic Judaism had become the mainstream form of Judaism, and was himself one of its great authorities. Partly because of his authority and partly because of the cultural climate of the age, his work had wide-ranging effect on Jewish communities throughout the Islamic world and even beyond it.

As the first important rabbinic figure to write extensively in Arabic, Saadia may be considered the founder of Judeo-Arabic literature. Besides writing on Jewish law, a natural topic for a rabbinic authority, he also translated the Bible into Arabic and wrote an extensive Arabic commentary on it, an unusual project given the secondary position of the Bible in rabbinic education in his time. His Bible commentaries are the first by a rabbi to be deeply influenced by philosophy, and his *Book of Beliefs and Opinions* was the first systematic Jewish theological treatise ever written. Through these works, Saadia gave official status to the philosophical analysis of the Jewish tradition. Saadia also polemicized energetically against rabbis whose views he opposed and against sectarians, writing some of his polemical works in both Arabic and Hebrew. He composed poetry for the synagogue in Hebrew, which by his time was the only language being used in synagogue services, but he chose Arabic as the language of his textbook for the guidance of liturgical poets. Thus, Saadia may be said to have Arabized rabbinic Judaism not merely through his choice of the Arabic language, but by adapting the rabbinic tradition to the best of contemporary intellectual life.

Saadia's lifelong effort to harmonize Jewish traditions with the Hellenistic philosophical and scientific ideas that had become accessible through the Arabic language marks the beginning of an intellectual trend that became characteristic of Jews in the Islamic world at a time when Islam was at the forefront of Western civilization. This work would be carried on by Arabic-writing rabbis as long as the Islamic world retained its lead. As Muslims in this period were the vanguard of the intellectual life of the Western world, so the Jews within the Muslim world were in the vanguard of Jewish intellectual life worldwide.

In his religious polemics, Saadia defended the Bible against the attacks of rationalist critics who had pointed out contradictions and logical fallacies in Scripture. Even more important were his polemics against the Karaites, a movement within Judaism whose name means "the people of Scripture." This movement had been founded in late eighth-century Iraq by Anan ben David, who sought to overthrow the authority of the geonim by declaring the whole history of rabbinic Judaism to be a fraudulent distortion of the principles of the Jewish religion. Anan's intention was to reinstate the Bible as the sole religious authority, with every individual free to interpret it independently, limited only by the accumulated traditions of the Karaite community itself. This approach was appealing to Jewish communities, such as those of distant Persia, who were not firmly under the sway of geonic authority, but its very nature led to fragmentation. Anan's successors in the ninth and tenth centuries, men like Benjamin al-Nahawendi and Daniel al-Qumisi (who brought the movement to Palestine), modified his doctrine somewhat, developing their own tradition of biblical interpretation and making their own compilations of ritual traditions and legal codes, mostly in Arabic.

The Karaites' devotion to biblical studies made them pioneers in the study of Hebrew grammar and the manuscript traditions of the Bible, as well as energetic authors of commentaries on the Bible. It was in the tenth century that the Hebrew text of the Bible was authoritatively fixed, if not by Karaites, at least as a result of the impetus lent to this kind of work by their influence.

Karaism did not rebel against rabbinic Judaism in order to relax the complexity and rigidity of rabbinic law; it was from the beginning a rather rigid and even ascetic variety of Judaism. Nevertheless, it attracted followers, many of them well-to-do, in all the territories ruled by Islam, and it became so widespread that it was recognized as an alternate variety of Judaism, so that talmudically oriented Jews acquired the distinguishing title "Rabbanite." Though the two groups considered each other heretical, their adherents intermarried in this period. But because Rabbanites were generally recognized by Islamic governments as the authoritative spokesmen for Judaism, given the antiquity and prestige of such institutions as the exilarchate and the academies, they were eventually able to suppress the Karaites, without, however, completely eliminating them. The movement declined in the Muslim East in the twelfth century, but remained active in Egypt until modern times. It flared only briefly in Islamic Spain. It had an important community in Palestine and Byzantium, concentrated around Constantinople; from there it spread, in the seventeenth and eighteenth centuries, to the Crimea and Lithuania, where it existed until modern times. Small Karaite communities still exist in Israel, Turkey, and elsewhere.

After Saadia, the Jewish community of Iraq gradually declined in importance relative to other Diaspora communities as the Islamic Empire broke up into regional Islamic powers and as Iraq lost its dominant position within the Islamic world. The geonim of the tenth century sent appeals to other Diaspora communities for contributions that would enable them to maintain their institutions, but the last gaon to enjoy international authority was Hai of Pumbeditha, who died in 1038.

One of the Islamic regions that was flourishing just as Iraq was entering its decline was Spain, which the Muslims had conquered in the eighth century. This conquest saved the tiny Jewish community from a regime that had treated them with particular severity (see chapter 3). Under the benevolent rule of Islam, the Jews of the territory prospered along with the country as a whole, which quickly freed itself from the control of the empire. By the tenth century, the local ruler assumed the title "caliph," asserting formally his independence of an empire that was already far advanced in decay. His capital in Córdoba became a magnificent metropolis and for a time ranked as one of the great cities of the Islamic world, attracting wealth as well as artists and scholars. The economic success and the growing sense of a distinctive regional identity and pride benefited the Jews as well, some of whom became wealthy through the manufacture of textiles and through trade.

In the middle of the tenth century, a Jew named Hasdai Ibn Shaprut rose to prominence as a courtier in service of the caliph in Córdoba. He is the first example of a type of leader typical of Islamic Spain, the courtier-rabbi; such men held positions of power and influence in public life and also took responsibility for Jewish communal affairs. Many of them were learned in the religious tradition, and some of them participated personally in the extraordinarily vibrant literary and intellectual life of Islamic Spain. Hasdai used his power to look after the interests of the Jewish community of Islamic Spain, and he used his wealth and influence to create a circle of Jewish writers and scholars in Córdoba. He particularly encouraged the writing of Hebrew poetry, serving as patron to two poets whose work marks the beginning of the medieval golden age of Hebrew literature.

Poetry written in Hebrew had always been an important part of the Jewish liturgy, and there was a continuous tradition of composing new liturgical poetry (we have mentioned Saadia's efforts to encourage this practice), but there was no tradition of using Hebrew for nonliturgical purposes. As the Jews adopted the manners and customs of the Muslims, they acquired a taste for Arabic poetry, which was immensely popular wherever Arabic was spoken or studied. In the Arabic-speaking world, poetry was not considered merely entertainment; it even played an important role in public life as a vehicle for publicity and propaganda. Hasdai's poets adopted these functions of poetry, but used Hebrew instead of Arabic, since they were writing for the internal use of a small class of cultured Jewish aristocrats. This adaptation of Arabic literary manners can be seen as a continuation of the trend begun by Saadia of joining the Jewish tradition to the intellectual and literary currents of the Islamic world. Soon, poets were writing in Hebrew about most of the topics that were fashionable in Arabic: love, wine drinking (although prohibited by Islam, wine drinking was a favorite theme of Arabic poetry), friendship, personal and public affairs. Although the fashion for secular Hebrew poetry spread to other parts of the Arabic-speaking world, its greatest productions were by Hebrew poets living in Muslim Spain.

One of the most powerful and interesting of the courtier-rabbis was Samuel the Nagid (993–1055 or 1056), who achieved prominence in Granada in the eleventh century, when Islamic Spain had fragmented into many small kingdoms. According to legend, Samuel came to the notice of the court through his mastery of the ornate Arabic literary style used in diplomatic correspondence. Through personal charm and mastery of political skills, he became the indispensable adviser of the prince of Granada and, for a time, de facto ruler of the little state. He had some military responsibility as well, for he wrote many poems in Hebrew, describing the battles he witnessed between the troops of Granada and such neighboring states as Seville and Almería. In addition to his courtly responsibilities, he led an active literary career, writing books on religious law and Hebrew grammar and a great deal of poetry on a wide range of topics. Within the Jewish community, he came to be viewed as a kind of ideal figure because of his versatility, urbanity, learning, and loyalty to the community. Muslims also respected his abilities, but resented the power that he, a *dhimmi*, wielded over non-Muslims. Samuel was able to keep this discontent in check, but his son Yehosef, who inherited his position at court, was not, and in 1066, Yehosef was killed in a great uprising against the Jews of Granada. This riot was a nearly isolated event in the history of Islamic Spain and in the Muslim world in general during this period, for the position of Jews was generally quite secure. It serves as a reminder that, while the Jews may have been tolerated by Islam, they were nevertheless regarded as alien.

The massacre of Granada was, however, a harbinger of far worse troubles that the next century would bring. Beginning in 1146, the fanatical Almohads, an extremist Islamic sect from Morocco, arrived in and gradually took control of Spain, outlawing both Judaism and Christianity in their territories. This was only the second case in the history of Islam of a governmentally organized campaign against *dhimmis* (the first will be mentioned presently), and it was destructive and traumatic for the Jews. Although the Almohads eventually relaxed their rules, the damage to Jewish life was permanent, since it spelled the end of one of the most successful and creative Jewish communities. A number of the Jews who left Islamic Spain fled to Provence, bringing with them their distinctive Judeo-Arabic tradition, to the great benefit of intellectual life in this previously more insular community (see chapter 5).

Many Jews were able at least to remain within the Iberian Peninsula because by the time of the Almohad persecution, the Christian kingdoms of the north, never completely conquered by the Muslims, had begun expanding into Muslim territory. The king of Castile took Toledo in 1085. The Jews were welcome in the new Christian territories, and many found refuge there, so that for a time it appeared—contrary to the general pattern—that Christian rule was more benevolent to the Jews than that of Islam. This favorable state would not endure, as we shall see in the next chapter.

One of the Córdoban Jewish families that fled the Almohad persecution was that of a judge named Maimon, whose son, known today as Maimonides (1138–1204), would become the most famous Jew of the Islamic age. Maimonides was only about ten when the family left Spain, first for Morocco, then for Palestine. As an adult, he settled in Egypt, where he made his distinguished career.

Egypt had long been an important center of Jewish life. In the tenth century, it came under the control of the Fatimid dynasty, which built the city of Cairo as its capital. The founder of the dynasty, like Abd al-Rahman in Spain, took the title "caliph" as an assertion of his independence; one of his main advisers was a Jewish convert from Islam. The Jews thrived under the moderate rule of the Fatimids, who generally also controlled Palestine as well as Egypt, and who granted the Jews considerable communal autonomy. For about a century, the regime recognized the rabbinic academy at Ramle, in Palestine, as the highest Jewish authority of the realm; when the province of Palestine was lost to invading Turks in 1071, an official called "the head of the Jews" became the chief Jewish authority. The only significant difficulties the community had experienced occurred during the reign of the unstable Fatimid ruler al-Hakim II (ruled 1007–21), who adopted measures to humiliate his Christian and Jewish subjects, but these rules were soon rescinded by al-Hakim himself and did not cause the community any long-lasting trauma. In 1171, a few years after Maimonides' arrival, Egypt came under control of the Ayyubid dynasty, headed by the renowned Saladin, whose regime also accorded the Jews benevolent treatment for most of its duration. Under both Fatimids and Ayyubids, a few Jews reached positions of power in court.

The Egyptian Jewish community in the age of Maimonides is the best-documented of all medieval Jewish communities because of the survival of a *geniza* in one of its synagogues. A *geniza* is a storage room for discarded books and written materials. Such storage rooms were necessary because the Jews considered it sacrilegious to destroy any document in which the name of God appeared, lest the name itself be mutilated. Because references to God were common even in writings not dealing directly with religious matters, the practice of storing old writings rather than destroying them was extended to anything written in Hebrew letters and created a disinclination to discard any written material at all. Books and documents no longer needed were either buried in cemeteries or stored indefinitely in a *geniza*. The old city of Fustat, originally south of Cairo but now incorporated into it, was home to the famous Ben Ezra synagogue, which had a storeroom of this type continuously until the late nineteenth century.

This storeroom came to the attention of European book collectors in the course of the nineteenth century. When it was opened and systematically explored in 1897, it was found to contain manuscripts of literary works of all kinds—commentaries on the Bible and the Talmud, *responsa*, poems, prayer books, philosophical and scientific works—that had lain there since the Middle Ages and that permitted a much broader view of Jewish intellectual life in the Middle Ages than had previously been possible. But even more remarkable was the discovery in the *geniza* of an unheard-of quantity and variety of documents—personal and business letters, commercial contracts, bills of sale and lading, marriage contracts, writing exercises, book lists, inventories, and amulets. This discovery made it unexpectedly possible to view everyday life in medieval Egypt from the tenth century to the thirteenth century, not only of Jews but of Muslims, too, with a degree of detail that is not available even from Islamic sources. The material is vast, fragmentary, hard to decipher, and difficult to access, being scattered among the libraries of Europe and the United States, so that the study of it, a century after its discovery, is still far from complete. The recently renovated Ben Ezra synagogue may be visited in Cairo.

When Maimonides arrived in Egypt in 1165, he was an outsider who had to overcome the opposition of the local Jewish communal leaders in order to achieve a position of authority in the community. Eventually, he was recognized as Egypt's prime rabbinic authority, though it is not certain whether he actually held the title "head of the Jews." He did become a figure of international stature whose opinion was sought from all over the Mediterranean world, even from Christian Europe; his prestige brought him into conflict with the later geonim in Iraq, who saw him as usurping their already reduced authority. His reputation rested not only on his mastery of religious law, but also in his expertise in philosophy, science, and medicine. He became the personal physician to one of Saladin's viziers, traveling each day from Fustat to Cairo in order to care for the vizier's wives and children.

Maimonides was a supreme exemplar of the rabbinic type created by Saadia: an expert in religious law completely involved in contemporary intellectual life, whose writings embrace both the Jewish tradition and the sciences. His enduring reputation and authority rest primarily on two works: his code of Jewish law, written in Hebrew and organized according to an original and logical scheme, and his philosophical treatise called *The Guide for the Perplexed*, written in Arabic and designed to assure Jewish students of philosophy that the Jewish tradition was philosophically defensible. The latter became the most famous book of medieval Jewish philosophy, but its approach was too advanced for communities that were not Arabic-speaking and that therefore had not yet been touched by Greco-Arabic philosophical ideas. In addition to these major works, Maimonides also wrote medical treatises and a treatise on logic; these were purely philosophical works intended for non-Jews as well as Jews.

The Palestinian Jewish community, which was again ruled by Egypt after Palestine was reconquered from the crusaders by the Ayyubids, remained relatively unimportant during all this period. It had its own rabbinical academy, at first in Tiberias, later in Ramle, which tried to contend for authority with the academies of Iraq. Early in the ninth century, the head of this academy had attempted to restore the patriarchal prerogative of establishing the calendar for Diaspora Jewry, but this attempt had been quashed by Saadia. Palestine remained, for Jews and for Muslims, a bit off the beaten track.

For Muslims, this situation changed when the crusaders arrived in 1099. For almost two centuries, the territory was contested between Muslims and Christians, who wanted to restore the Holy Land to Christian control. The Christians succeeded in creating a kingdom of Jerusalem, which lasted from 1099 to 1187, and they were not expelled from the region completely until 1291. Jews were not permitted to live in the city itself, but were permitted to visit, and they were not persecuted elsewhere in the crusader territories of Palestine (as they had been by the crusaders crossing Europe in 1096; see chapter 5). Their status was about the same as that of the Muslim inhabitants of the territories occupied by the crusaders. Thus, the Crusades had little immediate impact on the Jews of the Middle East.

But the Crusades started the Islamic world on a long process of deterioration that would eventually have a deleterious effect on the status of the Jews. The rapid conquest of Persia and Byzantium in the seventh century, the tremendous extent and wealth of the Islamic territories, their great cities with their countless mosques and schools, the fame of their scholars, and the brilliance of their intellectual production—all these successes had lent the world of Islam the confidence to tolerate its subject peoples and to leave its *dhimmis* to lead their lives in peace. Though the empire had begun to fragment politically as early as the ninth century, the independent and quasi-independent states that emerged long remained powerful and confident. But now, Islamic power began to fray. Sicily was conquered by the Normans even before the Crusades began (1091). The invasion of the crusaders in the East coincided with the progressive loss of Spain—one of Islam's greatest treasures—to Christian conquerors in the West (the process lasted, for practical purposes, from 1085 to 1248). And the Crusades opened the way for such Italian city-states as Venice, Pisa, and Genoa to take control of trade in the eastern Mediterranean. By the end of the thirteenth century, the Muslims had been driven out of Europe, the coast of North Africa was under constant attack by Europeans, and the Mongols had embarked on their long march across Asia. In 1258, Baghdad fell to the Mongols, putting an end to the caliphate and to any remaining pretensions to an Islamic Empire. The balance of power and wealth was shifting in favor of Christian Europe.

Islam reacted partly by turning against its non-Muslim subjects, Christians and Jews alike. The discriminatory rules of the Pact of Umar, generally neglected in the past, were now enforced with rigor. Jews and Christians had to wear distinguishing clothing; they were prohibited from riding even on donkeys within cities; churches and synagogues were vandalized; and Jewish physicians lost the right to treat Muslim patients. Jews and Christians found themselves ever more harassed and humiliated and subjected to the contempt and violence of the mob. With the progressive decline of the Islamic world's economic power in the fourteenth and fifteenth centuries, the conditions of the *dhimmis* deteriorated to the point that many of them simply converted to Islam. The results of these pressures may be gauged by the fact that by 1481, Alexandria, once one of the most important centers of Jewish life in the world, had only sixty Jewish families remaining.

The laws of Islam continued to protect the *dhimmis'* lives, and there were no massacres. The Mongol conquest of Baghdad even brought about a brief amelioration in the condition of the *dhimmis*, for the Mongols, not being Muslims, abolished "*dhimmi*" as a legal category. Not only did they have no religious prejudice against Christians and Jews, but they needed them as supporters. One early Mongol ruler even had a Jewish physician and scholar as a vizier. But the prominence of such Jews sometimes led to riots among the Muslim population, and when the Mongols converted to Islam in 1295, they restored the discriminatory rules of the Pact of Umar with the zeal of converts. Given the prevailing atmosphere of intolerance and economic stagnation, the literary and intellectual productivity characteristic of the heyday of Islam could not be sustained. Judaism in the central Muslim territories stagnated.

In Egypt, the Turkish and Circassian Mameluk rulers (1250–1517) discriminated against not only *dhimmis* but also, among others, Muslims who were not of the ruling class. This situation exacerbated the hatred of non-ruling-class Muslims toward the *dhimmis*, their inferiors on the social ladder. Regulations for distinguishing Jews and Christians from Muslims and excluding them from public life were constantly renewed and ingeniously expanded, and a climate of hostility toward "infidels" existed that would have been inconceivable in the days of Islamic expansion.

Golden Age Poetry

The Jewish aristocrats of Muslim Spain lived very much like the Arab aristocrats of the age. Their houses had gardens where they would entertain fellow grandees with outdoor nighttime wine parties. At these parties, Arabic and Hebrew poetry was recited, sometimes sung to the accompaniment of musical instruments. Not all Jews thought that this was appropriate behavior. The ambivalence of one participant is expressed beautifully in a poem by Dunash ben Labrat, which describes with great enthusiasm a party that was held in Córdoba in the tenth century, but also expresses the poet's compunctions about participating in it.

> There came a voice: "Awake!
> Drink wine at morning's break.
> 'Mid rose and camphor make
> A feast of all your hours,
>
> 'Mid pomegranate trees
> And low anemones,
> Where vines extend their leaves
> And the palm tree skyward towers,
>
> Where lilting singers hum
> To the throbbing of the drum,
> Where gentle viols thrum
> To the plash of fountains' showers.
>
> On every lofty tree
> The fruit hangs gracefully.
> And all the birds in glee
> Sing among the bowers.

continued

The cooing of the dove
Sounds like the song of love.
Her mate calls from above—
Those trilling, fluting fowls.

We'll drink on garden beds
With roses round our heads.
To banish woes and dreads
We'll frolic and carouse.

Dainty food we'll eat.
We'll drink our liquor neat,
Like giants at their meat,
With appetite aroused.

When morning's first rays shine
I'll slaughter of the kine
Some fatlings; we shall dine
On rams and calves and cows.

Scented with rich perfumes,
Amid thick incense plumes,
Let us await our dooms,
Spending in joy our hours."

I chided him: "Be still!
How can you drink your fill
When lost is Zion hill
To the uncircumcised.

You've spoken like a fool!
Sloth you've made your rule.
In God's last judgment you'll
For folly be chastised.

The Torah, God's delight
Is little in your sight,
While wrecked is Zion's height,
By foxes vandalized.

How can we be carefree
Or raise our cups in glee,
When by all men are we
Rejected and despised?"

Dunash ben Labrat, translated by Raymond P. Scheindlin, in *Wine, Women, and Death: Medieval Hebrew Poems on the Good Life* (Philadelphia: Jewish Publication Society, 1986), pp. 41–42.

The deterioration in Jewish life was not so marked in northwest Africa. Once the fanaticism of the Almohads died down, in the course of the twelfth century, the discriminatory rules were applied with less rigor. The communities of what is now Tunisia and Algeria were stable, and were even invigorated by an influx of population when Jews began fleeing there from nearby Christian Spain in 1391 (see chapter 5). Among the refugees were a number of scholars and rabbis who revived the region's intellectual life. This immigration had a favorable effect on Jewish life in Morocco as well. Here, the Merinid dynasty, which ruled in Fez from 1286 to 1465, was more tolerant of *dhimmis* than were their Muslim subjects, and even had Jewish courtiers. But the populace shared the intolerance toward *dhimmis* that had become normal in the Islamic world by that time. Around

Judeo-Arabic Language and Literature

With the important exceptions of Ladino and Yiddish, Diaspora Jews generally have spoken the language of their environment. Accordingly, after the Muslim conquests, when most Jews of the world came under Islamic rule, they behaved exactly as their non-Jewish neighbors did, and gradually exchanged their traditional languages—Aramaic, Greek, Berber, and Latin—for Arabic. Soon they were writing in Arabic as well, and by the tenth century a Judeo-Arabic literature had come into existence.

When Jews wrote in Arabic, they generally used the Hebrew, rather than the Arabic, alphabet. The reason was probably that the Hebrew alphabet was the one that came most naturally to them. Education in those early times always began as religious education. For the Jews, this meant learning to read Hebrew first, and therefore literacy in Hebrew was quite widespread among the Jews. They generally knew the Arabic script and could use it when writing for the use of non-Jewish readers, but for communicating with fellow Jews, there was no reason to go to the trouble.

Judeo-Arabic literature includes works on theology, philosophy, and Hebrew grammar; commentaries on the books of the Bible; and rabbinical decisions on religious law. There are also books in Judeo-Arabic on scientific subjects such as medicine and astronomy. There is even a book in Judeo-Arabic on how to write Hebrew poetry.

But there is a great deal of writing in Judeo-Arabic that is not literature. Much of the material preserved by the *geniza* (see text) consists of letters, inventories, and other everyday kinds of writing, and these are written in the vernacular Arabic of everyday affairs. Such documents afford a precious glimpse into the lives of ordinary people in the medieval Mediterranean world and allow us to imagine medieval people speaking in their own voices.

After the Middle Ages, when Jews in many Muslim countries came under greater restrictions and were often forced to live in closed communities,

Judeo-Arabic did develop into a specifically Jewish dialect. Popular religious books were composed in this dialect, as well as poems on the lives of biblical characters and religious songs for use at weddings and other communal events.

1438, a special walled quarter, called *mellah*, was set aside for the Jews of Fez to protect them from the riots that had already caused considerable unrest. This pattern repeated itself throughout Morocco, with the result that the Jews were progressively segregated from the population at large, and what began as a protective measure ended as a kind of isolation. Nor were the *mellahs* always effective protection. In 1465, there was a wave of massacres throughout the kingdom when a Jew was appointed vizier, a perfect case study in the disparity between the attitudes of the regime and the populace toward the Jews.

The second half of the fifteenth century completed the process of change in the Middle East and in Jewish history that had begun with the Crusades. A new force now appeared in the region, sweeping away the decadent old regimes and replacing them with a new and vigorous Islamic state. This new force was the Ottoman Turks, the last and most important of the series of invaders from central Asia that had included the Mongols. After progressing through Asia Minor, the Ottomans took Constantinople in 1453, the prize that Islam had coveted since the seventh century. They went on to take Palestine and Egypt in 1517 and subsequently to seize Iraq and much of the north African coast. These conquests put an end to over a thousand years of Byzantine history. By this time, the Jews had been expelled from Spain and most of western Europe; the advent of the Shiite Safavid dynasty in Persia in 1502 reduced that formerly important Jewish community to marginality. But the rise of the Ottomans would provide the opportunity for a new flowering of Jews in the newly ascendant world of Islam.

The synagogue in Worms, often known as the Rashi-Synagogue, dating from the eleventh century. Destroyed on Kristallnacht (the night of November 9–10, 1938), the building was reconstructed in 1961. Photo © Frank J. Darmstaedter. Courtesy of the Jewish Museum, New York.

FIVE

The Jews of Medieval Christian Europe

(Ninth century to 1500)

The Origins of Ashkenazic Jewry

There was an important Jewish community in Rome in antiquity, and Jews first appear to have entered other parts of western Europe in the first century C.E. following the lines of Roman settlement. Thus, from the early part of the first millennium C.E., there are traces of a Jewish presence in Spain (which is treated in a separate section of this chapter), Provence, and various parts of Gaul. But the Jews do not seem to have created continuous settlements in these places in Roman times, except perhaps in Spain. The first important Jewish community we encounter in western Europe is in Sicily and southern Italy, which until 1091 was under the control of the Byzantine Empire. From the ninth century on, this community was important enough to have its own academies for the study of rabbinic law in Bari, Oria, and Otranto, as well as liturgical poets, some of whose works are still recited today by Ashkenazic Jews. The works of these poets have preserved the memory of persecutions by the Byzantine emperors Basil I in 874 and Romanus I Lecapenus in 943.

TIMELINE

T I M E L I N E

JEWISH HISTORY		GENERAL HISTORY
Final expulsion from France	1394	
Tortosa disputation	1413–14	
Pope orders censoring of Talmud	1415	
	1431	Burning of Joan of Arc
	1453	Constantinople conquered by Turks
	1457	Gutenberg prints first surviving printed book
	1469	Marriage of Ferdinand and Isabella, permitting union of Castile and Aragon
Blood libel of Trent	1475	
	1480	Inquisition established in Spain
Expulsion from Spain	1492	Conquest of Granada, discovery of America
Mass forced conversion of Jews in Portugal	1497	

The Frankish kings, especially Charlemagne (ruled 768–814), his son, Louis the Pious, and their successors, encouraged Italian Jews to migrate to Provence and the Rhineland. They were eager to have in their territories a community of traders who could develop commerce in a region whose economy was completely agricultural. The thriving Jewish communities that were established in this period along the Rhine, in towns such as Cologne, Mainz, Worms, and Speyer, became the nucleus of the permanent Jewish settlement of western and central Europe. This region was called *Ashkenaz* in Hebrew, and its Jews therefore are called Ashkenazic. (We shall see in chapter 7 how Ashkenazic Jewish culture was later carried to eastern Europe and America, where it is now the dominant form of Judaism.)

Already in the origins of Ashkenazic Jewry, we can observe a peculiarity that in time would come to have a deleterious effect on their relationship to the non-Jewish world. The Jews had been brought to western Europe as clients of a ruler because of their skills as merchants and businessmen. Being neither landowners nor peasants, they were not part of the feudal hierarchy but were directly dependent for their legal status on a king, baron, or bishop. This made them anomalous in feudal Europe, where a person's status was defined by land. Jews were sometimes granted fiefdoms, as in the south of France and in England at the time of Richard the Lion-Hearted, but on the whole, wherever the feudal system prevailed, Jews either never came into possession of land or were sooner or later driven from it.

This special status was the foundation of the lasting social and economic differences between the Jews and the European masses; reinforced by the difference in religion, it marked them as a natural object of distaste even in good times, and as an object of hatred in bad times. Their status gave them privileges, but it also made them pawns in the shifting constellation of power between nobility, clergy, and the mob. Even an honorable lord could not always protect them; a venal lord might exploit their dependency on him as a means of extorting payments, and a needy lord might simply expel them in order to confiscate their property.

The separation of the Jews from the land had the further consequence that they were concentrated in towns and active mostly in business and crafts. This, too, might seem advantageous, as it afforded them economic opportunities not available to the peasantry. But with the growth of cities in the course of the Middle Ages, they were gradually edged out of these fields by the culturally and numerically dominant Christians and were excluded first from the crafts, then from most respectable business activities.

But the consequences of the Jews' special status emerged only gradually and unevenly throughout western and central Europe; in the time of Charlemagne and Louis the Pious, the Jews, though socially, politically, and religiously different from their neighbors, were not yet objects of opprobrium. They prospered and spread geographically eastward to central Europe and westward to France and England. They had rabbinic academies of their own beginning around 1000, when a family of rabbis known as Kalonymus moved from Lucca in Italy to Mainz. Scholarship was more limited to the Talmud and Jewish law in the

Ashkenazic world than it was in the cosmopolitan Arabic-speaking world; the intellectual climate was not favorable to the kind of cross-cultural fertilization that produced a Saadia in Iraq. But the study of the Talmud was pursued with a single-mindedness that was productive in its own way. Its most famous product was the commentary on the Talmud produced by R. Solomon b. Isaac (commonly known as Rashi, 1040–1105), which has no peer from the Arabic-speaking world and which remains an indispensable tool of Talmud study until our own day.

Talmud study in this period was not merely the academic activity that it became in the modern period. The semiautonomous status of the Jews in both the Islamic and the Christian world meant that the Jewish courts had full jurisdiction over Jewish business activities, and therefore rabbis, as legal authorities, were a vital component of commercial life. The existence of a uniform legal system for all Jewish communities, together with the existence of a common written language—Hebrew—greatly simplified international transactions for them and lent them an edge in international trade.

Relations between Jews and Christians remained more or less stable until near the end of the eleventh century, when pressure began to build for a crusade to rescue the Christian holy sites in Palestine, especially the Holy Sepulchre, from the hands of the Muslims. The religious enthusiasm directed violently against the distant nonbelievers came to be directed also against the Jews, for as some Christians argued, "Here we are going to make war against the infidels in the Holy Land, when we have infidels in our own midst." When the mobs of the First Crusade began to sweep eastward across Europe in the spring of 1096, among their early victims were the Jews of the Rhineland communities. Local lords and church authorities on the whole tried to live up to their legal obligation of defending their Jewish clients, but they lacked the forces to prevent the onslaught. The result was widespread massacres and forced baptisms. Rather than risk falling into the hands of the Christian mobs, many Jews committed suicide, the men killing their own wives and children first and then themselves. This was the first

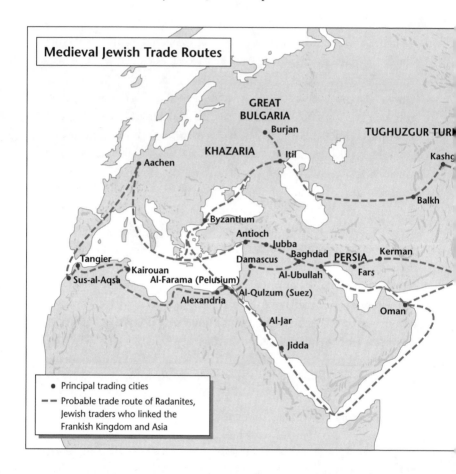

Medieval Jewish Trade Routes

GREAT BULGARIA

Burjan

KHAZARIA

TUGHUZGUR TUR[

Aachen

Itil

Kashg

Balkh

Byzantium

Antioch

Jubba

Tangier

Damascus   Baghdad   PERSIA   Kerman

Sus-al-Aqsa   Kairouan
Al-Farama (Pelusium)   Al-Ubullah   Fars

Alexandria   Al-Qulzum (Suez)

Oman

Al-Jar

Jidda

• Principal trading cities
-- Probable trade route of Radanites,
Jewish traders who linked the
Frankish Kingdom and Asia

great trauma suffered by Ashkenazic Jewry, but there was far more in store. The Second and the Third Crusades brought their own horrors. In England, the Jews of York committed mass suicide in 1190 rather than fall into the hands of the warriors of the Third Crusade, an event still commemorated weekly in many Ashkenazic synagogues.

Hostility now became the normal attitude of the average European toward the Jews. This hostility was partly grounded in fear. The ordinary illiterate and superstitious medieval European peasant saw

the Jews, with their strange customs, odd religious practices, and mysterious Hebrew prayers, not just as social and economic outsiders, but as weird practitioners of black magic directed both against man and God, perhaps even agents of the devil. This attitude came to its fullest expression in the blood libel, the widespread belief that Jews regularly murder non-Jews, particularly children, in order to use their blood for magic or religious rites, especially for Passover. The blood libel had arisen as far back as Hellenistic times, when it was directed by pagans against Christians as well as Jews, but it achieved its fullest and most destructive form in medieval Christian Europe. For Christians, the central religious rite was the mass, in which, they were told, wine and bread were changed into the blood and body of Christ. Their priests regularly taught them that the Jews, in their perverse wickedness, had spilled the blood of their savior. Against the background of these ideas, it was natural for the credulous masses to imagine that the Jews practiced diabolical counter-rituals involving blood. It was likewise rumored that Jews would steal communion wafers and torture Jesus by sticking pins in them and by otherwise defiling them. Sometimes Jews were accused of using the wafers for unholy magical rituals.

The first full-fledged blood accusation was made against the Jews of Norwich, England, in 1144. They were accused of capturing a Christian child named William before Easter and hanging him on Good Friday in a reenactment of the torture and crucifixion of Christ. They were supposed to have performed this ritual in fulfillment of an alleged agreement among world Jewry that a Christian child should be killed each year. The Jews of Norwich were massacred. Similar accusations were subsequently brought against Jews all over Europe. The accusation took a particularly sinister turn when the belief became widespread that the Jews used the blood of a slaughtered Christian child to make the Passover *matzot* (wafers eaten in lieu of bread during the eight days of the festival). The details of the accusations varied, but the consequences were similar: Whole Jewish families, sometimes whole Jewish communities were killed, often by being burned alive. The most famous cases occurred in Gloucester (1168); Blois (1171); Vienna (1181); Saragossa (1182); Fulda (1235); Lincoln (1255)—commemorated by Chaucer in *The Canterbury Tales*, in connection with his own fictional tale of a blood libel—Munich (1286); Trent (1475); and Avila (1491). This last case was known as that of "the Holy Child of La Guardia"; it was concocted by those in Spain who were campaigning for the expulsion of the Jews, and it had the gravest possible political consequences.

Christian intellectuals, even in the Middle Ages, did not give credence to the blood libel, and in the sophisticated Islamic world in this period, the blood libel and the image of the Jew as ally of the devil were unknown. Christian kings and the upper Christian clergy did what they could to defend the Jews against the outlandish accusations. After the Fulda blood libel of 1235, the Holy Roman Emperor Frederick II established a commission to study it; the commissioners quite correctly pointed out how absurd it was to accuse the Jews, whose religious law prohibited them from eating even an egg with a blood spot on it, of eating human blood for ritual or any other purpose. In 1249, Pope Innocent IV condemned the blood libel. But parish priests and preaching friars were constantly inciting their listeners to hold the Jews responsible for the original crucifixion and to believe that the Jews were still reenacting it at every opportunity. Thus, the blood libel could not be quashed, and has continued to surface, even in modern times. (We shall see in chapter 6 how it emerged in the Islamic world in 1840 and in chapter 7 how it was revived in czarist Russia as recently as 1913.)

Several historical processes contributed to the further deterioration of the condition of the Jews in western and central Europe in the twelfth and thirteenth centuries. During the Crusades, Italian republics such as Venice gained a monopoly in Mediterranean trade, reducing the usefulness of European Jewry in that field. In many cities, control of manufacture, crafts, and commerce had come into the power of the guilds, professional organizations for each specialty regulating not only the conduct of the profession and the professional lives of their members, but their social and religious lives as well, such that Jews were ordinarily excluded. The economic position of the Jews of the northern Italian states was somewhat more favorable. But the enhanced power of the papacy during this period resulted in ever-tightening ecclesiastical control of the Jews and constant legislation to regulate their relations to their secular overlords, to the Church, and to individual Christians.

The key to the Jewish policy of the popes in the territories under their control was the old principle that the Jews should be permitted to live in poverty and humiliation, but were to be protected in their lives and property. On their accession, popes would issue an edict renewing these guarantees, but the terms would vary. For example, when Innocent III renewed the Jews' privileges, in 1199, he added the provision that they could not collect on loans made to Christians if the Christian debtor went on crusade. The strong popes of the period would also use occasional Church councils to issue legislation affecting the Jews. The Third Lateran Council, in 1179, was an important milestone, since it revived some long-neglected restrictions on the Jews, some of which were designed to bring about the social separation of Jews and Christians. Jews were prohibited from having Christian servants or employees, Christians were prohibited from living in Jewish neighborhoods, and the testimony of a Christian was to be accepted against that of a Jew. The Fourth Lateran Council, in 1215, took a decisive step further toward the segregation of Jews by creating the hated Jewish badge, which labeled every single Jew as a shameful outcast. It also prohibited Jews from holding public office and from appearing in public on Easter and certain other holy days.

Both Councils enacted commercial legislation that contributed to the decline of the Jews' role in economic life. Particularly fateful was the ruling of the Third Lateran Council that prohibited the taking of interest in loans between Christians. Since the prohibition did not apply to Jews who lent money to Christians, the entire field of moneylending was practically abandoned to the Jews just at a time when the process of their exclusion from other economic opportunities was nearly complete. The prohibition of taking interest did not eliminate the need for loans, which were essential for economic growth and the waging of war, besides being the lifeline of the poor. It was this attempt to purify Christian behavior of usury that turned the Jews into the hated pawnbrokers of medieval Europe. The Fourth Lateran Council limited the amount of interest that Jews could exact on loans and also ruled that when a Christian debtor forfeited property to a Jewish creditor, the Jewish creditor had to continue paying tithes on the property to the churches. The net effect of all this legislation was to reduce the Jews, by the end of the thirteenth century, to penury and to turn them into a class of peddlers, traders in second-hand goods, and pawnbrokers.

In his determination to enforce the domination of the Church, Pope Innocent III waged war on the heretical sects of the Catharites and the Waldensians in Languedoc and Provence. To help in stamping out these heresies, he created the Inquisition, which would play such an important role in Spain and Portugal from the last part of the fifteenth century on. Innocent also authorized the creation of the Franciscan and Dominican orders of monks; the Dominicans were particularly assigned the responsibility of prosecuting heresy and preaching orthodox Christianity to the non-orthodox. Both orders were to contend with the Jews and to incite Christians against them in the coming centuries.

The thirteenth century also saw efforts to undermine Judaism as a religious system, as learned Jewish converts to Christianity now began to bring the Talmud to the attention of Christian scholars. The Talmud was considered offensive to Christianity because, having been compiled long after the death of Jesus, its existence implied a Jewish claim to religious validity after the Jewish religion had supposedly been superseded. The Talmud also contains a number of passages derogatory to Jesus and to Christianity. Pope Gregory IX officially condemned it in 1233. It was put on public trial in 1242 at the instigation of a Jewish apostate named Nicolas Donin, and all copies that could be found were burned. In 1263, the king of Aragon instituted a public disputation intended to convince the Jews of the falsity of their religion on the basis of the Talmud itself and the associated rabbinic literature (see later).

In 1232, the books of Maimonides were burned in Montpelier by the Dominicans. This event was partly the result of a cultural clash within the Provençal Jewish community. It had been less than a century since the Arabic-speaking refugees from Almohad Spain had imported into Provence their worldly manners and broad philosophical training; many Provençal Jews were captivated by the ideas introduced by the newcomers, but others defended what they saw as the old tradition. The philosophically advanced works of Maimonides aroused controversy (lasting well into the next century and involving Spain as well); the traditionalist faction denounced them to the Dominicans, who, though charged to extirpate Christian heresy, presumably could be counted on to recognize Jewish heresy as well.

The slow and painful process now ensued by which the Jews were gradually expelled from all of western Europe.

In England, Edward I declared all debts to Jews void in 1275 and prohibited the Jews from moneylending, thus depriving them of one of their few remaining sources of livelihood. He imprisoned the leaders of the community and demanded a huge ransom for them; once the ransom money was in his hands, he expelled the Jews from the kingdom in 1290. It would be four centuries before they would be readmitted.

In France, Philip the Fair followed Edward's example in 1306, seizing the Jews' property and then expelling them from the country. They were permitted to return in the following reign, but in 1320, an unauthorized popular movement known as the Shepherd's Crusade destroyed some Jewish communities, and the next year, 5,000 Jews were burned alive for supposedly poisoning the wells. By 1322, there were hardly any Jews left in all of France. The Jews were definitively expelled from France in 1394.

The expulsions of the Jews from France drove many of them to Provence, which was not yet part of the kingdom. Thanks to the refugees who had arrived from Spain in the twelfth century, Provence had become an important center of Jewish intellectual life, in which talmudic study of the Ashkenazic type was combined with philosophical study and literary activity of the Judeo-Arabic type. In the twelfth and thirteenth centuries, it incubated the kabbalah, a form of mysticism that would become a major force in Jewish intellectual life, spreading first to Spain and eventually worldwide. But after Provence was attached to France in 1481, the entire Jewish community was gradually forced into exile.

Many of the Jews of Provence found refuge, amazingly, in an enclave of their own country. One county of Provence, the Venaissin, and the city of Avignon had been the property of the popes since the early thirteenth century, and the popes resided in Avignon from 1309 to 1377. As the chief authorities of Church law, the popes in this period strictly enforced Church policy protecting the Jews' right to minimal survival. The Jewish community of Provence thus came to be compressed into Avignon and a few towns in the vicinity, and there, over centuries, it acquired a distinctive character and traditions of its own, surviving until the end of the nineteenth century.

Between 1348 and 1351, Europe was terrorized and decimated by the Black Death, which wiped out a third of the population of Europe, not discriminating between Jews and Christians. The panicky populace expressed and sought to allay its fear by means of extreme religious fervor. In the climate of hysteria, the rumor circulated that the Jews had caused the plague by poisoning drinking wells. One by one, the Jewish communities, especially in central Europe, were rounded up and destroyed or expelled. As his predecessors had done in the case of the blood libel, Pope Clement IV repeatedly attempted to quash the absurd claim that the Jews, who were dying alongside the Christians, could possibly have been responsible, but it was impossible to satisfy the masses except with the Jews' blood. The Jews gradually drifted back, but their lives were restricted, miserable, and unstable. In the course of the fifteenth century, they were expelled from the various German states of central Europe. The largest and most shocking expulsion was from Spain at the end of the fifteenth century (discussed later).

Meanwhile, at the southeastern end of the Europe, the Jews of the Byzantine heartlands—the Balkans and Asia Minor—continued to bear the harsh anti-Jewish Christian regime, unlike their coreligionists of Palestine and Egypt, from whom the burden had been lifted by the Muslim conquests. The community survived and came to be known as the Romaniot community. Legislation further restricting their ability to consort with Christians was enacted by Justinian II in 692. The most successful Byzantine Jewish community was not the one in the East, but the one in Sicily and southern Italy, already described at the beginning of this chapter. Popular anti-Jewish sentiment was aroused by the iconoclastic controversy, which rocked the

This selection is from a poem by Eleazar of Mainz, one of the great rabbis of medieval Germany, whose wife and children were killed in the aftermath of the Third Crusade:

> . . . *Let me speak of my big daughter Bellet.*
> *Thirteen she was, and shy as a bride;*
> *knew all the prayers and hymns from her mother—*
> *modest, pious, lovely, and clever.*
> *Modeled herself, pretty girl, on her mother,*
> *making my bed, taking my shoes off at night.*
> *Handy at housework was Bellet, and honest;*
> *served God, spun, sewed and embroidered.*
> *Pious, faultless, always well-meaning—*
> *she would sit quietly, listening, as I discoursed on Torah . . .*
> *She was killed with her mother and her sister on the night of the*
> *twentieth of Kislev.*
> *I was sitting at peace at my table—*
> *two pieces of filth came, killed them as I looked on—*
> *wounded me, my disciples, my son.*
>
> *Now let me speak of my little daughter.*
> *She already was saying the Shema—just the first lines—every night.*
> *At six she was spinning and sewing,*
> *embroidering, entertaining me with her singing.*
> *Alas for my wife, alas for my daughters!*
> *I mourn, I lament—how have my sins caught up with me! . . .*
> *My sons and my daughters—all dead!*
> *Woe to me for my pious wife!*
> *Woe to me for my sons and my daughters, I mourn them . . .*

> *But You, God, are just, and I am ashamed.*
> *God is the righteous one, I am the sinner.*
> *Whatever You grant me, I thank You,*
> *sing You my hymns,*
> *bow to You, and bend my knee.*

Byzantine Empire from about 726 to 843; those within the empire who attempted to eliminate icons from Christian worship were accused by their opponents of being the tools of the Jews, whose worship does not tolerate the use of images, and this accusation subjected the Jews to violent attacks.

The persecutions in Byzantium under Basil I and especially under Romanus I Lecapenus, mentioned earlier, induced many Byzantine Jews to flee to Khazaria. This militant little kingdom had been established by the seventh century by a pagan Turkic people known as the Khazars; it was located in the region north of the Caspian and the Black Seas and had its capital at Atil, on the Volga. Remarkably, the ruler of this kingdom and his whole ruling class converted to Judaism, probably around 740. The Byzantine rulers did their best to try to destroy the Khazar kingdom, but could not press too hard for fear of reprisals against the kingdom's Christian minority. The existence of the Khazar state was a source of great comfort for Jews worldwide; it signified to them that, though they had lost their homeland in Palestine and though they were at best a tolerated minority in the Islamic world and at worst a persecuted minority in the Christian world, God had not forgotten them, but had granted them one place where they were their own masters. News of the Khazar kingdom reached Spain in the tenth century, and Hasdai Ibn Shaprut, the leading Jewish figure of that community (see chapter 4), initiated a correspondence with Joseph, the contemporary Khazar king. It was just during this period that the Khazar kingdom reached the fullest extent of its sway, but in 965 it received a crushing blow from the rising Russian power of Kiev. It was still in existence in the twelfth century, but after that we lose sight of it.

The Jews of Christian Spain

We have already followed the extraordinary success of the Jewish community of Islamic Spain, and we have seen how the arrival of the Almohads in the 1140s put an end to the period of their greatest flourishing. The Muslims had never succeeded in controlling the entire peninsula; there always remained pockets of Christian control, especially in the area around Barcelona in the northeast and the Asturias in the northwest. By the late eleventh century, the little Christian kingdoms were expanding southward; Toledo was conquered by Alfonso VI of Castile in 1085, the first major event in the long process of the Christianization of Spain. This process was completed for all practical purposes by 1248, by which time all of the Iberian Peninsula was in Christian hands except for Granada and its territory. This territory remained an independent Muslim kingdom until 1492.

The expansion of Christian rule in Spain spelled opportunity for the Jews. They knew the land, its inhabitants, and especially its language, Arabic, and many of them had experience in its administration, especially in the area of taxation and finance. The new Christian rulers were in need of skilled administrators to help them control and govern a population that would naturally be looking for opportunities to subvert their rule. Muslims might look to neighboring Muslim states for help in restoring Muslim control; Jews had no one to look to for support except the ruler himself. Thus, the pattern of Jewish life in the rest of medieval Christendom was also established in Christian Spain: The Jews were clients of the rulers, who could be counted on to protect them from the masses—up to a point. For a long time, this arrangement worked well for the Jews of Spain, and the Christian kingdoms seemed like a haven. In addition, the Christian rulers of

The Main Jewish Communities of the Iberian Peninsula after the Reconquest

Communities after the Reconquest

Spain were generally rather independent in their responses to the demands of the popes, and they often failed to enforce regulations emanating from Rome regarding the treatment of Jews.

The Jews were also a valuable cultural resource in Christian Spain. Arabic remained the language of high culture and the key to Greek science and philosophy, since the books of the ancients were available only in Arabic or Hebrew translation. The presence of Jewish and Christian scholars together made Spain a hub for the study of the works of the ancients and a center for the translation of their books. Jews teamed up with Latin-speaking churchmen in the work of translation. A Jewish scholar might read aloud the Arabic translation of a

Greek work, translating into Castilian as he read, and the Christian scholar would translate the Jew's Castilian dictation into Latin as he wrote. Or the Jew might work from a Hebrew translation that had been made from the Arabic version of a Greek text. This activity, a harbinger of the Renaissance, became an important route for the transmission of Greek writings to the Latin-speaking monasteries and universities of the West. It was encouraged especially by Alfonso X of Castile (known as Alfonso the Wise, ruled 1252–84), who supported many cultural and scientific projects. Alfonso had Jewish courtiers among his advisers and Jewish astronomers among his protégés.

In Aragon, the other great state of Christian Spain, the Jewish community was somewhat more conservative and its position somewhat less favorable. Barcelona, which had an important Jewish community, had never been Arabized, and its region, Catalonia, had always had important ties to southern France. It was therefore more like the rest of Christian Europe, and its Jews closer to Ashkenazic Jews in outlook. During this period, this region served as a kind of bridge between Ashkenazic and Spanish Jewry, with scholars traveling back and forth between Narbonne or Lunel in "Provence" (for the purposes of Jewish culture, this term includes not only Provence proper but the entire Mediterranean part of France) and Gerona, just north of Barcelona. Here an important religious academy existed in the thirteenth century, where talmudic studies were pursued in the Ashkenazic manner, and the kabbalah, which had originated in Provence (see earlier), was disseminated to the rest of Spain. One of the leaders of this academy was Rabbi Moses ben Nahman (also known as Nahmanides, 1194–1270), a famous talmudist and mystic who, though personally opposed to some of Maimonides' philosophical opinions, attempted to play a moderating role in the controversy over his writings and the permissibility of the study of philosophy that flared repeatedly in thirteenth-century Provence and Spain. His disciple and successor, Solomon Adret (c. 1235–1310), all but entirely banned the study of philosophy.

Under James I of Aragon, the Jews of the region came under pressure to convert. Induced by the Dominicans and a Jewish apostate named Pablo Christiani, the king himself presided over a disputation between the two religions in 1263, having summoned Nahmanides to represent the Jewish side. It was a dangerous position for the rabbi to be in, since anything he said in refutation of Christian doctrine could be interpreted as an insult to Christianity. Though even the king admitted that Nahmanides acquitted himself well, the rabbi was forced to flee for his life and ended his days in Jerusalem, where the synagogue he is said to have built is still standing.

In Castile, Jewish intellectual life retained its ties with the illustrious Arabic tradition, though it naturally came to absorb elements from the Christian environment. Here too, kabbalah came to be an important area of religious and intellectual life, achieving classic formulation in the Zohar, a large collection of mystical treatises, including a mystical commentary on the Torah written by Castilian scholar Moses de Leon (c. 1240–1305); this work did not achieve truly widespread dissemination until the sixteenth century.

Even the enlightened king Alfonso X had included in his law code, the *Siete Partidas*, the harsh anti-Jewish measures of the Fourth Lateran Council, and toward the end of his reign he turned on his Jewish advisers, imprisoning and killing some, and nearly ruining the Jewish community of Toledo with his exactions. After his reign, the position of the Jews in Castile gradually deteriorated, although their lives were generally stable during the first half of the fourteenth century. Jews continued to hold royal appointments, especially in the spheres of finance and tax collecting; the most famous example in this period is Samuel Halevi, who was close to Pedro I (known as "The Cruel"); the lovely synagogue he built in Toledo is one of the few Spanish synagogues from the Middle Ages that is still standing.

But the preaching orders of monks were active in Spain throughout the fourteenth century and did much to undermine the Jews in the eyes of the population. When Spain, like the rest of Europe, was hit by the

The Zohar

Though the Zohar became the most influential classic work of Jewish mysticism, it represents but one of several distinct mystical forms that Judaism has taken over the millennia. It is actually not a single book but a whole library of mystical commentaries on the Bible and mystical treatises composed mostly during the last third of the thirteenth century. The books are interwoven with one another, so that one breaks off and gives way to a second, and then resumes; sometimes parts of two different books appear side by side in parallel columns or with one as an inset on the page.

The main author of the Zohar was Moses de Leon, who composed his work in Aramaic, the language of the Talmud and some other ancient Jewish books, but which the Jews had stopped using centuries earlier. The reason for this tour de force was that Moses de Leon wanted the book to appear not as his own composition, but as an ancient work that he had discovered. He claimed that the author was Simeon bar Yohai, a wonder-working rabbi of the second century C.E., and this attribution, though often questioned, prevailed until this century. Nevertheless, some of the traditions embedded in the Zohar probably are considerably more ancient than the thirteenth century.

The Zohar elaborates in a nonsystematic but insistent way the idea that each word of the Torah refers to one of the myriad aspects of God as He is manifest in the universe. God Himself is hidden and unreachable, but different aspects of His inner being take the form of manifestations, called *sefirot*. These *sefirot* are related to one another as are the limbs of a human being, so that God manifests Himself to the world as a kind of supernal man. But the *sefirot* are constantly shifting and changing both in their own nature and in their relations with one another, and these changes determine the course of the cosmos. The words of the Torah, in their true signification, refer to the *sefirot* in their varying aspects; the Torah is thus not simply a collection of stories and laws but a kind of blueprint of the Deity, or even a mysterious name of the Deity. The interaction of the *sefirot* determines the course of life on earth, but conversely, the behavior of mankind has an effect on the *sefirot* themselves, and therefore on God. Man's purpose is to restore, through the correct performance of rituals and by leading a life of holiness, the perfection of God that was disturbed by a primordial cataclysm that brought about the creation of the world. Man and God thus exist in a kind of mutual interdependence.

Black Death in 1348, the Jews were the target of mob hysteria, which the preachers helped to direct against them. Intense anti-Jewish preaching by a Dominican monk led to a violent attack on the Jewish community of Seville in 1391; this violence quickly caught on all over Spain and resulted in thousands of Jews being killed (as much for their property as out of religious zeal) or forcibly baptized. Many fled the cities for the countryside or fled the country altogether for North Africa, where their presence enriched the cultural life of the existing Jewish communities. But the outstanding and most unusual result of the atmosphere of hysteria that prevailed in 1391 was mass conversion to Christianity, a phenomenon unprecedented in Jewish history.

This event precipitated the long and painful slide of Spanish Jewry toward its extermination a century later. With pressure to convert unremitting, there arose alongside the Christian majority and the Jewish minority a third community consisting of new Christians, or *conversos*. Many of this constantly growing group became sincere Christians, and after a generation or two, their descendants may have had only dim memories of their Jewish origins. Some, though completely Christianized, continued to maintain some relationship with their unconverted families or continued to practice some Jewish customs, whether merely out of habit, superstition, or vestigial loyalty to their past.

Conversion opened the path of opportunity for many Jews. Some even became prominent churchmen. Rabbi Solomon Halevi, under the name Pablo de Santa María, actually rose to the rank of bishop of Burgos. Joshua of Lorca, under the name Gerónimo de Santa Fé, persuaded antipope Benedict XIII to hold a disputation at Tortosa. Unlike the comparatively intellectual atmosphere of the Barcelona disputation that had been sponsored by James I of Aragon, this one was a humiliating yearlong harangue. From 1413 to 1414, a battery of monks lectured the rabbis and the communal leaders of Aragon that the Messiah had already come and that this was proven by the Jewish texts themselves, while the Jewish representatives, severely restricted in what they were permitted to say by way of reply, could do little to keep the event from becoming a debacle. The result of this farce was that a number of the Jewish disputants simply gave up and converted, a development that had the very demoralizing effect on the Jewish community that the debate's organizers had been counting on.

During Spanish Jewry's last century, the Jewish communities, reduced in numbers and wealth, became a less prominent feature of Spanish society. New Christians, on the other hand, were everywhere, occupying positions in court and church that had never been accessible to them before. Now the distaste that had formerly been directed at the Jews was diverted to them. They were accused of converting solely in order to advance their own ambitions and to take control of the country. Those who retained some Jewish observances were accused of being insincere in their Christianity. Those who maintained relationships with their Jewish families were accused of backsliding into Judaism. The entire class of *conversos* came to be seen as potentially subversive to Christianity. Only Old Christians were considered real Christians; the New Christians were seen as being merely Jews in disguise. This idea took on a racial coloring in the notion of "Purity of Blood," which came to be seen as the criterion for acceptance into society. By the end of the fifteenth century, tensions were high again, this time directed at the *conversos* more than at the Jews themselves.

It was the problem of the *conversos* that led Ferdinand and Isabella to introduce the Inquisition into Spain. Their marriage, in

1469, had led to the union of Castile and Aragon—in effect, creating the kingdom of Spain. They were determined to extend their rule to Granada, the still-unconquered outpost of Islamic sovereignty, and to unify the peninsula religiously. The Inquisition, it will be remembered, was an investigative body of the Church designed to detect and prosecute heresy; the Church had never outlawed Judaism per se. Therefore, Jews as such were not the object of the Inquisition's attention, but New Christians could be denounced to the Inquisition under suspicion of not being sincere Christians, of having reverted to Judaism, or of being otherwise deviant in their Christian beliefs or practices.

The Inquisition was introduced into Spain in 1480. (It was not fully established in Portugal until 1547.) It was eventually extended to Spanish territories in the New World; incredibly, it lasted until 1821 in Portugal, and was not definitively abolished in Spain until 1834. A Christian could be denounced to the Inquisition either for observing Jewish customs or for appearing to be insufficiently Christian in behavior. Once arrested, the accused were usually examined under torture; if they confessed, they were required to denounce relatives and friends. Only rarely were the accused released from custody, and when they were, they were often physically broken and materially ruined. Persons found guilty and who refused to repent were burned alive; those who repented were given humiliating penances and were often reduced to penury besides. Convicted heretics could escape being burned at the stake by a last-minute confession, which entitled them to be strangled instead.

The system was inherently corrupt. The Church had great incentive to prosecute suspects, since their property could be confiscated if they were convicted. The Inquisition was also a useful tool for anyone of rank who wanted to eliminate an enemy, since a whisper in the ears of the inquisitors could bring about the person's arrest and ruin or death. The Church satisfied its own moral standards by scrupulously avoiding carrying out the death penalty; instead, convicted heretics were turned over to government officials for execution. The executions were often performed at great autos-da-fé, elaborate and colorful public spectacles that were extremely popular with the masses and the nobility alike.

Thus, the Inquisition did not officially concern itself with Jews. But after the expulsion of the Jews from Spain, and especially after the expulsion from Portugal, many of those New Christians whom it prosecuted actually were crypto-Jews, persons who had been baptized so as to be able to remain behind, but who kept up their old religious practices in secret. Such crypto-Jews were called Marranos (said to derive from the Spanish word meaning "pig").

Even after the establishment of the Inquisition, Ferdinand and Isabella had two Jewish counselors and financiers in their court, Don Isaac Abrabanel and Don Abraham Seneor. These men did their best to dissuade the monarchs when, in 1492, soon after the conquest of Granada, they determined on the expulsion of the Jews; despite the Jewish courtiers' efforts, the edict of expulsion was signed on March 31, and as of August 1 it became illegal for a Jew to set foot on Spanish soil. Some Jews became crypto-Jews, many fled overseas, and many others fled across the border to Navarre or Portugal. In Portugal, Judaism was not outlawed until 1496, but the expulsion from Portugal did not make as clean a break as the expulsion from Spain. When the Jews attempted to leave Portugal, the king halted the departures and had them all forcibly baptized on March 19, 1497. But because the Inquisition was slow to be established in Portugal and even slower to obtain full powers, it was safer and easier to be a crypto-Jew in Portugal than in Spain, and therefore the Portuguese New Christians and Marranos retained their ties to Judaism longer. In the next two chapters, we will find many of these Portuguese Marranos rejoining the Jewish people in other lands.

Thus, the greatest of all medieval Jewish communities was dispersed. The Jews of Spain were heirs to a long continuous culture that was different in many ways from that of Jews elsewhere in medieval

Europe. Having had a distinctively Arabic coloration before the Christian conquest, they became Spanish along with the Christians, as the Spanish culture and identity gradually came into being in the course of the late Middle Ages. Aware of and proud of their distinctiveness, they called themselves Sephardim, after *Sepharad*, the Hebrew name for Spain; and they retained their distinctiveness in their particular Diaspora communities, whose fortunes we shall follow in the next chapter.

The Jewish Merchant. Sketch of a Jewish gentleman of Persian origin living in Ottoman Turkey; he was called Mordecai in Hebrew, Murad in Turkish. Photo of sketch © Suzanne Kaufman. Courtesy of the Library of the Jewish Theological Seminary of America, New York.

SIX

The Jews in the Ottoman Empire and the Middle East

(1453 to 1948)

The effect on Jewish life of the expulsions from Spain and Portugal extended far beyond the fate of the particular families that were forced out of the Iberian Peninsula after 1492. Little by little, the Jews were expelled not only from Iberia but from other Spanish possessions as well, including Sicily, Sardinia, and parts of Italy. Refugees would sometimes be admitted to a place, only to be expelled again in the course of the sixteenth century. Marranos who had remained behind in Iberia, especially in Portugal, continued to leave Iberia throughout the sixteenth and seventeenth centuries out of fear of the Inquisition. The age was one of constant movement, and the problems of the Marranos—salvaging the wealth of some and relieving the poverty of others, finding them new homes, integrating them into existing Jewish communities, and solving the religious problems created by their having been or lived as Christians—dominated Jewish life in the Mediterranean world and, a bit later, in the Netherlands (see chapter 7) for a long time to come.

But even as the Jews of Spain were enduring their difficult final century, changes were under way in the eastern Mediterranean that

TIMELINE

JEWISH HISTORY		GENERAL HISTORY
	1453	Ottoman Turks capture Constantinople
Beginning of mass emigration of Spanish Jews to Turkey	1492	
	1498	Vasco da Gama discovers route to India
Palestine conquered by Ottoman Turks	1516	
	1517	Ottoman Turks conquer Egypt
	1520–66	Suleiman the Magnificent sultan of Turkey
Suleiman the Magnificent completes building the walls of Jerusalem, still standing	1542	
Inquisition fully operative in Portugal	1547	
Joseph Nasi created duke of Naxos	1566	Selim II becomes sultan of Turkey
Isaac Luria in Safed	1569–72	
Persian Jews forcibly converted to Islam	1622	
	1639	Ottoman Turks capture Iraq from Persia
Shabbetai Zevi proclaims himself Messiah	1665	
	1683	Ottoman Turks besiege Vienna
	1798–1801	Napoleon occupies Egypt, fails to capture Palestine
	1821	Greek war of independence
	1830	France conquers Algiers and Morocco
Palestine taken by Muhammad Ali of Egypt	1831	
Position of chief rabbi created for Ottoman Empire	1836	
Jews granted Turkish citizenship	1839	Westernizing reforms in Turkey
	1854–56	Crimean War between Russia and Turkey, France, and Britain
Damascus blood libel	1840	
Turks appoint first chief rabbi in Jerusalem	1841	
Tunisian constitution grants Jews full civil rights	1857	
Alliance Israélite Universelle founded in Paris	1860	
Moses Montefiore visits Morocco	1863	
Jews of Algeria become French citizens	1870	
	1908	Young Turk Revolution
	1914–18	World War I
Salonika fire	1917	
	1923	Ottoman Empire becomes modern Turkey
	1932	Iraq becomes independent
	1945	Formation of Arab League
Anti-Jewish violence throughout Middle East	1947	

would enable them to reorganize and flourish as an exile community. The Ottoman Turks, who had emerged from central Asia a century and a half earlier and conquered the Balkans and Hungary, took Constantinople in 1453, putting an end to the Byzantine Empire; they soon took control of Syria, Palestine, and Egypt, and later, Iraq and most of North Africa. The Ottoman Empire injected new life into the stagnant and fragmented Middle East and became a vigorous competitor and antagonist of Christian Europe, where the modern states were just coming into being. As the Ottoman Empire expanded, it inherited first the Greek-speaking Jews of the old Byzantine Empire and the mostly Arabic-speaking Jewish communities of the Middle East; when the disaster befell the Jews of Spain, it gladly welcomed the Spanish-speaking exiles. The sultans considered the Jewish exiles an economic asset to their expanding nation, which was strong in the military and agricultural arts but deficient in commercial experience, international connections, and linguistic skills, all of which the exiles from Spain could supply. Sultan Bayazid II is reported to have been incredulous that Ferdinand should be considered a shrewd ruler when, by expelling the Jews, he had impoverished his own country and enriched that of his enemies.

As long as the Ottoman Empire was burgeoning under a series of vigorous rulers, it permitted its subject peoples considerable religious freedom. The discriminatory regulations that had so humiliated the *dhimmis* during the long decline of the Islamic Middle East were neglected, and having paid the special *dhimmi* taxes, the Jews were left to govern their own affairs. Local authorities may occasionally have mistreated the Jews, but on the whole, the age of Ottoman ascendancy, through the mid-sixteenth century, was a new golden age for Spanish Jewry.

The Spanish Jewish exiles soon came to dominate the existing Jewish communities of the Ottoman Empire. Not all the newcomers were Sephardim, for the Ottoman Empire attracted Ashkenazim as well. But thanks to their sheer numbers and their pride in their

Spanish heritage, the Sephardim took control of Ottoman Jewry and lent it a distinctively Spanish coloration. These changes did not occur without intercommunal strife. Important Sephardic communities sprang up in Constantinople, Salonika, Edirne, Smyrna, and many other cities; in some of them, especially Salonika, the Sephardim dominated not only the local Jewish communities, but the life of the city as a whole. The number of the original Sephardic refugees was continually augmented by new refugees from Spain and Portugal, and later from Italy, as the expulsion was successively extended, first to the Spanish possessions there, and in 1569, to most of the Italian papal territories.

A particularly striking feature of Ottoman Jewry was the dominance of the Spanish language over the affairs of the Jewish community. In Spain, the Jews had not had a distinctive language; they spoke substantially the same dialects as their neighbors, though interspersing their speech with Hebrew terms when referring to Jewish customs and employing some expressions of their own. In the Ottoman Empire, they joined a heterogeneous society in which many religious and linguistic groups, such as the Armenians and Greeks, coexisted in major cities, as in Constantinople, in relative harmony; there was no common language that the Jews felt under pressure to adopt. Thus, it was only natural for them to continue speaking Spanish in their new settlements, and the Ottoman Jews came to be seen as a Spanish-speaking community. The Sephardim also carried their language to the Arabic-speaking territories conquered by the Ottomans, such as Palestine, Egypt, and Iraq, though in these linguistically more homogeneous territories, many Jews continued speaking Arabic. In time, the Spanish of the Ottoman Jews developed a character of its own—it remained somewhat archaic, compared with the more rapidly developing Spanish of the homeland, and it acquired an admixture of words of Turkish and Greek origin—and evolved into a distinctively Jewish language known as "Judezmo" (Jewish) or "Ladino" (Latin). It is still spoken by an ever-diminishing number of speakers, mostly in Israel. The pride that the

Sephardim cherished for their Spanish culture is reflected in the fact that they continued to stay abreast of literary developments in Spain, which entered its own golden age in the sixteenth century. This link is attested to by the translations of contemporary Spanish works into Hebrew that began to appear in the East.

Salonika was, alongside Constantinople itself, the metropolis of Sephardic life and culture; though it remained a major Jewish center until World War II, its greatest flourishing was in the sixteenth century. As in many cities of the Ottoman Empire, the Jewish community of Salonika was actually composed of many distinct communities. The original Romaniots had been joined by Bavarian Ashkenazim in the fifteenth century, and they were followed by Jews expelled from Spain, Portugal, Italy, France, and North Africa. Each group established its own community named after its place of origin—Sicily, Calabria, Mallorca, Lisbon, etc.—with its own synagogue and a complete panoply of communal services for its members. The communities were able to work in concert to issue common ordinances when necessary, and the rabbis sometimes issued joint rulings, as when they declared in 1514 that Marranos should be considered complete Jews with respect to divorce and marriage law. The Jews of Salonika were engaged in international trade, jewelry manufacture, weaving, and the dyeing of wool and silk. Salonika Jews established the first printing presses in the Ottoman Empire, and their scholars produced a flood of rabbinic *responsa,* poetry, scientific works, and kabbalistic writings—even a trilingual edition of the Bible in Hebrew, Castilian, and Judeo-Greek. Besides the usual schools, or yeshivas, they also established a school for singing and another for medicine, natural science, astronomy, and other subjects, adopting the Renaissance ideal of the universally cultivated scholar to the traditional ideal of the learned rabbi. This intellectual breadth, so different from the Ashkenazic preoccupation with Talmud, was typical of Sephardic Jewry at its height, as it had been of their ancestors, the Arabic-speaking Jews of Islamic Spain.

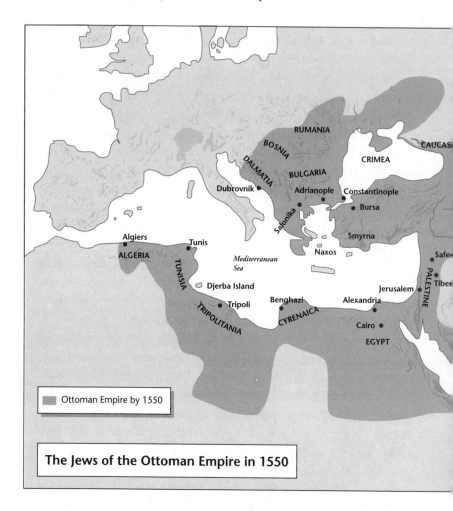

The Jews of the Ottoman Empire in 1550

Conditions under Ottoman rule were favorable to individual Jews as well as to communities. Wealthy, cosmopolitan Sephardim with connections throughout the Mediterranean that might include Marrano relatives in Spain, Portugal, Italy, the Netherlands, and even France were well placed to engage in both commercial and diplomatic affairs. Jews were particularly useful to the government, partly because of these connections and because of their linguistic skills, but

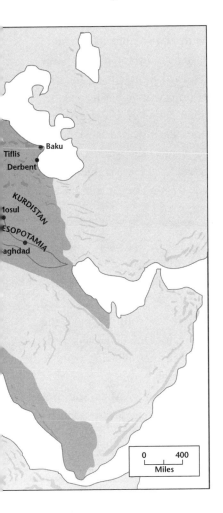

also for the traditional reason that their loyalty could be counted upon: Even the most ambitious Jewish aristocrat could not aspire to seize power, and there was no Jewish state to whom Ottoman interests might be betrayed. Jews could be especially useful in dealing with Spain, one of the empire's chief rivals, for while they had deep familiarity with that country and its language, there was not the slightest chance that they retained any loyalty to a regime that had treated them so brutally. By the middle of the sixteenth century, many individual Jews had risen to positions of power and influence as doctors, financiers, diplomats, and statesmen, and the Sephardic grandees of the Ottoman Empire reestablished, on an even larger scale, the pattern that had existed in Spain in both its Muslim and Christian phases, in which wealthy, cosmopolitan Jews held prominent positions in public life and at the same time were deeply involved in community affairs.

The most powerful Sephardic grandees of the era were Doña Gracia Nasi (c. 1510–69) and her nephew, Don Joseph Nasi (1524–79). Doña Gracia had been born in Portugal to Spanish Jews who had probably fled there in 1492, had been forcibly converted with the other refugees (see chapter 5), and had become Marranos.

She married a Marrano businessman with connections in Antwerp. After his death, she left Portugal with her family for England, the Low Countries, and Italy, where she returned to practicing Judaism openly. During this period, she engaged in extensive business activities, providing credit to the Holy Roman Emperor Charles V and King Francis I of France. At the same time, she provided assistance to Marranos seeking to escape Portugal. In Venice, she was denounced to the Inquisition by her own sister and had to flee to Istanbul, where she and her capital were welcomed by Sultan Suleiman the Magnificent in 1553.

With her upon leaving Portugal was her Marrano nephew, João, the son of a royal physician. After leaving Portugal, he continued his studies in Louvain and then joined the family business in Antwerp. While still a young man, he came to the attention of some of the most powerful men of the age, including Charles V, Francis I, and the future Emperor Maximilian. He was able to use connections in the Ottoman court to secure the sultan's support for Doña Gracia's release from Venice. Joining her there in Istanbul in the following year, he also reverted to Judaism under the name Joseph Nasi.

In Istanbul, Doña Gracia continued helping Marranos and attempting to subvert the Inquisition, patronizing Jewish scholars and founding Jewish religious institutions. One of her most ambitious activities on behalf of the Jewish people was her attempt, in 1556, to organize a boycott by all the Jews of the Ottoman Empire against the city of Ancona to punish it for treacherously burning twenty-four Marranos after having granted them permission to revert to Judaism. Had the boycott succeeded, it would have had a devastating effect on the city, but the conflicting Jewish interests could not be rallied behind it, and it failed.

Joseph had supported Prince Selim in his struggle against his brother Bayazid for the throne, and on the prince's accession as Selim II, Joseph became one of his closest advisers. Though, as a Jew, Joseph could not hold any official court position, Selim rewarded him with lofty titles and extensive powers, making him duke of Naxos and its archipelago, and later, count of Andros. Joseph had already obtained the extension of a grant that Doña Gracia had obtained from the sultan, conceding to her certain rights in Tiberias, and so was also, in effect, lord of Tiberias and its environs. Don Joseph attempted to turn Tiberias into a center for the manufacture of wool and silk, hoping thereby to benefit both the local economy and that of the empire. He imported mulberry trees and Jewish refugees from the Italian papal states to plant and cultivate them, so that the region flourished briefly. But Don Joseph never visited the place, and his plans for its economic development did not bear fruit.

Don Joseph's plan for Tiberias may have been the nucleus of a larger plan to solve the problem of the Marranos by creating a refuge for them in Palestine. He had collaborated in Doña Gracia's activities on behalf of the Marranos, attempting to induce the city of Venice to give one of the city's islands as a refuge for them. Later, when the Turks went to war with Venice over Cyprus, he was promised the kingship of the island in the event of a Turkish victory, and he may have had thoughts of using the island as a political solution to the Marrano problem. But after the Turkish defeat at Lepanto (1571), his career went into eclipse.

The brief flourishing of Tiberias was only a hint of the general revival experienced by the Jewish communities of Palestine and Egypt after the Ottoman conquest in 1517. These communities, impoverished and depressed, like all the Jewish communities under Mameluk rule (see chapter 4), suddenly sprang to life, thanks to the influx of the Spanish refugees. Gaza, Hebron, and Acre revived, as did Jerusalem— the construction of the massive walls that still surround the Old City was begun in 1537—and we have already noted the brief prosperity of Tiberias. But the most important of the revived Palestinian communities was Safed, in the Upper Galilee, a town that had never before been a major center of Jewish life, but that now became one of the most influential religious centers of the Jewish world.

The upheaval of 1492 had religious as well as political consequences, for it spurred many Jews to intensive reflection on the
meaning of the Jewish condition and brought about an intensification of mystical religious thought. Many Jews of a pietist cast of mind
were drawn to the academies of Safed, where the central figure was
Rabbi Isaac Luria (known as the Ari). He devised a new approach to
the great mystical classic of Spain, the Zohar, by which he attempted
to explain the sufferings of the Jews as cosmic events bound up with
the very nature of the Deity and Jewish ritual as a means of redeem-
ing God Himself and bringing about the messianic age. His ideas
were disseminated by his disciples to all parts of the Ottoman Empire
as well as to Italy and the rest of Europe. Kabbalistic rituals and
prayers devised in Safed were spread, along with Luria's thinking, to
other parts of the Jewish world and were incorporated into the liturgy
even by nonmystics; some of these rituals are included in prayer
books in general use today. The extent to which these innovations
were accepted as part of mainstream Judaism may be judged from the
fact that one of Luria's associates was Rabbi Joseph Caro
(1488–1575), author of the authoritative code of Jewish law, who was
himself subject to mystical visitations.

In the wake of the expulsion, such eschatological speculation was
accompanied by messianic movements. An impostor named David
Reubeni appeared in Italy and Portugal in the 1520s. He claimed to
be a prince of the lost Israelite tribes, which he said were living in
Ethiopia, and that he had been commissioned by God to liberate the
Holy Land from the Turks. In Portugal, he won many adherents
among the Marranos, including Solomon Molcho. Together they
went to Italy and managed to get an interview with Pope Clement
VII, whom they tried to persuade to permit the formation of an army
of Marranos; Molcho narrowly escaped being burned at the stake.
Later, they met with Charles V at Regensburg, apparently in order to
urge him to call upon the Jews to fight the Turks. This time, Molcho
did not escape; he was burned at the stake by the Inquisition in

Mantua, and Reubeni was sent back to Spain, where he probably died in an auto-da-fé in 1538.

The seventeenth-century messianic movement centering on Shabbetai Zevi was the one that had the greatest impact by far. Zevi, a kabbalist, was born in Smyrna in 1626. Expectation was widespread that the Messiah would come in 1648; in the wake of the failure of these expectations and the disaster of the Chmielnicki persecutions in the Ukraine (see chapter 7), Zevi came to believe that he himself was the expected messiah. After acquiring some followers, he performed weird ceremonies in which he publicly pronounced the ineffable name of God, and was excommunicated. He traveled to Constantinople, Salonika, Cairo, and Jerusalem, gathering adherents, including the mysterious Nathan of Gaza, who shaped Sabbateanism into a mass movement. In Smyrna in 1665, Zevi proclaimed 1666 as the messianic year. Jews from all over the Ottoman Empire and even Christian Europe acclaimed him; important rabbis and competent communal authorities, Ashkenazic and Sephardic alike, took him seriously. He went to Constantinople to open the messianic age by dethroning the sultan, but was, predictably, arrested and imprisoned in Gallipoli, where multitudes flocked to honor him and to await his signal to begin the journey to the Holy Land. But the sultan decided to put an end to his pretensions by offering him the choice of conversion or death, whereupon Shabbetai Zevi converted to Islam.

Shabbetai Zevi's apostasy was a blow to the morale of all the Jewish communities of the Ottoman Empire and Christian Europe. Nathan of Gaza attempted to salvage the situation by claiming that it was part of Zevi's messianic plan, a necessary descent into the world of darkness, where he would vanquish the force of evil; many Jews clung to the promise of salvation by telling themselves that it was merely a ruse. Even after Shabbetai Zevi died in 1676, Nathan of Gaza tried to keep the movement alive, maintaining that Shabbetai had gone into hiding in a higher sphere, having been absorbed into the "supernal lights." Such claims secured the movement an afterlife, especially in Turkey, Italy, and Poland. Many of Shabbetai's adherents in Turkey followed him into apostasy, practicing Islam in public and Judaism in secret while awaiting his return; this group, known as the Dönmeh, still exists in modern Turkey. In the eighteenth century, a Polish Jew named Jacob Frank revived the movement, claiming that he was an incarnation of Shabbetai Zevi and preaching a bizarre and antinomian blend of Zoharic, Christian, and Muslim ideas before converting to Islam. But the overall effect of the collapse of the Sabbatean movement was demoralization, as communities remained long divided between pro-Sabbateans and anti-Sabbateans.

The demoralization of the Jews of the Ottoman Empire corresponded to the empire's general economic and cultural decline. The central government's control over the provinces had begun to weaken as early as the end of the sixteenth century. The cordiality shown to the Jews by the sultans of the mid-fifteenth to the mid-sixteenth century abated, beginning with the reign of Murad III (1574–95), the first Ottoman sultan to enforce the discriminatory regulations against the Jews; he extorted money from the Jewish community by threatening to massacre them all, then rescinding the decree in exchange for a bribe.

As the seventeenth century progressed, these negative tendencies worsened. A stagnant economy impoverished most people, and given the weak control exercised by the central government and the unchecked rule of predatory local authorities, all minorities suffered from insecurity and abuse. The empire's failure to conquer Vienna in 1683, followed by the progressive loss of Hungary and much of the Balkans, led to demoralization. Islamic society drew inward, losing its earlier proud cosmopolitanism and becoming religiously more conservative. In the Arab countries, the ruling Turks treated the Arabs with contempt, the Arabs responded by pouring their own contempt on the *dhimmis*, and religious tensions ran high. In many places, Jews practically lost the protection of the law. Since the regulations governing the construction and number of synagogues came back into force,

Safed

Safed is a picturesque town in the mountainous Upper Galilee region of Israel, inhabited today by artists—who are perhaps attracted by the view and the town's quaintness—and by the intensely pious, who are attracted to its concentration of tombs of famous mystics.

Until the expulsion of the Jews from Spain, Safed had only a small Jewish population. Refugees began to arrive after 1492, and especially after Palestine was conquered from the Mameluks by the Ottoman Turks. At that time, conditions in Jerusalem were less favorable to immigrants, but the towns of the Galilee were more welcoming, and in the course of the sixteenth century, a number of scholars and mystics made their homes and established schools there. Among them were Joseph Caro, a Spanish rabbi who had spent most of his life in Salonika. He was the author of *The Prepared Table*, the code of religious law still considered authoritative by Orthodox Jews. But he was, in addition, a mystic who kept a diary in which he recorded nocturnal visitations by the Mishnah, monitoring and guiding his spiritual life. Another scholar-mystic who immigrated to Safed was Solomon Alkabetz, the author of a hymn to the Sabbath bride, still sung today in synagogues throughout the world on Friday nights. Caro's disciple in Safed was Moses Cordovero, who married Alkabetz's sister. He formulated a rule of life for a mystical brotherhood of Safed pietists, requiring that the members meet in pairs every day to discuss their spiritual lives and every Friday to talk over the deeds of the preceding week; that they confess their sins before every meal; and that they speak in Hebrew among themselves. Under the influence of such men, Safed turned into an otherworldly place dominated by scholarship, prayer, and nontraditional, extreme ascetic practices such as midnight vigils and extended fasting.

Stories were told of the mystics' heroic acts of piety. One Joseph de la Reina was said to have used his knowledge of mystic lore to lure Satan into his power. He was on the point of destroying Satan and bringing about the

continues

messianic age, when he accidentally allowed the enemy to escape, so that the world has since remained in its fallen state.

The most romantic of these mystical figures was Rabbi Isaac Luria, known as the Ari, one of the few Safed mystics who was of Ashkenazic origin. He had spent his youth in Cairo, where his teacher was supposed to have been the prophet Elijah himself. Immigrating to Safed, he established his own circle of disciples and became the hero of a cycle of folktales. He was said to be a superhuman being whose face shone like the sun, and master of all sciences who knew the language of trees, birds, and angels. He was said to be able to tell by looking at a person what transmigration his soul had undergone before coming into this world and what his mission was on earth, and what animals, insects, birds, and stones embodied the souls of the wicked of earlier ages. He could tell the past and the future and could assign penances for sins committed in a previous existence. Luria died in 1572, Caro in 1575, Alkabetz in 1584; thereafter, Safed fell behind Jerusalem in importance as a center of Jewish religious life. But it has never lost its mystical aura.

Ottoman Jews turned to holding services in private homes. These grim social conditions continued well into the nineteenth century.

Another reason for the decline of Jewish prosperity in the Ottoman Empire was the decrease in the flow of Iberian refugees to the empire after the sixteenth century, when Holland and Italy became their preferred goal. This decline deprived the empire's Jews of a supply of new forces that might enable them to recover, and it reduced their contact with western Europe just when the latter was in a state of rapid expansion and modernization. The Ottoman Jews gradually lost their advantage to the Greeks in the field of trade, and to the Armenians in banking. By the end of the eighteenth century, most of the Jews in the Ottoman Empire and in the adjoining Islamic territories were living in poverty and degradation.

Some Jews were able to prosper even under these unfavorable conditions, thanks to the system of "capitulations." These were the treaties designed to permit the establishment of commercial colonies for international trade; they were negotiated by foreign countries with business interests in the empire and permitted these countries to extend extraterritorial rights to their subjects in the empire. Since Jewish and Christian middlemen were essential for the transactions of these colonies, the protection of the foreign country, as well as exemption from some taxation, was extended to them, giving some Jews the advantage of a relationship with a European country. But in the long run, the system favored Greek Orthodox and Armenian businessmen, who were protected by Russia, and French Catholics, who were protected by France, for the European powers tended to shift business to their own coreligionists.

Napoleon's invasion of Egypt in 1798 marked the beginning of greatly intensified intervention on the part of the countries of Christian Europe and of the long process through which the Ottoman Empire became the modern Middle East. This process had a profound effect on the region's Jews.

Conscious of the weakness of the Ottoman Empire and afraid that its collapse would upset the balance of power in Europe, some of the European powers pressured the empire into introducing a number of reforms. These reforms were designed to strengthen the control of the central government and to assure the rights of the varied subject peoples; some of them had wide-ranging effects on the status of the Jews. In 1839, the empire extended civil equality to non-Muslims. In 1856, it decreed that non-Muslims could no longer be referred to abusively in official documents. Finally, in 1876, it granted full citizenship to all Ottoman subjects. This was a major break with the past, for an individual's status in Islamic lands had always been determined by religion and by membership in a religious community. But the new concept of citizenship emanating from the West could not immediately be put into effect throughout the empire, particularly in its Arab provinces.

The steps that were taken to tighten central control also affected the Jews. The power of the Jewish communities declined somewhat, since now that the Jews were officially citizens of the empire, the jurisdiction of the rabbinical courts was reduced. On the other hand, a central rabbinical authority was created—the office of grand rabbi, or *hakham bashi* (the institution had existed briefly in the sixteenth century)—and the religious communities were organized into the millet system, in which each non-Muslim religious community became an officially recognized autonomous body whose members were represented to the state through designated communal leaders. The purpose of these institutions was to strengthen the control of the central government, but the effect was partly to bestow political and legal equality and official recognition. The special tax paid by *dhimmis* was also abolished, and non-Muslims were included in local advisory councils.

With the relaxation of the Ottoman hold on North Africa, with its large Jewish communities, parallel changes to the Jews' legal status occurred there, too, but under quite different circumstances. In 1830, France occupied Algeria and subsequently established protectorates over Tunisia and Morocco. France soon absorbed Algeria, and by 1870, after a series of partial measures in their favor, granted the Jews the rights of French citizens. Tunisia, under somewhat Westernized Muslim rulers, maintained reasonably official liberal policies toward the Jews even before the establishment of the French protectorate; but because of the resistance of the Muslim population, the Jews continued to live as members of a religious community rather than as citizens. Most Tunisian Jews would have preferred French to Tunisian citizenship, but this did not become possible until after World War I.

But in Morocco, the mistreatment of the Jews was so extreme that it attracted attention in western Europe. Under pressure from a European delegation, the sultan issued a vague promise of amelioration, but he withdrew it as soon as the delegation had left the country. The proclamation of the French protectorate was accompanied by the massacre of Jews in Fez. The Jews of Morocco never did receive French citizenship, but their conditions improved somewhat under the protectorate.

Egypt was officially an autonomous province of the empire, but under its nineteenth-century pashas it behaved fairly independently. The physical security and material well-being of the Jews improved along with that of the country, which modernized somewhat more rapidly than its neighbors. But the Jews did not achieve full civil equality in Egypt until 1882, after the British occupation.

In Syria, tensions between the various religious communities ran high at all times, but it was the much larger and more prominent Christian population that bore the brunt of the tension. On the other hand, the Syrian Christians shared the Muslims' hatred for the Jews, and it was they who imported European-type anti-Semitism into the region. The Muslims of the Middle East had held non-Muslims in contempt and treated them uncivilly, but until the nineteenth century they had not known the demonizing myths that had been cultivated in medieval Christian Europe. In 1840, the first serious blood libel appeared in the Middle East; this was the Damascus Affair, in which a Jewish barber was accused of killing a monk in order to use his blood for Passover. Jewish children and leaders of the Damascus community were imprisoned, and under torture, some confirmed the accusation. Riots occurred in Rhodes, Beirut, and Smyrna, as Muslims joined Christians in attacking the Jews. The French consul supported the accusation; the Syrian Jews appealed to the Jewish communities abroad for help, and the matter quickly became an international event that was tied to the interests of the various Western powers in the Middle East. England intervened on behalf of the Jews, sending Moses Montefiore, an immensely wealthy British Sephardic philanthropist, to the region. After delicate negotiations, he managed to get a statement from the sultan denouncing the blood libel.

The condition of the Jews of Yemen, which was as miserable as that of the Jews of Morocco, did not improve at all in the nineteenth century, when the country suffered from the collapse of the rule of law and all non-Muslims were vulnerable to exploitation, extortion, and attack. They continued in unrelieved misery and total discrimination until the community emptied out soon after the establishment of the State of Israel. In Iraq, the situation of the Jews was so bad that wealthy Baghdad families such as the Sassoons fled to India or Australia.

In Iran, the establishment of the Shiite form of Islam as the state religion in the sixteenth century was particularly unfavorable for the Jews, as the clergy had almost unlimited power and all non-Muslims were defined as ritually unclean. Their status improved slightly toward the end of the nineteenth century under the influence of Western ideas and under pressure from Western institutions.

In the course of the nineteenth century, the Jews of the Middle East became progressively more Westernized and urbanized. Jews were drawn to great cities such as Cairo and Alexandria, and traditional patterns of life inherited from the Middle Ages began to break down. Generational splits developed as the young adopted European dress and patterns of culture and women began to leave the home to take part in cultural life. The modernization of the Middle Eastern Jews was abetted by the Alliance Israélite Universelle, which was founded in Paris in 1860 in order to work for the emancipation, welfare, and improvement of Jews worldwide, especially in the French territories of the Middle East. For this purpose, it established an extensive system of schools for religious and secular education in Hebrew and French throughout the Ottoman Empire and North Africa, as well as an agricultural school in Palestine. These schools taught secular and religious subjects and provided for the Jews who chose them the same cultural advantages as were available to Christians through the missionary schools established by Western Christian denominations. Though many Jews continued to send their children to traditional religious schools, the Alliance schools managed to produce a class of Westernized and prosperous Middle Eastern Jews.

The Jews' legal status, economic situation, and educational level slowly improved in the course of the century, but their relations with the Muslim majority did not. In part, this was because the Jews welcomed Westernization as a window of escape from oppression, poverty, and backwardness, while the Muslims saw it as colonialism and exploitation. The Muslims, who for centuries had denied the Jews a minimally dignified existence and had treated them with vilification and contempt, now saw the Jews' welcome of Western interests as treachery. Mired in their traditional poverty, they resented the success of the Jews and the Christians. Thus, the improvement of the legal and economic position of the Middle Eastern Jews actually undermined their social position and physical security.

The struggle of the various Christian populations of the Balkans for freedom from the Ottoman Empire, beginning with the Greek uprising in 1821, unleashed considerable ethnic strife (which, at the end of the twentieth century, continues to be a catastrophic problem in the region). The successive uprisings of Greeks, Rumanians, Bulgarians, and Serbs each involved the killing of Jews, and once independence was achieved, no pressure from the West succeeded in securing the Jews' protection. The persecution intensified during the Balkan wars of 1912–13. When the Jewish quarter of Salonika burned down in 1917, the Greek government refused to permit the Jews to resettle their ancient district and instituted other discriminatory edicts against them. But remarkably, even during this period of insecurity and decline, Sephardic culture bloomed, as Jewish newspapers appeared in all the major cities of the Balkans and the Ottoman Empire in French, Turkish, and Ladino, and Ladino culture flourished, especially in the fields of fiction, folk poetry, and music.

In World War I, the Jews of Algeria, who were French citizens, fought vigorously for their country, but the Tunisian Jews, who were not French citizens, were reluctant to fight, especially in the face of the anti-Semitism of the French officials in Tunisia. Palestinian and

British Jews, with the reluctant support of the British authorities, organized the Jewish Legion to help England fight the Turks.

World War I spelled the end of what was left of the Ottoman Empire, which, in 1923, became Turkey, consisting of little more than Anatolia. A modern regime with strict separation between state and religion, Turkey gave all its citizens, including the Jews, equal rights and religious freedom. The Jews of the other Middle Eastern countries were far less fortunate. While most of these countries came under the control of European powers, the patterns and trends that had affected Jewish life before the war continued in force, with conditions varying from country to country. Morocco, which had become a French protectorate just before the war, was one of the few in which the condition of the Jews actually improved, though they continued to be classified officially as *dhimmis*. But elsewhere, conditions deteriorated, as intensifying Arab nationalism put the Jews of the Middle East in an increasingly difficult position.

Arab nationalism envisioned the establishment of Arab states free of European influence, in which citizenship would be based on Arab identity and Islamic religion. Because of its predominantly Islamic and Arab nature, the Jews generally saw this movement as a threat to themselves. In some countries, non-Zionist Jews tried to position themselves as "Arab Jews," but met with little success. When the British occupied Iraq in World War I, both the Jews and the Christians begged the British, whom they saw as their saviors, not to reinstate an Arab government, or at least to grant them British citizenship. During the period when Iraq was a British mandate, Jews and Christians served in the civil service and a Jew even became a cabinet minister; but when Iraq attained its independence in 1932, it became impossible for a non-Muslim to hold a government position. In Algeria, which was torn between Arab nationalists and Francophiles, the Jews sided firmly with the latter, and in their personal lives they tended toward radical assimilation. In Egypt, which was more Westernized and cosmopolitan than most of the other

Middle Eastern states and less caught up in pan-Arab national sentiment, the Jews did participate in public life, and some affiliated with
the nationalist party and even served in the parliament. But in general, the Jews saw their interests as lying more with the Western powers than with the Arab states.

For some Middle Eastern Jews, the solution to the problem of
national identity was Westernization. This approach was encouraged
by the ubiquitous Alliance Israélite Universelle, with its program of
self-improvement through the adoption of French culture. Radical
Westernization came most naturally to the Jews of Algeria, whose
legal status as French citizens permitted them to identify themselves
as French and to seek assimilation, an approach that also recom-
mended itself to many Jews in France itself. Like assimilationist Jews
in France, they were not always accepted as French by non-Jews and
had to face the particular hostility of the French colonists in Algeria.
Their response to this hostility, paradoxically, was to embrace French
identity all the more fervently.

Many Middle Eastern Jews found the solution in Zionism. This
movement, which aimed at reconstituting the Jewish people as a
nation-state and establishing that state in Palestine, arose among
Ashkenazic Jews toward the end of the nineteenth century (for
details, see chapter 10), but it had a natural appeal to many Middle
Eastern Jews. These Jews had always had closer links to the Land of
Israel than the Ashkenazim, partly because many of them lived in
closer geographical proximity to it, and partly because during the
centuries of Ottoman rule, most Middle Eastern Jews had been part
of the same political and cultural sphere as Palestine. Sephardic Jews
had begun to settle in Palestine early in the century as artisans, entre-
preneurs, and founders of agricultural colonies. Later in the century,
they were joined by non-Sephardic Middle Eastern Jews from such
places as Yemen and Bukhara. These migrations occurred independently of the Zionist movement, which began only toward the end of
the century, among Ashkenazic Jews.

Egyptian Jews founded a number of Zionist organizations, and after World War I, the arrival of Palestinian Jewish refugees in adjacent Egypt stimulated more intense Zionist activity there. Moroccan Jewry, less Westernized and more traditionally religious, embraced the Zionist idea enthusiastically, but the opposition of the influential Alliance Israélite Universelle and the failure of the European Zionists to understand fully the conditions of Middle Eastern Jewry limited its organizational effectiveness. Algerian Jewry was naturally unreceptive to Zionism, given the prevailing tendency toward assimilation to French national identity. Zionism had better success in Tunisia. It was at first strong in Syria and Lebanon, especially after Palestinian Jewish refugees arrived there during World War I. It was slower to become organized in Iraq, where a combination of forces—the established conservative Jewish merchant class, the British mandatory authorities, the Alliance, and rising Arab nationalism—forced its adherents to maintain a low profile. By the late 1920s, the rise of Arab nationalism, first in Syria, Lebanon, and Iraq and later in other countries, together with the European orientation of the World Zionist Organization, led to the waning of Zionist activity.

Tension over Zionism became severe beginning in 1929, when a riot in Jerusalem brought the Palestinian national movement to the attention of the Arab nations and led to wild and widespread accusations against the Palestinian Jews. Arab nationalism came ever more into conflict with Jewish national aspirations. It also exacerbated the strain between the people of the Middle East and the Western colonial powers, damaging further the position of Middle Eastern Christians and Jews. Arab nationalism took a sinister turn when it began to emulate European fascism. Nazi Germany was an appealing model for Arab nationalists because of its hostility to England and France, the chief colonial powers active in the Middle East, and because it provided a model of extreme nationalism. European fascism carried with it a virulent strain of anti-Semitism, which, building on the traditional Christian demonization of the

Jews, cultivated a myth of an international conspiracy to bring the world under Jewish control. By the late 1930s, the anti-Semitic classic *Protocols of the Elders of Zion* and Hitler's *Mein Kampf* (minus its anti-Arab passages) were circulating in Arabic translation (for the former, see chapter 8; for the latter, chapter 9). By the end of the decade, with sabotage against the property of Jews a routine feature of life, the position of the Jews in many Middle Eastern countries had become untenable. In the hope of normalizing relations, Jewish community leaders disavowed Zionism; the leaders of Egyptian Jewry stressed their own Egyptian patriotism and tried to promote Egypt as a model of peaceful Jewish–Arab cooperation. But there was little the Jews could do against events that were being generated by much larger historical forces.

The German invasion of the Balkans during World War II put an end to Jewish life there, for the Germans were implacable in their policy of extermination of the Jews. (For the fate of the Jews of the Balkans and Greece, including Salonika, see chapter 9.) The war left the Jewish communities of Egypt and Yemen relatively unharmed, but the position of Iraqi Jewry deteriorated badly, especially after a massacre of Jews in Baghdad in 1941.

In North Africa, the Tunisian Jews came under direct German control, but the occupation was too brief to permit the invaders the kind of destruction that they visited upon occupied Europe. Despite the history of French anti-Semitism in Algeria and the discrimination suffered by the Jews of Morocco, the Jews of northwest Africa saw clearly that their interests were with the Allies, and they experienced the fall of France in 1940 as a terrible blow. Algeria and Morocco came under the control of the French Vichy government. Algerian Jews were stripped of their beloved French citizenship, and the anti-Jewish laws of the Vichy regime were strictly applied against all the Jews of northwest Africa. The French Vichy government legislation concerning Jews was not put into effect in the French protectorates of Syria and Lebanon. Perhaps surprisingly, the sultan of Morocco declared himself opposed to the anti-Jewish legislation, and he is said to have attempted to appeal to French authorities in favor of the Jews of Morocco. The liberation of these territories in 1942 and 1943 did not bring immediate relief to the Jews, as Vichy officials in many cases remained in control of the administrations of the countries involved.

World War II not only convinced most Jews of the Middle East that it was pointless to continue to hope for normal relations with the local population, but it also disillusioned them toward the European powers, to whom they had formerly looked for support. The result was the intensification of Zionism among the region's youth. But Zionism and Arab nationalism continued to move toward confrontation. Anti-Zionist and anti-Jewish riots occurred in Egypt, Libya, and Syria. When the United Nations voted to partition Palestine between Jews and Arabs in November 1947, a wave of violence spread throughout the Middle East. Only Morocco was spared.

The end of Jewish life in the Arab world (except for Morocco) came with the establishment of the State of Israel in 1948. The Libyan and Yemeni Jewish communities quickly emptied out completely, the Jewish population mostly migrating to Israel. The Iraqi Jewish community soon followed. Many Syrian Jews moved to Lebanon, a relatively cosmopolitan and tolerant multiethnic state, and many went to Israel. In Egypt, the lower classes went to Israel, while some of the rich moved to Europe or America, but most of the middle and upper classes stayed in Egypt, and for them, conditions did become somewhat normalized. Large numbers of Jews from Morocco also came to Israel, not so much because of oppression but out of sheer messianic enthusiasm generated by Israel's victory over the Arab League. The Jews of the modern, secular state of Turkey, which was created out of the Ottoman Empire after World War I, continue to thrive, but in greatly diminished numbers.

Thus, by the middle of the 1950s, the Jewish communities of the Middle East had been reduced to insignificance.

Early Hebrew Printing

The invention of modern typography is traditionally dated to 1440. The first printed Hebrew books that bear a date appeared in Italy in 1475, but there were Jewish printers in Rome as early as the preceding decade. Most early Hebrew printed books were produced in Italy, but Hebrew presses existed also in Spain and Portugal in the fifteenth century. Jewish refugees of the expulsion in 1492 carried their fonts with them from Iberia to Morocco, Italy, and Turkey, and introduced printing there.

The Ottoman rulers prohibited printing by Muslims, considering it to be a source of subversion. They allowed Jews to engage in printing as long as they did not use Arabic type, the script used both for Arabic and Turkish at the time. (Printing in Turkish became legal only as late as 1727.) Spanish Jewish refugees established the first printing press in the Ottoman Empire at Constantinople in 1493, and from there, printing spread to other Ottoman cities and to Egypt. Don Joseph Nasi was an important patron of printing, and his widow maintained a press in Constantinople.

Italy remained the main center of Hebrew printing during the first half of the sixteenth century, with the two important competing firms of Gershom Soncino and Daniel Bomberg, a Christian printer in Venice who specialized in Hebrew books. Soncino shifted his operations to the Ottoman Empire in 1527; it was Bomberg who accomplished the monumental achievement of printing the first complete edition of the Talmud, in 1520–23. When Pope Julius III had all available copies of the Talmud burned and prohibited the publication of any new editions in 1553, the Italian Hebrew presses went temporarily into decline, but Venice soon revived as one of the main centers for the production of Hebrew books.

The interior of the synagogue of Florence, built in 1882. Photo © Suzanne Kaufman. Courtesy of the Library of the Jewish Theological Seminary of America, New York.

SEVEN

The Jews of Western Europe

(1500 to 1900)

The changes in European society and intellectual life that began around 1500 had a profound effect on the Jews. The expansion of the European economic system provided a perfect vehicle for the economic improvement of a people who for centuries had been relegated to moneylending, as this formerly despised profession became transmuted into the respected field of investment. The rise of mercantilism and capitalism in the seventeenth century made fiscal expediency a more important criterion for toleration than religion. The early modern period also laid the foundations for the gradual breakdown of the intellectual monopoly of the Church, through humanism and the Reformation, and later through the Enlightenment, which undid the theological underpinnings of religious discrimination against the Jews. The latter part of the period also saw changes in political thought, making it possible to think of Jews as individual citizens of the state rather than as members of a corporate entity called the Jewish community. These changes would achieve full expression only in the period after 1700, but the foundations were laid in the early modern period.

TIMELINE

JEWISH HISTORY		GENERAL HISTORY
	1510–20	Reuchlin-Pfefferkorn controversy
Ghetto established in Venice	1516	
	1517	Martin Luther begins Reformation
	1523–84	Clement VII pope
Inquisition begins in Portugal	1531	
Solomon Molcho burned	1532	
	1544	Luther attacks Jews
	1545	Beginning of Council of Trent
Jews expelled from papal states	1569	
Burning of Talmud in Rome	1553	
Censorship of Hebrew books begins	1554	
First extant decree of the Council of Four Lands	1580	
	1581	Netherlands becomes independent of Spain
Marranos settle in Amsterdam	1590	
	1618–48	Thirty Years' War
	1649	Puritan Revolution in England
Menasseh Ben Israel in London	1655	
Excommunication of Spinoza	1656	
	1689	Locke argues for extending religious toleration to Jews
Joseph II of Germany and the Holy Roman Empire issue Edict of Tolerance	1782	
Death of Moses Mendelssohn	1786	
	1789	French Revolution
France grants civil rights to Jews	1791	
Assembly of Jewish Notables and Sanhedrin in France	1806	End of Holy Roman Empire
	1814–15	Congress of Vienna
Hamburg temple opened	1818	
Hep! Hep! riots	1819	
Beginning of large German immigration to U.S.	1836	
Moses Montefiore knighted	1837	
	1848	Revolutions in many European countries
Alliance Israélite Universelle founded in Paris	1860	
Ghetto of Rome abolished	1870	
	1870–71	Franco-Prussian War
Dreyfus Affair begins	1893	
	1914–18	World War I

We have seen that in the course of the Middle Ages, the range of occupations open to Jews in much of Christian Europe had been so reduced that hardly anything was left them but moneylending, usually on the small scale of pawnbroking, and trading in secondhand goods. This restriction enabled some Jews to accumulate capital and turned them into experts in the management of money and investments. Expulsions and forced migrations scattered members of individual Jewish families and communities all over the Western world, giving Jews international contacts that could easily turn into business connections. Finally, for all the cultural differences between Ashkenazim and Sephardim, several factors—their common status as outsiders, their shared minority religion, and their common written language, Hebrew—put them in a good position to mediate business connections between Christian Europe and the Islamic Middle East. Thus, as miserable as was the condition of the Jews worldwide at the beginning of the sixteenth century, the basis for their economic recovery was already in existence.

The waves of persecution and expulsion that began with the Crusades had gradually driven the Jews of central Europe eastward toward Poland and Lithuania, especially during the thirteenth and fourteenth centuries, but the mass exodus that shifted the focus of European Jewry to eastern Europe began only in the late fifteenth century. The migration was the product of intensified rejection by the West but also of a welcoming attitude on the part of the rulers of the East. Just as the Ottoman sultan was encouraging the fleeing Sephardim to settle in his territory because of their high education level, their skills, and their international business connections, so the kings and nobles of Poland were encouraging the Ashkenazic Jews to settle in their territories, and for similar reasons.

Poland in the fifteenth century (with Lithuania, with which it was linked in this period) was a major European power, but it lacked the manpower and business expertise for the management of large estates and long-distance trade. The need was especially great in the East, where Polish nobles owned huge tracts of land with thousands of villages that they did not wish to manage themselves or even to inhabit. Jews became the noblemen's managers and representatives among the native population, another variation on the pattern of the Jews having a special relationship with the overlord and living alongside, but not forming part of, the populace. By 1600, Jews had settled whole districts and were engaged in crafts, agriculture, trade, tax farming, and customs collection. After having been nearly completely excluded from economic life in central and western Europe, they found in Poland and Lithuania a haven of normalcy in eastern Europe parallel to the one found by the Sephardim in the Ottoman Empire.

Like the Sephardim, the Ashkenazim also carried the language of their homeland with them to their new home. Like other medieval Jews, the Jews of Germany had always spoken the language of their environment, but since they came to Poland as a class separate from both the rulers and the peasants, they lived mostly among themselves and did not use the language of their neighbors within their own circle. Their retention of German is a further indication of the small degree of their social integration into the population of eastern Europe. The German spoken by the Jews had already incorporated some Hebrew words and expressions; in eastern Europe, it gradually absorbed Slavic elements and came to be different enough from German to acquire its own name, Yiddish. As are Ladino and Judeo-Arabic, Yiddish is written in the Hebrew alphabet.

Thanks to their improved economic conditions, the Ashkenazim were now freer to develop intellectually; most of their intellectual energy went into traditional talmudic scholarship, which acquired enormous prestige. Important academies flourished in Lublin, Poznan, and Cracow, and the great trading fairs of Lwów and Lublin became academic recruiting centers for these academies. A near-exclusive devotion to talmudic scholarship remained the hallmark of Ashkenazic religious practice until recent times.

As Jewish communities proliferated in eastern Europe, they were granted wide autonomy, which reached full expression in the remarkable Council of the Four Lands, a kind of Jewish parliament that regulated Jewish life in eastern Europe. This institution, a lay body that included rabbinical representation, supervised thousands of individual communities through a network of regional organizations, effectively governing the Jews of eastern Europe from 1580 until the early eighteenth century. Its prestige lent its decisions influence even among communities of western Europe, where there was no organization of comparable scope.

Eastern European Jewry sustained a severe setback in 1648, when the Cossacks of the eastern Ukraine, supported by Ukrainian peasants and Crimean Tatars, revolted against the Poles under the leadership of Bogdan Chmielnicki (1595–1657). The Orthodox Ukrainians slaughtered Polish nobles and Catholic clergy, and they were particularly vicious toward the Jews, who were the hated tax collectors and managers of the estates that the peasants farmed. Sometimes the Jews, offered the opportunity to save themselves by converting to Christianity, reenacted the behavior of their ancestors in the First Crusade, killing themselves and their families. The revolt spread west and north, amid fearful massacres and atrocities; the disorders lasted until 1655, when the Russians and Swedes invaded Lithuania. Each time, the Jews were victims. The Jewish population of Poland was significantly reduced both by the slaughter and by the resultant migration back to western Europe. Polish Jewry recovered by the end of the century, but its morale was damaged. The enthusiasm of eastern European Jewry for Shabbetai Zevi and his messianic movement (see chapter 6) was probably a result of the trauma; news of his apostasy was all the more crushing a blow.

In central Europe, the Humanist movement of the fourteenth and fifteenth centuries revived the study of ancient languages and cultures, and under the influence of these studies, scholars began to free themselves somewhat from the influence of Church doctrines. Some turned their attention to the Hebrew text of the Bible, Jewish Bible commentaries, and later Jewish writings, especially the kabbalah. Thus, Hebrew came to be integrated into High Renaissance scholarship alongside Latin and Greek. An odd example of this Christian commitment to Judaic texts occurred in 1513, when a Christian scholar named Johannes Reuchlin defended the Talmud in an ecclesiastical court against a former Jew named Pfefferkorn, who had tried to have all copies in the Holy Roman Empire confiscated. Reuchlin's prestige helped to make the study of Hebrew respectable among Christian scholars. But even Reuchlin was true to the medieval Church's negative attitude toward the Jews, and other Humanists, such as Erasmus, saw too-intensive cultivation of Hebrew scholarship as a danger to Christianity. Thus, although Humanism made Christian scholars more aware of Jewish traditions, it did not have any directly beneficial effect on the life of the Jews.

The Reformation, begun by Martin Luther in 1517, instead of encouraging Christian tolerance toward Judaism, actually heightened anti-Jewish attitudes among the Christian clergy. Early in his campaign, Luther included in his critique of the Church its persecution of the Jews, assuming that his attack on the popes and his appeal to the authority of the Bible would win Jews over to Christianity. When it did not, he turned on them as "disgusting vermin," urged Christians to treat them with enmity, and endorsed their expulsion from various German states.

The Church's reaction to the reformers' challenges, the Counter Reformation (which may conveniently be dated from the Council of Trent, convoked in 1545), was an even greater step backward. As we have seen, the medieval popes, as the executors of the official Church policy that granted the Jews a meager tolerance, had generally been their protectors. The humanist popes of the Renaissance in the early sixteenth century had been especially favorably inclined toward the Jews, as had many of the ruling families of the great Italian cities, such as the Medici in Florence, the Gonzaga in Mantua, and the House of Este in Ferrara. Now, in the popes' struggle to regain control of Christendom, they included the Jews in their attack on all religious deviancy.

Perhaps surprisingly, the Council of Trent did not deal specifically with the Jews, but the Jesuit order, founded in 1541, conducted an aggressive campaign to convert them. The Church dealt the Jews of Italy a particularly severe blow in 1555, when Pope Paul IV ordered the Jews of Rome and other papal territories to be segregated into ghettos—walled-in neighborhoods where all of a town's Jews were required to live, cages for Jews with gates that were locked from sunset to sunrise. In a small town, the ghetto might consists of no more than a single overcrowded, unsanitary street with a gate at both ends. The first ghetto in Italy, established in Venice in 1516, lent its name to all ghettos subsequently founded (the word means "foundry" in Venetian dialect; this was the name of the neighborhood in Venice that was first designated for the confinement of Jews). Walled Jewish neighborhoods already existed in some towns outside Italy, notably Frankfurt. They now became a standard feature of Jewish life, first in the papal territories of Italy and Provence, then in most of the major Italian cities. The building of ghettos continued until 1732.

In the reactionary climate of the Counter Reformation, the Inquisition was now on the lookout for Marranos fleeing Iberia for Italy and reverting to Judaism; since Italy was no longer safe, many of them now moved on to the Ottoman Empire, as we saw in chapter 6, where we also saw how the pope withdrew the protection of the Marranos of Ancona, and with what bloody result. Jews in the papal territories had to wear a distinctive badge and a yellow hat, were forbidden to own real estate, and were expelled from smaller towns where they had lived for centuries. Censorship was imposed on the Hebrew books being printed in profusion on the Italian presses.

But even the harsh restrictions of the Counter Reformation did not prevent the flourishing of Italian Jewish life and culture. By the time of the Renaissance, Italian Jewry had become a rather heterogeneous group. The original Jews of Byzantine Italy (see chapter 5) had spread over the peninsula and had been joined by various migrant groups: German Jews fleeing persecution and expulsion in the thirteenth and fourteenth centuries; Spanish and Portuguese Jews expelled from Iberia at the end of the fifteenth century; and Jews from the Ottoman Empire who had turned westward in pursuit of trading opportunities in the

sixteenth century. Known as Levantine Jews, this last group formed a fourth community alongside the Italians, Ashkenazim, and Sephardim. In the larger towns, all four groups maintained their separate identities; in the ghetto of Venice, one may still visit the old German, Spanish, Italian, and Levantine synagogues. Finally, throughout the sixteenth century, Marranos kept arriving from the Iberian Peninsula.

As in central Europe, the Italian Jews were largely expelled from the craft and merchant guilds and subsisted mainly by pawnbroking and trade with the Near East, though there was no uniformity, and in many places Jews were admitted to a variety of professions. Nevertheless, pawnbroking often provided the entire raison d'être of a Jewish community. In order to provide small loans to the poor, individual Jews were often granted a contract, known as a *condotta*, by local governments to live in a place for a stipulated number of years on the condition that they would establish a pawnbrokerage. In some places, Christian charitable loan societies were also established, specifically with the intention of putting the Jews out of business or inducing them to reduce their rates of interest. But in many towns, the Jewish pawnbroker and the charitable loan society existed amicably, side by side.

The *condotta* principle functioned on a larger scale as well: In big cities, where there was a need of capital for investment, whole communities of Jews would be granted a *condotta* so as to make available the capital for larger ventures. (This situation is the background to Shakespeare's play *The Merchant of Venice*.) The arrangement had to be renewed at fixed periods, and at each renewal, the terms would be negotiated between the Jewish community and the local authority.

One of the most interesting features of Jewish life in the Italian Renaissance is the extent to which the Jews, even after being segregated into ghettos, adopted the manners, tastes, intellectual activities, and pastimes of this colorful age. As it had been in the golden age of Hebrew in Spain, Hebrew poetry was a vehicle of social and communal life as well as a form of entertainment, but in Italy, Jews wrote poetry in Italian and Spanish as well. In a Jewish adaptation of Renaissance literary taste, the sermon was developed into a formal oration; for the first time, Jewish preachers compiled and published their sermons. Musicians abounded, especially string players, and choral music was much cultivated, even in the synagogues; Salomone de' Rossi composed secular music for the court of Mantua as well as motets for the synagogue. Judah Sommo wrote the first play in Hebrew. Young people organized races; rabbis had to debate whether it was permitted

Jewish Businesswomen

Though Doña Gracia was the most powerful Jewish woman in early modern times, she was not the only woman of her time to achieve extraordinary success in business. Another outstanding example was Benvenida Abrabanel, a niece of the great rabbi and courtier Don Isaac Abrabanel, whose attempt to intercede with the Catholic monarchs is mentioned in the main text of this book. The aristocratic Abrabanel clan fled Spain in 1492 and settled in Naples. There, Benvenida married her cousin, Samuel Abrabanel, a son of Don Isaac, who had become a financier to the king of Naples. Benvenida was so well educated that she became the tutor of Eleonora, a daughter of the Spanish regent and later the wife of one of the Medici dukes of Florence.

Benvenida was an active partner in her husband's banking career. In his will, Samuel made Benvenida his general heir, overriding the Jewish legal tradition that a man's heirs are his sons, in order to make her the head of the family business. Samuel explained his decision by stating that his own wealth was derived from her great dowry, which had been his start-up capital, and that he trusted her to run the household and business more than he trusted his sons. For his sons and their three daughters, Samuel only left fixed bequests and provided that Benvenida should pass the inheritance on to them as she would see fit.

By the time of Samuel's death, in 1547, the Jews had been expelled from Naples, and the family was settled in Ferrara. In that year, Benvenida successfully negotiated several banking contracts with the duke of Florence, who granted her and one of her sons permission to open a network of banks in the towns of Tuscany. Her relationship with Eleonora continued, and she was occasionally present at the ducal court in Florence, as were many other Spanish nobles.

Most Italian Jewish women, like most Christian women, were poor or very humble folk who worked at silk spinning or wool making in their homes. But there was also a middle class, which included women like

Ginevra Blanis, who lived in the ghetto of Florence. Ginevra was matriculated into the Florentine Silk Guild, not as a humble silk spinner, but as a manufacturer of silk cloth. In her testament of 1574, she made bequests to the Florentine Jewish community for the instruction of poor Jewish boys; for the maintenance of ten Jewish paupers; to provide dowries for eight Jewish girls; and, to adorn the synagogue, "twenty gold coins to be spent for a silver candelabra and a curtain for the Torah Ark, which the Jews shall promise to call mine."

to play ball on the Sabbath and whether it was permitted to play tennis at all, since tennis matches were the occasion for betting, which might be considered a prohibited form of gambling. Gambling with cards and dice was common enough to be a social problem; Rabbi Leone de Modena, one of the greatest preachers of Venice in the early seventeenth century, was addicted to it to the point of ruination, as he ruefully confessed in his memoirs. Yet with all their engagement in secular pleasures and general literature, the basis of education in the Italian Jewish community remained the basic works of the Jewish tradition—the Bible with its commentaries and the Talmud with its commentaries—together with the classics of the rational philosophical tradition, as well as the Zohar and other kabbalistic works.

Western Europe gradually became more hospitable toward the Jews in the last part of the sixteenth century. In 1579, the Low Countries freed themselves from the control of Catholic Spain sufficiently to grant freedom of religion. In the following year, Portugal was annexed by Spain and the lax Portuguese Inquisition became much stricter in its quest for crypto-Jews. This combination of events created a stream of New Christians and Marranos from Portugal to Amsterdam, which was later augmented by a flow of Spanish Marranos. Thus, Amsterdam, during the period of its great flourishing in the seventeenth century, was home to so many Jews and had such a rich Jewish life that it came to be referred to as "The Dutch Jerusalem." In the mid-seventeenth century, the Sephardim were joined by German Jews, and the two communities existed side by side, though it was the Sephardim who lent the community its particular color. Many of the Marranos who reached Amsterdam had formerly been doctors, lawyers, government officials, and churchmen; such intellectuals found a natural home in the Netherlands, which, in its great period of economic expansion, was also a center of Humanism. Jews were welcome primarily on account of their business skills and connections; they played an active role in the country's economic expansion. Jewish businessmen invested in the East and West India Companies and traveled to such remote places as Surinam, Curaçao, and Dutch Brazil. (This was to be the source of the first Jewish immigration into New York; see chapter 8.) By the late seventeenth century, the Jews of Amsterdam received permission to build a new synagogue. The magnificent Portuguese synagogue inaugurated in 1675, one of the finest buildings in Amsterdam at the time, may still be visited.

The new intellectual currents of the modern era affected Jewish life in the Netherlands to a greater degree than in many other Jewish communities. Holland in the later seventeenth century was a center of heterodox religious ideas, philosophical freethinking, and general intellectual ferment. The Dutch Jewish community organization (*mahamad*) tended to impose a strict communal discipline and tried to control the books published by members of the community, but could not prevent Jews from reading books in Spanish and Portuguese. The rigidity of the *mahamad* jarred against the atmosphere of religious toleration typical of the Netherlands in the seventeenth century, and there were troubling cases of rebellion. A poignant case was that of Uriel da Costa, a Portuguese New Christian who converted to Judaism and fled to Amsterdam to join the Jewish community there. But he had had doubts about religion even in Portugal, and in Amsterdam his freethinking led to his excommunication by the Amsterdam *mahamad.* Twice he begged for reconciliation with the community; on the second occasion, the penance to which he was ordered to submit was so humiliating that he committed suicide after undergoing it.

More significant was the case of Benedict Spinoza (1632–77). After receiving a thorough rabbinic education, Spinoza had studied the great medieval Jewish philosophers such as Maimonides and went on to study such modern philosophers as Descartes. He became a member of a philosophical circle, many of whose members, like many thinkers of his time, rejected divine revelation altogether as a source of knowledge, insisting on the priority of reason. Since these principles implied the rejection of the divine authority of the entire Jewish tradition, Spinoza was excommunicated in 1656. Spinoza went on to write his *Tractatus Theologico-Politicus*, which includes a fundamental critique of Judaism and, by implication, of Christianity. The work was very influential as a statement of philosophical deism, and Spinoza's works became a touchstone of heresy among both Jews and Christians.

The prosperous city of Hamburg also became hospitable to Jews, especially Sephardim, toward the end of the sixteenth century. In the 1590s, a dozen families of Portuguese Marranos arrived, intending to engage in trade. They were made welcome until it became evident that they were Jews, upon which the clergy tried to have them expelled. But their presence was considered so advantageous that the Hamburg senate permitted them to stay. The community prospered, especially in the seventeenth century, when Spain's policy of directing its trade away from Amsterdam to Hamburg gave it a great trading advantage; for a time, Hamburg became the second most important Sephardic community in Europe. German Jews were largely excluded from Hamburg until the mid-seventeenth century.

England began to readmit Jews in the second half of the seventeenth century, though without overtly reversing the expulsion of 1290. A small number of Marranos had been present in the country since the time of Elizabeth I; her own physician was a Marrano who was sensationally executed on suspicion of trying to poison her. Marranos increased in numbers and economic power during the reign of Charles I (1625–49), when the question of their toleration arose. The Puritan revolution of 1649 paved the way for toleration, because of Puritan admiration of the Old Testament and because Oliver Cromwell thought that Jewish commerce would be to the country's benefit. On the other hand, the clergy feared that the Jews would undermine Christianity, and the merchants feared Jewish competition. In 1650, Rabbi Menasseh Ben Israel (1604–57) of Amsterdam petitioned the English parliament to allow the Jews to enter England and to practice their religion openly, and in 1655, he came in person to England to present his petition to the government. Cromwell gave the informal guarantees that permitted the formation of a small Sephardic community in London. Charles II also confirmed the authorization of a Jewish presence in England, convinced that their economic benefit to the country as a whole was more important than protecting the English merchant class from competition; by the end of the seventeenth century, it was possible to be openly Jewish in England.

The Thirty Years' War, which devastated Europe from 1618 to 1648, actually encouraged the growth of the Jewish communities of central Europe. The Holy Roman Emperors and the rulers of the individual German states needed huge amounts of money to finance the war. Not only were Jewish businessmen capable of raising the cash; there was actually an advantage in borrowing from them, since they could often be paid back cheaply in concessions and privileges, such as the right to live in places or do business in areas formerly closed to them. These conditions intensified when the Swedes invaded Germany in the course of the war; the kings on both the Catholic side and the Protestant side defied the attitude of the populace, borrowing from the Jews and granting them residence privileges out of sheer self-interest. Thus, Jewish communities in central Europe increased in number and in economic significance.

The Thirty Years' War marks the beginning of wide Jewish involvement in state finance and in the provision of military supplies on a large scale. From this period come the first cases of "court Jews," individuals wealthy enough to supply the needs of the princes of the myriad tiny German states that formed after the Thirty Years' War; such court Jews would remain a notable presence in Europe until the mid-eighteenth century. Jews brought into the petty German-speaking courts as financiers and financial advisers gradually found their duties expanding into other areas, until they were indispensable. Wealthy Sephardim in Holland and Hamburg also emerged as important figures in the financial affairs of Spain and Portugal, despite these countries' particular hostility to Jews. Such Jews were often exempted from some of the restrictions that Jews normally had to endure; they might receive titles and honors, and sometimes might even socialize with their masters. But they were sometimes dropped by their Christian masters when their usefulness was at an end, and they were an obvious object of hostility by the Christian masses. A hallmark of their activity was that these men were leaders in the internal affairs of the Jewish community and used their influence to ameliorate the conditions of its members and to protect the Jews against attacks.

An outstanding example was Samuel Oppenheimer (1630–1703), who obtained the financing and organized the distribution of supplies to the Austrian troops that fought the French in the 1670s and defended Vienna when it was besieged by the Turks in 1683. In 1700, a mob stormed his house and destroyed his records, and the government refused to repay its debts to him, with the result that he died bankrupt. Another famous example was Samson Wertheimer (1658–1728), who financed the military operations of Austria and its German allies and was presented with a gold chain at the coronation of Emperor Charles VI in 1711.

The masses of Jews in this period were still poor; large numbers of them wandered between central and eastern Europe in quest of a livelihood as peddlers, beggars, and even bandits. The itinerants presented local communities with a serious social problem and were a burden on their charitable resources. Nevertheless, by the eighteenth century, the growing economic power of individual Jews and changes in the intellectual climate in western Europe at large were working together to bring about more favorable attitudes toward the Jews. Skepticism, deism, and other Enlightenment philosophies broke the monopoly of Christianity over the intellectual life of the West, opening the way to an evaluation of Judaism and of the Jewish condition free of the burden of theological opprobrium (though individual leaders of the Enlightenment such as Diderot and Voltaire remained contemptuous of Judaism as a superstitious, obscurantist system, and of Jews as ignorant and clannish). New conceptions of statehood and citizenship emerged in which the state was coming to be seen as made up of individual citizens governed by a single set of laws, rather than a network of autonomous and semiautonomous bodies (including the Jewish community). These principles did not immediately come into full effect, but to the extent that they did, they were favorable to the Jews as individuals, allowing them to improve their economic, social, and political conditions.

At the same time, these tendencies that were favorable to Jews as individuals tended to weaken the Jews as a community. The opportunities available to individuals served to attenuate communal control, and multitudes responded to their freedom by loosening their ties to the Jewish community and the Jewish tradition or abandoning them altogether in favor of French or German or other national identity. This conflict between the centrifugal forces operating on individuals and the centripetal needs of the community became a characteristic problem of Judaism in the modern era.

In an age rife with new political theories, many intellectuals turned their attention to the problem of the Jews in society, and many thinkers envisioned the Jews being absorbed into the body of the state, if they could only be properly educated. The Austrian emperor Joseph II, for example, was eager to "improve" the Jews, make them more useful for society, and prepare them for full civil rights—if they should come to deserve them. In 1782, he reduced their tax burden somewhat and took steps to encourage their social and linguistic assimilation. His approach may seem rather patronizing, but it was a considerable improvement over the earlier one, that the Jews deserved to be kept in misery. This approach to the Jewish problem was adopted—usually in the form of lip service—by several enlightened monarchs of the eighteenth century.

An even more positive approach was formulated by the English political philosopher John Toland, who argued in 1714 that merely granting the Jews civil rights would turn them into more useful and productive citizens. This opinion was shared by Gotthold Ephraim Lessing, one of the German Enlightenment figures most sympathetic to the Jews, who argued that the Jews should be treated equally simply because they were human beings, in spite of their religious and social distinctiveness. He was influenced in his thinking about the Jews by Moses Mendelssohn (1729–86), a German Jewish philosopher who managed to straddle both the Jewish world and the world of the Enlightenment. Mendelssohn, who was completely at home in contemporary philosophy and played an active role in contemporary intellectual life, also took seriously the project of salvaging Judaism as an intellectual system. He reformulated the basic ideas of Judaism in the spirit of the Enlightenment, arguing that, far from being a debased religion, Judaism actually embodied the highest ideals of the age. Through his writings and his personality, Mendelssohn impressed many influential non-Jewish thinkers as an embodiment of the Enlightenment notion that the power of reason, common to all human beings, could civilize even a backward people.

Mendelssohn contributed to the project of attempting to "improve" his fellow Jews by translating the Bible into German in order to provide them with a model of the correct use of the language and having his translation printed in Hebrew letters so that it would be completely accessible to them. He also influenced a generation of Jewish intellectuals to convey the ideas of the Enlightenment and modern ideas in general to the Jewish masses through journals and books written in Hebrew. These writers were known as the "Enlighteners" (*maskilim*, in Hebrew).

The French Revolution, after some initial hesitation, offered Jews a perfectly clear choice: They could enjoy the full civil rights of

Frenchmen if they were willing to become acculturated as Frenchmen and to give up the corporate status they had had throughout the Middle Ages. Napoleon modified this position somewhat. In 1806, he convoked an Assembly of Jewish Notables and a mostly rabbinical body called the Sanhedrin to give religious sanction to the Assembly's resolutions. This Sanhedrin ruled, among other things, that the Jews had a religious duty to regard the state in which they were born or had settled as their fatherland; it confirmed the love of French Jews for other Frenchmen; it condemned usury; and it declared the priority of French courts over Jewish courts. Having thus undone the principle of Jewish corporate status, the Sanhedrin was adjourned.

This was a decisive moment in the history of Judaism, for it was the first time that a body of Jews officially defined themselves as constituting a religion rather than a people. Having thus established the basis for the treatment of Jews as equals, Napoleon then partially revived the medieval system by creating a central organization to represent them collectively and to supervise the implementation of his plans for them. Finally, Napoleon created regional associations subordinate to the Ministry of Religion for the supervision of Jewish life in France, known as "consistories."

Napoleon later effectively reversed his position on the Jews' equality as citizens of the empire by subjecting them to some discriminatory laws; furthermore, the Jews' acquisition of citizenship did not alter the traditional odium that the French felt, especially for the German-speaking Jews of Alsace. Nevertheless, Napoleon was regarded by the Jews as a great liberator, and the legal position of the Jews in France generally continued to improve throughout the nineteenth century. Conditions were especially favorable for the Sephardic Jews of France's southwestern territories, mostly highly acculturated descendants of Marranos who had fled adjoining Spain centuries earlier.

The emancipation of the Jews of France was extended to Italy and to the German territories occupied by Napoleon in his wars of conquest and was eventually grudgingly extended to the Jews of Prussia in 1812. But the fall of the Napoleonic empire was accompanied by a reaction; the Congress of Vienna refused to ratify the rights that the Jews had acquired under the empire, and 1819 saw violent anti-Semitic riots called the "Hep! Hep!" disturbances. Jews participated actively in the liberal revolutions that swept Europe in 1848, but the failure of the movement again set back the process of full emancipation. It was only in the second half of the nineteenth century that the Jews were granted full civil rights in central Europe: in Italy, with the unification of the country in the course of the 1860s; in Austria-Hungary, through the constitution granted in 1867 by Emperor Franz Joseph I; and in Germany, after many fits and starts, in 1871, soon after the unification of the German states and establishment of the German Reich. In England, the process was considerably less protracted; early in the nineteenth century, Jews had virtually all the rights of Englishmen except that of holding public office, and that watershed was crossed in 1858, when Lionel Rothschild was seated in the House of Commons.

Having thrown off their disabilities, the Jews of Europe rapidly joined the general European population in its numerical growth and material improvement. Their numbers now outstripped by far the numbers of the Jews of the Middle East, whose story was told in the preceding chapter. With the secularization and commercialization of society, large numbers of Jews were able to take up new occupations or to practice their traditional occupations on a much larger scale. Jews turned from being peddlers to storekeepers to businessmen; from talmudic scholars to lawyers, doctors, and even German teachers (though professorships were still only rarely available to them). Within a few decades, they had left the ghettos and joined the growing bourgeoisie. A few had success on a grand scale, lending money and underwriting bonds for whole countries, as their predecessors, the court Jews of the seventeenth century, had done for the princes of the German states. Such were the Rothschilds of Frankfurt, the Pereiras of France, and the Bleichroeders in Prussia. Baron de Hirsch, a Jewish estate owner in Bavaria, financed railroad construction.

That not all elements of society were prepared to accept the Jews as fellow citizens was a discovery that assimilated Jews were repeatedly forced to confront. The depth of anti-Semitic feeling, even among the intellectual leaders of enlightened French society, was revealed by the case of Alfred Dreyfus. Dreyfus was a high-ranking Jewish officer in the French army who, in 1893, was charged with treason and convicted on the evidence of documents later proved to have been forged. The case and the cover-up by the French military establishment became an international cause célèbre, especially with the intervention of the novelists Emile Zola and Anatole France, who called worldwide attention to the injustice done to Dreyfus by the French military establishment. Dreyfus was eventually vindicated, but not before he had served five years on the Devil's Island penal colony.

The radical changes in the Jews' status had a profound effect on the internal life of the community. Now that Jews were no longer subjects but voluntary members of the Jewish community, many chose to leave its control. Some went so far as to convert to Christianity, partly in order to smooth their paths to the opportunities now within their reach, partly simply in order to conform to the dominant trend in society. But even the many who did not go to this extreme length relaxed their ties to the Jewish community, became lax in religious observances, and gave priority to European education over Jewish education. In many cases, this was a principled decision; now that Judaism was reduced from the status of a national identity to that of a religion, it could not sustain the loyalty of persons who were genuinely attracted by the secular culture of the age or by Christian spirituality. In other cases, the falling away from tradition was simply the product of apathy in a world in which conformity to tradition could no longer be compelled.

Enlightened Jewish religious leaders attempted to counter these destructive tendencies through religious reform. Strongly influenced by the arguments that had been marshaled in favor of political emancipation, they aimed at re-creating Judaism as a religious and ethical system externally resembling German Protestantism; they wanted to minimize the national element in Jewish identity, the rituals that were associated with that identity, and any religious behavior that tended to mark the Jews as superstitious aliens. On a practical level, they revised the synagogue service to make it more dignified and rational, introducing the use of the German language for sermons and even for some prayers. They renamed the synagogues "temples," using the word that had always been reserved for the Temple of Jerusalem, and implying the abrogation of the age-old messianic dream that the Temple destroyed by Rome would one day be rebuilt for a newly reunited Jewish people. Radical reformers wished to abolish all religious impediments to integration with non-Jews, such as the dietary laws and the prohibition of mixed marriages. The first reformed synagogue was the Hamburg temple, founded in 1818, which issued a reformed prayer book based on the Portuguese rite and including prayers in German instead of Hebrew.

A new historical school of Jewish scholarship emerged, which also contributed to the modernization of Jewish religious traditions documenting the changes that Jewish rites, traditions, and doctrines had undergone over the centuries. This approach provided historical precedent for further change, for it demonstrated that all rites were not equally sacred, while at the same time it provided historical criteria for demonstrating which elements were truly constant in the Jewish tradition and therefore less amenable to change. Among the great representatives of this trend was the somewhat radical but extremely learned rabbi-historian Abraham Geiger (1810–74).

Changes in the synagogue rites occasioned much controversy within the German and Austrian communities, and several synods of German rabbis were held in the mid-nineteenth century to try to iron out the principles of reform. But unanimity could not be achieved, and the outcome of the controversy was the existence, side by side, of Orthodox and Reform congregations in the German-speaking countries, and, after 1840, in London as well. But even Orthodoxy gradually modified itself under such leaders as Samson Raphael Hirsch (1808–88), who labored to find a new intellectual

The Rothschilds

The name Rothschild, the famous family of financiers and philanthropists, derives from the red shield (German, *roter Schild*) that hung in front of the family home in Frankfurt in the sixteenth century. They rose to prominence in the eighteenth century, when Mayer Amschel Rothschild came to the attention of William IX, future ruler of the German state of Hesse-Kassel, as a supplier of coins and antiques for the ruler's collection. Mayer Amschel gained the confidence of William, who was heir to one of the greatest fortunes of Europe, and was able gradually to increase his share of the ruler's financial transactions. When William was exiled because of Napoleon's victory at Jena (1806), he entrusted a large part of his fortune to Mayer's son Nathan, in London, who made a fortune of his own in the process of purchasing securities for William and protecting his interests. Nathan became a central figure in the London stock exchange, lending money to the British government to finance the troops of Wellington, who were fighting the French in Spain. His brother Jacob (also called James), who had taken up residence in Paris, was able to help him transport the huge sums needed for this purpose through the heart of France. Meanwhile, the father and his eldest son, Amschel Mayer, stayed behind in Frankfurt; another brother, Salomon, established the family business in Vienna, and yet another brother, Karl, did the same in Naples.

The main Rothschild enterprises were embodied, throughout the nineteenth century, in three separate firms, founded by Mayer Amschel (Germany) and his sons Nathan (London) and James (Paris). All three engaged in vast financial enterprises on behalf of their governments, supported their national Jewish institutions, and provided for general charities. Many of the descendants of the five Rothschild brothers married other Rothschilds, and their affairs were often linked, but in spite of the popular misconception, the Rothschild firms of Germany, France, and England were discrete operations.

The German branch supported the orthodox community in the dispute over Jewish reform; its house in Frankfurt was attacked during the Hep!

Hep! disturbances and during the 1848 revolution. Its head for much of the nineteenth century was Mayer Karl Rothschild, who was pro-Prussian in the struggle between Prussia and Austria that led up to the unification of Germany; he was elected to the North German Reichstag and later was appointed to the Prussian House of Lords. This branch died out in 1901. The French firm, Rothschild Frères, pioneered in developing railroads. It energetically supported the activities of the French Jewish community, and one of its members, Edmond de Rothschild, gave crucial support to the early Jewish settlements in Palestine. During the occupation of France in World War II, all the French Rothschilds managed to escape the Germans' efforts to capture the family; one member joined the Free French and ended the war as an adjutant to De Gaulle's military governor of Paris. The British firm was headed, after the death of the founder, Nathan, by Lionel Nathan Rothschild, who, in 1847, became the first Jewish member of Parliament, and whose son, Nathaniel, became the first Jewish peer. Though Nathaniel did not incline toward Zionism, his son, Lionel Walter Rothschild, was a Zionist and was instrumental in securing the Balfour Declaration.

Although some Rothschilds continue to support Jewish causes, their involvement in Jewish affairs has on the whole diminished since World War II; assimilation to the non-Jewish world has had a similar effect on the Rothschilds as it has had on other Jews.

basis for the tradition. A middle position emerged when Zacharias Frankel (1801–75) broke with the Reformers. Like them, Frankel rejected the literal truth of traditional religious doctrine, but he differed in not being able to reject the national component of Jewish identity as expressed in traditional ritual observances. He became the ideological founder of Conservative Judaism, the third trend, which, however, did not become an important force until the following century, in the United States.

The Jews of an Eastern European shtetl on the Sabbath. "The Sabbath" by Leopold Pitichowski. Photo © Suzanne Kaufman. Courtesy of the Library of the Jewish Theological Seminary of America, New York.

EIGHT

The Jews of Eastern Europe and the United States

(1770 to 1940)

Eastern Europe

The condition of eastern European Jewry lagged far behind that of the Jews of western Europe.

When Poland was partitioned between Prussia, Austria, and Russia in the 1770s, the greater part of its huge Jewish population fell to Russia, which until then had excluded Jews. In order to control this huge population of "infidels," Jews were permitted to reside only within the territories that they already inhabited and in some territories recently annexed from Turkey that the Russians wished to colonize. This area was called the "Pale of Settlement." This restriction, with modifications, would remain officially in effect until the Russian Revolution. In 1804, Czar Alexander I issued the Jewish Statute, which promised "maximum liberties, minimum restrictions." It authorized admission of Jews to Russian schools and permitted Jews to open their own schools if they were operated in Russian, Polish, or German. But it prohibited them from residing or leasing land in villages and from selling alcoholic beverages to peasants.

TIMELINE

JEWISH HISTORY		GENERAL HISTORY
	1447	Poland and Lithuania united
	1518	Jurisdiction over Polish serfs transferred from king to landowning nobility
Jurisdiction over Polish Jews transferred from king to nobility	1539	
Rise of Council of the Four Lands	1580	
Chmielnicki massacres	1648	
First Jews arrive in New York	1654	
	1655	Poland becomes involved in Russian-Swedish War
Eastern European Jewry affected by Sabbatean movement	1665	
Death of Baal Shem Tov	1760	
End of Council of Four Lands	1764	
Jews of eastern Poland under Russian rule; Vilna rabbis excommunicate Hasidim	1772	First partition of Poland
	1776	Independence of the U.S.
Jewish merchants admitted to guilds in Russia	1778	
Russian Jews expelled from villages to towns	1782	
	1789	French Revolution; ratification of U.S. Constitution
Catherine the Great establishes Russian Pale of Jewish settlement	1791	Bill of Rights adopted in U.S.
	1795	Third partition of Poland eliminates Poland altogether
	1812	Napoleon invades Russia
Reform congregation founded in Charleston, South Carolina	1824	
Cantonist decrees in Russia	1842	
	1848	European revolutions generate large immigration of German-speaking Jews to U.S.
	1861–65	Civil War in United States
Pogrom in Odessa	1871	
Union of American Hebrew Congregations founded	1873	
Beginning of mass migration to U.S. from eastern Europe	1881	Assassination of Czar Alexander II
Kishinev pogrom	1903	

TIMELINE

JEWISH HISTORY		GENERAL HISTORY
Peak of Jewish immigration to U.S.	1906–9	
Beilis trial in Russia	1911–13	
	1914–18	World War I
	1917	Russian Revolution
End of mass immigration of Jews to U.S.	1924	
	1939	Beginning of World War II

Later, steps were taken to expel the Jews from the villages altogether, isolating them from the peasants; having first been penned inside the limited territory of the Pale, the Jews were now to be packed into the towns. This expulsion encouraged the expansion of the Jewish market towns—*shtetls,* as they were called in Yiddish—with their economy of small shopkeepers, craftsmen, and peddlers centered on the market-place, homes to the vast majority of the eastern European Jewish population. Only a handful of Jews were able to enter Russia as large-scale businessmen, and a Jewish city proletariat emerged only slowly.

After Napoleon's defeat, Alexander's pretensions to enlightened despotism gave way to the reactionary attitude emanating from the Congress of Vienna, and his repression of the Jews became more severe. His successor, Nicholas I (ruled 1825–55), hit upon the plan of ridding the country of the Jews by using the army as a vehicle for assimilating them into the general population. He established a quota of Jewish male youths to be supplied for military service. The normal term for eighteen-year-olds was twenty-five years, but Jewish children were taken from their families at the age of twelve and trained in special units called Cantonist battalions until they reached the age of eighteen, when their regular service began. During their training, efforts were made to convert them to Russian Orthodoxy. This edict caused great bitterness within the Jewish community, for community leaders responsible for its implementation quite naturally protected their own children by filling the quota with children of the poor.

Another measure aimed at assimilating Jewish youth was the establishment of modern schools for Jews, with a curriculum embracing both religious and secular studies, but designed to bring them nearer to the Christians and weaken their attachment to traditional beliefs. Most Jews perceived the assimilationist motive behind the curriculum and the schools never attained any great popularity, but the few graduates would later form the nucleus of a Jewish intellectual class in Russia. Other measures were taken by successive czars to encourage assimilation by rewarding the more assimilated Jews and penalizing others.

But even within the Jewish community, there were those who saw the benefits of modernizing the system of education and the Jewish way of life. The Jewish Enlightenment movement, which had begun in Germany under the influence of Moses Mendelssohn and his disciples, reached eastern Europe as well, via Galicia, the part of southern Poland that had fallen to Austria at the time of partition. The Jews of the great cities like Lemberg and Brody were in closer contact with German language and culture than were the Jews of the Pale of Settlement, and though strictly Orthodox, some were able to accommodate Western learning and to impart it in Hebrew, making it possible for eastern European young people to get a glimpse of modern literature and science. For thousands of yeshiva students, who were well versed in Hebrew but stultified by the limited scope of the traditional curriculum, such books were a window into an exciting and somewhat dangerous new world. The village freethinker and the yeshiva boy caught with a Hebrew novel hidden inside his enormous Talmud folio-volume became celebrated folk-types. The Hebrew textbooks, novels, and poetry of the mid-nineteenth century laid the foundations for modern Hebrew literature and the revival of Hebrew as a spoken language toward the end of the century. In the latter third of the century, Yiddish, too, emerged as a modern literary language, especially through the works of Shalom Abramowitsch (1835–1917), known by his pen name of Mendele Mokher Seforim, and Sholem Rabinovitz (1859–1916), known by the pen name Sholem Aleichem.

The masses of eastern European Jews were untouched by the religious reform that swept western European Jewry, but among them, too, were several religious trends. In the eighteenth century, Hasidism arose, a popular religious movement tinged by mysticism. Founded by Israel Baal Shem (c. 1700–60), Hasidism, which swept first the Ukraine, then other Slavic territories, was a corrective to the excessively intellectual Talmudism that had formerly dominated eastern European Jewish piety. Though theoretically grounded in the kabbalah, on a practical level it catered to the common man, stressed

Yiddish

Yiddish is essentially a dialect of German that the Ashkenazic Jews brought with them from western Europe as their centers of population shifted progressively eastward in the course of the Middle Ages. Since the Ashkenazic community itself originated in Italian- and French-speaking territory, this Germanic dialect always contained some Romance words and sounds, a handful of which are still present in modern Yiddish. But Yiddish became truly distinctive when the Jews made contact with Slavs in Bohemia and then in Poland. Jews who were already living in these territories at the time of the eastward migrations of Ashkenazim were speaking a Judeo-Slavic language. This language gradually disappeared (much as the Romaniot spoken by the Jews of the Balkans would later be overwhelmed by the Spanish spoken by the refugees who arrived in waves after the expulsion from Spain in 1492). But through the interaction of the immigrants with the established Jewish population, many Slavic elements entered Yiddish. From 1500 to 1700, as the Jews of eastern Europe became more and more separated from German-speaking territories, their language became ever more distinctive. The Hebrew and Aramaic elements in Yiddish—not only terms connected with religion, but words denoting all kinds of ordinary activities—also increased in number and importance. Such elements were always present in the speech of the Jews; they were familiar from widely studied religious texts such as the Bible, its commentaries, and the Talmud and its commentaries, works that deal not only with religious themes but also with everyday life.

After about 1700, the Jews remaining in the German-speaking world tended to assimilate linguistically to ordinary German, so that western Yiddish gradually disappeared. In eastern Europe, by the middle of the nineteenth century, a Yiddish press began to appear, together with a modernizing literature; eventually, schools were established in which Yiddish was the language of instruction, and Jewish social and administrative organizations were formed using Yiddish as the normal language of operations. But the social forces favoring the integration of Jews into European life were unfavorable to Yiddish, as they were to other aspects of Jewish identity. Most urban eastern European Jews adopted Russian or Polish in the early twentieth century, though important Yiddish-speaking institutions continued to exist in the cities through the 1930s. The shtetls, where Yiddish remained the main language of the Jews, lost population between the world wars and were liquidated by the Germans in World War II. Soviet policy, which for a time had encouraged Yiddish culture as one of many national languages of the Soviet Union and as the instrument of a new Jewish proletarian culture, turned against Yiddish and other forms of Jewish life in the late 1930s; the war destroyed much of the Yiddish-speaking population and their cultural institutions; and the Soviet Union finished the process by actively suppressing Jewish culture, beginning in 1948.

Yiddish was brought to America on a large scale by the huge eastern European immigration between 1880 and 1924. Though the immigrants were nostalgic for the shtetls from which they had come, they were more eager to take advantage of the opportunities offered by America than they were to preserve their native culture, and they encouraged their children to master English, even at the cost of a painful generation gap. Though most sent their children to afternoon classes for Jewish education, the education such children received usually consisted of a watered-down version of the kind of education the parents had received in the shtetl, stressing the reading of prayers and study of the Torah in Hebrew. Hebrew also gained status in Jewish education at the expense of Yiddish because of its revival as a spoken language in Palestine; to the extent that American Jewish children learned any Jewish language, it tended to be Hebrew. By the third generation, few descendants of eastern European Jews knew more than a handful of Yiddish words.

Outside of the United States, a small secular Yiddish press and theater still exist in Israel, Argentina, and Canada. Yiddish continues to thrive as the everyday language in only one community: that of the ultra-Orthodox, especially in New York and Jerusalem. The academic study of Yiddish is widely

continues

pursued in German universities, where it is considered an essential witness to medieval German. In the United States, the study and documentation of Yiddish is particularly encouraged by YIVO, an organization for the scientific study of Yiddish, founded in Vilna in 1925 and centered in New York since 1940.

ecstatic worship, and idealized naive forms of religious expression. Its leaders were charismatic rabbis, called *zaddikim*; they established courts in the shtetls and accepted homage from their adherents, who often came from great distances as pilgrims in quest of inspiration, advice, or simply a blessing. Some zaddikim claimed or were rumored to be able to perform miracles; many were treated by their followers like royalty and acquired considerable wealth.

Hasidism was harshly attacked by the great scholar-rabbis of Lithuania, led by Elijah of Vilna (1720–97). The heads of the yeshivas of eastern Europe correctly saw Hasidism as an attack on their own authority and leadership. The Hasidim were excommunicated by their opponents, or *Mitnaggedim*, as they were known in Hebrew, and both sides sometimes denounced each other to government authorities. Though Hasidism began as a somewhat heterodox movement, it became a strong force for conservatism in the face of the modernizing tendencies of the nineteenth century and has emerged again quite recently as the most visible traditionalist force in Judaism.

The assassination of Czar Alexander II in 1881 precipitated pogroms, especially in the Ukraine, followed by more repressive regulations for the Jews under the reactionary Alexander III. The official government policy of anti-Semitism culminated in the May Laws of 1882, which expelled the Jews from villages and confined them to towns and townlets within the Pale of Settlement. By this time, enough exceptional Jewish businessmen and professionals had received permission to live in Moscow for a significant community to have established itself there and built a fine synagogue, known as the

Choral Synagogue, which is still standing. In 1891, the entire community was expelled from the city and the synagogue was boarded up. During the reign of Nicholas II (1894–1917), Russian reactionaries cultivated anti-Semitism as a weapon in their struggle against the liberalization of the absolutist regime. It was these circles that produced the slanderous *Protocols of the Elders of Zion,* a forgery purporting to demonstrate the existence of an international Jewish conspiracy aimed at acquiring world power.

Jews now began to leave Russia in a mass emigration to the Western Hemisphere that began around 1880 and continued for more than forty years. Specific events, such as the pogroms of 1881–82, the arbitrary decree of 1891, and the political upheavals in Russia between 1903 and 1907, contributed to this movement, but persecution was not the main cause, for large numbers of Jews also left Rumania and the eastern parts of the Austro-Hungarian Empire, where they were far safer than in the realm of the czars. The main cause was poverty. The Jews' numbers in Russia had increased to 5.8 million, but they were still excluded from Russia's great industrial cities and from agriculture. With a substantial population and no economic opportunity, large numbers were mired in hopeless misery. Underpopulated but potentially wealthy countries like Argentina and Canada were also hospitable to immigrants, but the United States was powerful, rich, and rife with opportunity; besides, it had a strong tradition of religious freedom and a successful Jewish community already. It was the destination of choice for the outcasts of eastern Europe.

Those who did not leave tried other solutions. Some converted to Christianity. This was not a very satisfactory solution, not only because it meant breaking with family ties, but also because the converts could not find social acceptance by Russian Orthodox society; prejudice against Jews was so ingrained that it had shifted from religion to race.

For some, socialism was an attractive solution. Many Jews had moved from the shtetls to the cities as laborers, and in some cities they formed a significant part of the proletariat. Under the brutal working

The Hasidic Masters

One of the most characteristic developments of eastern European Judaism was the emergence of zaddikim, the religious leaders of the Hasidic movement. The model for this type of leadership was Israel Baal Shem, a popular healer who prescribed magic formulas, amulets, and spells; led his followers in ecstatic prayer; and provided guidance, both practical and spiritual. Many were convinced that he had supernatural powers and visions. Some of his followers established themselves in different shtetls of eastern Europe, and many of them created long-lasting religious communities dominated by their descendants or disciples. Each of these communities had its own character, often deriving from the character and teachings of the founder. Within each community, a body of lore emerged in the course of generations, including the master's maxims and teachings, stories of his life and behavior (sometimes including miracle stories), religious melodies (usually without words), and rituals peculiar to the community. Many of these communities continue to exist, as long as 200 years after their founding.

The Baal Shem's chief disciples were Dov Baer (known as "the Preacher") of Mezhirech and Jacob Joseph of Polonnoye. Dov Baer was a Talmud scholar and mystic; he came to the Baal Shem for a cure after becoming ill from extreme ascetic mortifications, stayed on as his disciple, and later became his successor. Jacob Joseph elaborated a theory of the role of the zaddik, according to which the zaddik is like the head or eyes of a human body and the members of his community are like the feet; the community is a living organism in which all parts play an essential role in achieving true adherence to God, but the duty of the zaddik is to exercise influence over the others, and the duty of the others is to believe in him with absolute faith.

Shneur Zalman of Lyady, a disciple of Dov Baer, carried Hasidism into Lithuania. Denounced to the government by the Orthodox leadership there, he was tried at Saint Petersburg for treason and acquitted. The date of his acquittal is celebrated to this day by the followers of the movement he founded, now generally known as the Lubavitch Hasidim. This movement has experienced a remarkable revival in New York in the course of the last twenty years. Levi Isaac of Berdichev, who stressed even more than other zaddikim the importance of ecstatic prayer, was immensely popular; he is famous for his Yiddish prayers in which he addresses reproaches to God for the Jews' suffering. He traveled extensively with his followers in order to win Jews to Hasidism.

Other masters had a far less popular kind of appeal. Nahman of Bratslav, a grandson of the Baal Shem, held a radical notion of the zaddik, amounting to the idea that he himself contained the soul of the Messiah and that one of his descendants would actually be the Messiah. The stories that he told in order to teach this and other mystical doctrines are now considered to be literary masterpieces. But Nahman was a moody figure of complexity and ambivalence. He required that his followers make regular confession to him; unlike other zaddikim, he did not receive his followers every Sabbath and festival, but only a few times in the course of the year. His grave in the Ukraine was long the object of pilgrimage for followers of his movement, especially since the Ukraine became independent in 1991. Menahem Mendel of Kotzk preached a doctrine of spiritual perfection so uncompromising that it led him to rage at his disciples. Eventually, he locked himself in an isolation chamber adjacent to his house of study, where his followers would congregate, and for twenty years he was rarely seen by anyone.

conditions of the times, they were affected by leftist political thinking just as were the non-Jewish workers. Many Jews joined radical groups seeking internationalist-type solutions to social problems, hoping that the common interest of the working classes would render national identity irrelevant. Some made this transition successfully, but many either could not give up their Jewish identity or were shocked by pogroms into returning to Jewish identity. In 1897, the Jewish Workers' Alliance (Bund) of Russia and Poland was formed; later it became a constituent organization of the Russian Social-

Democratic Labor Party, representing Jewish interests within the party. The Bund walked out of the party in 1903 because of its insistence on national-cultural autonomy for the Jews, but it continued to function, organizing self-defense organizations to resist pogroms and fostering educational and cultural activities.

Zionism, or a combination of Zionism with socialism, was another widespread approach. It will be discussed in chapter 10 as background to the history of the State of Israel.

The decline of the czarist regime was accompanied by continual deterioration of the position of the Jews. A major pogrom occurred in Kishinev in 1903. On the day after the czar promulgated the manifesto of October 17, 1905, establishing a constitutional government, right-wing pogroms lasting a week occurred in more than three hundred cities. Even the blood libel was revived, with the government's blessing, in 1911. A Christian boy had been found murdered in Kiev; though the police themselves knew the perpetrators and their motive, a Jew named Mendel Beilis was accused of murdering the boy for ritual purposes, jailed for two years, and put on trial. The charges against Beilis caused a worldwide outcry similar to the one that had occurred in connection with the Damascus blood libel (see chapter 6) and the Dreyfus case (see chapter 7). Beilis was acquitted by a jury of fair-minded peasants, despite efforts on the part of the judge to hamper the defense. Then came World War I, which forced many Jews to relocate to get away from the war zone (the Pale of Settlement had to be abolished to make room for them) and destroyed many of the shtetls.

Thus, the Jews greeted the abdication of the czar and the establishment of a provisional government in 1917 as a miracle, for it seemed as if the burden of centuries would be lifted from them. When the Bolsheviks took power under Lenin, horrendous pogroms occurred throughout the country, especially in the Ukraine in 1918 and 1919; the only armed group that did not persecute the Jews was the Bolshevik Red Army, which actually punished some perpetrators of atrocities. Thus, the Jews came to see the Red Army as their protector, and some joined the Communist Party not out of commitment to Communism but out of a kind of Jewish activism. The Bolsheviks dissolved Jewish socialist and Zionist parties of various stripes, and members who wished to remain politically active had to join the Communist Party, which created its own Jewish section. Both the party and its Jewish section set about dismantling Judaism as a religion and merging the Jewish community into the new community of the proletariat.

This effort became a kind of Jewish civil war, conducted in Yiddish, in which communist Jews battled the Zionists, the Hebraists (Hebrew was condemned as the bourgeois language of the elite, in contrast to Yiddish, which was lauded as the proletariat language of the masses), and the religious. But the party itself shifted direction in the 1920s, when it began encouraging the myriad national cultures within the Soviet Union to develop socialism with local cultural characteristics and insisted that government and party activities be carried out in the local languages. Party resources were made available to the cultural organizations of many ethnic groups within the Soviet Union, and one of the results was the emergence of a state-supported flowering of Yiddish culture! Books and newspapers began to appear in Yiddish, and a few non-Russian Yiddish writers actually immigrated to the Soviet Union, hoping to participate in a renaissance. But it was too late. The readers of Yiddish were aging, and the young preferred Russian, because Russian society seemed to have more to offer. Russian Jews were just as happy to abandon the shtetl for the modern world as were their American cousins.

The desire to rehabilitate the impoverished Jews remaining in the shtetls dovetailed with this new interest in individual cultures and yielded the idea of creating Jewish agricultural colonies. These would provide a living for the Jews in cooperative settlements in conformity with socialist ideas, while at the same time permitting the development of a secular Jewish life. Jews themselves had experimented with agricultural colonies early in the century. Now, many new colonies were started, but they did not prove very successful, and when they were collectivized in 1928, many Jews abandoned them. Nevertheless, that year saw the undertaking of the most grandiose such experiment, apparently proposed by Stalin himself, a large-scale Jewish settlement in Birobidzhan. This Far Eastern territory the size of Belgium was billed as a "Jewish Land," with the hint that if it succeeded, it might be turned into a Jewish republic. In 1934, the area was declared an "autonomous Jewish region." But life there was hard, and Birobidzhan did not draw the Jewish masses. Then, Soviet policy turned against individual national cultures once again, including Jewish culture, in the late 1930s. The leaders of the Jewish sections of the party were accused of having nationalistic tendencies and purged.

The intensive industrialization of the Soviet Union under the first Five-Year Plan (1928–33) created work in the cities. Large numbers of Jews took advantage of this opportunity, thereby improving their lives considerably, but also abandoning what was left of traditional life in the process. Living among non-Jews and eager to improve themselves, they adopted Russian culture as their own. For all the differences between the Soviet Union and the United States, the trends in the two countries were analogous: As the Jews acculturated, many of them entered professions, literary fields, and even the military; quite naturally, they also intermarried. But in the Soviet Union, there were hardly any Jewish institutions left, and religion of any kind was discouraged by the state. Under the circumstances, Jewish religion, culture, and even identity began to evaporate.

Meanwhile, Poland had been reconstituted as an independent country after World War I, so that many of the Jews of eastern Europe were not directly affected by Russia's communist regime. Poland started off by guaranteeing the rights of its minority groups; but a number of factors combined to permit the continuation, even the intensification of the old anti-Semitic patterns. When Poland's troops entered the Ukraine in 1920, Jewish villages were attacked as if they were military objectives. In the course of the decade, the economic discrimination against Jews threatened to exclude them from the country's economic life, on the theory that the economy could only support either the "natives" or the Jews. In the 1930s, many industries in which Jews were prominent were nationalized and Jews were dismissed from the civil service. Despite the misery that resulted from these interwar policies, Poland's cities had a solid Jewish middle class, consisting of Jews who spoke Polish, dressed in the Western manner, and enjoyed a comfortable life. During this period, Jewish culture, in the form of Yiddish film, theater, and literature, had a brief flourishing.

The United States

Eastern Europe remained the Jews' chief center of population and culture until near the end of the nineteenth century, but the mass migration of Jews from Europe to America that began around 1880 gradually turned the American Jewish community into the dominant Diaspora community.

When the great migration from eastern Europe began, the United States already had an established Jewish community. The first Jewish settlers were twenty-three Sephardic Jewish refugees from Recife, a Dutch colony in Brazil, who arrived in New Amsterdam in 1654, after the Dutch lost the colony to the Portuguese. A short-lived Jewish community existed in Roger Williams's colony of Rhode Island, at Newport. It was refounded in the 1750s, and the handsome Newport synagogue built in 1763 is a national monument today. A Jewish convert to Puritan Christianity taught Hebrew at Harvard University in the eighteenth century and wrote a Hebrew grammar, the first book to use Hebrew type published in America. By mid-century, Jewish communities existed in Newport, New York, Philadelphia, Charleston, and Savannah. By the time of the Revolution, there were about 2,000 Jews in the colonies, mostly Ashkenazim, though Sephardic customs prevailed. But the level of religious learning was not high, and the pressures for assimilation were great.

Most of the Jewish settlers supported the Revolution; about a hundred are known to have fought in the war, and two, Aaron Lopez of Newport and Haym Salomon of Philadelphia, were involved in the war's financing. Salomon had been sentenced to death by the British for espionage and sabotage. In the course of the war, he advanced the Continental Congress the then-immense sum of $200,000 to provision the armies but was never able to recover the money and died bankrupt. The federal constitution adopted in 1789 eliminated religious tests and oaths for officeholders, making it possible for Jews to hold federal office (though the states only gradually eliminated such oaths; it was still impossible for a professing Jew to hold state office in New Hampshire as late as 1868). The adoption of the First Amendment, implying the separation of church and state, was for the Jews a grant of unrestricted freedom and equality.

The number of Jews in the United States was greatly augmented beginning in the 1830s by large-scale immigration of German-speaking Jews from Bavaria and Jews from Bohemia, Moravia, and Hungary; a few were political refugees from the 1848 revolutions, but most were peddlers and cattle dealers attracted by the cheap land and new cities in the United States. These Jews differed markedly from the Jews already present in being far less acculturated and far more traditional in their behavior and religious attitudes. They also differed from the majority of the non-Jewish European immigrants of that age in that they brought with them experience in trading and were thus ready to benefit from the need for mercantile skills at a time when retail trade was expanding rapidly. German Jewish peddlers clustered together in German-speaking neighborhoods in the cities (for example, the Lower East Side in New York), and they traveled throughout the country, establishing themselves as far away as California, where they served the gold prospectors. In New York, they quickly graduated from pushcarts to stores.

By the time of the Civil War, there were small Jewish communities throughout the United States, including the Midwest and the South, and many of the Jews in these towns had become substantial merchants. There was also the beginning of a secular Jewish organizational life, for B'nai B'rith was established in 1843 as a Jewish equivalent to such organizations as the Masons and the Independent Order of Odd Fellows. Later, other charitable, social, and fraternal orders were founded. Synagogues were founded, too, partly out of piety, partly as a link with the Old World. Most of these synagogues at first duplicated the manner of worship that had been practiced in the orthodox synagogues of the Old World, but they gradually adjusted themselves to a more American style by eliminating the separation of sexes, introducing the organ, and employing some English in the service. A Reform congregation was founded in Charleston, South Carolina, in 1824, and it was soon followed by Temple Emanu-El in New York. Such congregations were striving to develop a style and a ritual that would be in tune with conditions in the United States, reflecting the position of the Jews not as outsiders but as full members of society, even at the cost of breaking with traditional views and practices.

One of the great spokesmen of this approach to Judaism was Isaac Mayer Wise (1819–1900), who, after serving briefly as a rabbi in Albany, became rabbi of a Cincinnati synagogue, where he introduced Reform rites. From this position, he campaigned energetically on behalf of Jewish causes in a lifelong effort to complete the normalization of Jewish life in America. Wise founded a weekly newspaper, *The Israelite*. He tried to unify American Jewish religious institutions under his own leadership, but failed at first in the face of opposition both from the religious right, led by Isaac Leeser, and the religious left, led by David Einhorn.

In the Civil War, Jews generally took the same side as their neighbors, whether North or South. Strong abolitionist positions were publicly taken by only two rabbis, the Orthodox rabbi Sabato Morais of Philadelphia and the Reform rabbi David Einhorn of Baltimore.

After the war, Jews continued to prosper, mostly as retailers; they dealt extensively in clothing, owning more than three-quarters of the country's department stores. A small percentage were engaged in finance, but Jews were not yet prominent in this field. Yet despite their prosperity, Jews were still unable to gain acceptance in non-Jewish society. The members of the new Jewish middle class experienced the same need as that of the striving peddlers of the previous generation: to create their own social institutions parallel to the ones that continued to exclude them, both in the form of social clubs and charitable organizations. By the 1870s, these charitable organizations were extending aid to Jewish immigrants from eastern Europe.

But immigration from central Europe continued. By 1880, German-speaking Jews and Reform Judaism dominated American Jewry to such an extent that Reform Judaism was synonymous with American Judaism, and American Reform Judaism was the most radically reformed Judaism in the world. After his earlier failed attempt, Wise succeeded in organizing Reform Judaism nationwide by creating the Union of American Hebrew Congregations in 1873 and a seminary, the Hebrew Union College, in 1875. The principles of the movement were defined in the Pittsburgh Platform of 1885, which rejected virtually all traditional rituals and any national aspirations on the part of Jews and sought to redefine Judaism as a force for social justice.

The mass immigration from eastern Europe that began in the 1880s was one of the great population movements of Jewish history. It altered radically and permanently the character of American Jewry. By 1918, the Jewish community of the United States was the largest in the world; when the United States began to close its doors in 1924, the number of its Jews had risen to 4.5 million.

The immediate effect was the creation of densely populated Jewish districts in all the major cities of the United States, especially in older slum areas. The immigrants, mostly poor Jews from Russia, became workers, many of them in the garment industry, which quickly became a distinctively Jewish field. The brutal working conditions in the sweatshops where clothing was manufactured sparked Jewish involvement in the labor movement; with the growing industrialization of clothing manufacturing after the turn of the century and with the arrival of leaders of the Socialist Bund after the collapse of the first Russian revolutionary movement in 1906, unionism gained in strength.

The concentration of Jewish population in the big cities permitted a burst of cultural activity in Yiddish. Yiddish newspapers appeared, as well as theater, lectures, and, later, radio programs; there were even Yiddish music publishers. Yiddish cultural activity was primarily secular in content, but nostalgic for the folkways of the Old Country. It was fostered by the Yiddish press and the Jewish labor movement, especially the Workmen's Circle, which also provided social benefits. Help was also provided for immigrants by hometown associations (*landsmanshaftn*); hundreds of tiny synagogues sprang up to serve the immigrants. But this colorful period could not survive the process of acculturation that was so natural in a land that had no tradition of Jewish corporate existence and virtually no legal impediments for most minority groups. The children of the immigrants became Americanized as quickly as they could and largely left the immigrant neighbors and their nostalgia for the Old Country behind. But the immigration period left a mark on the character of big cities such as New York that was still noticeable through World War II and of which traces are evident to this day.

For the prosperous German Jews, who had worked so hard at becoming Americans and gaining acceptance by non-Jews, the eastern European arrivals posed a problem. The newcomers were from a backward part of Europe; they were poor and narrowly educated, and, though literate, did not speak English. The German Jews feared that their "outlandish" brethren would become an intolerable financial burden and a cause of anti-Semitism, which until then had amounted to little more than snobbishness on the part of non-Jews and exclusion of Jews from clubs, private schools, and fraternities. Furthermore, there were important differences of outlook between the two groups of Jews: The German Jews thought of themselves as full Americans who differed from other Americans only in religion (whether they had convinced the non-Jews of this is another question), whereas the eastern European Jews, habituated for centuries to being an unassimilable minority, still tended to think of themselves as strangers in the midst of another nation. Their Jewishness included religious practices but was not defined by them, for even after the majority abandoned or drastically reduced their religious practices, they remained a culturally cohesive group. Far more at home with Jewish traditions than the German Jews, but, unlike them, nearly strangers to high European culture, they did not share to the same degree the German Jews' aspiration to be accepted by non-Jews.

The German Jews took responsibility for helping the immigrants become settled and Americanized, partly so that the immigrants would not become a public embarrassment that would jeopardize their own status and partly because, despite all the differences, the German Jews did feel kinship with the newcomers. They established a network of charities and educational institutions to relieve the needs of the poor and to help them find work; in many cities, these charities became linked into federations of Jewish charities for joint fundraising and distribution of funds. (These federations still exist and still play an important role in American Jewish life.) They also engaged in an effective political campaign, in collaboration with liberal circles, to keep immigration open. Nevertheless, tensions arose between the two groups, for the Russians felt patronized by the Germans. As the numbers of Russian Jews increased and their economic status improved, they began to set a rather different tone for American Jewry from that of the Germans.

Some Jewish leaders worried that as a result of too-rapid acculturation, the younger generation was being lost to the twin seductions of radical social doctrines and materialism. New York's Jewish Theological Seminary of America was founded in the 1880s and was reorganized in 1902 under the leadership of Solomon Schechter to provide for the training of modern English-speaking rabbis who could appeal to this first native generation. Schechter was a distinguished academic scholar of Judaism who had taught rabbinic literature at Cambridge. As a religious leader, he strove to build institutions to propagate the kind of liberalized but historically correct Judaism that had been promoted in Germany by Zacharias Frankel. Thus, Conservative Judaism came into being as a third religious movement alongside Reform Judaism and the variety of Orthodox institutions established by the immigrants. As a middle-of-the-road movement, its natural appeal to second-generation Jews made it the largest of the three movements in the United States for much of the twentieth century.

Another important educational institution established during the immigration period was Yeshiva University, which included an elementary school, a rabbinical seminary, and after 1928, a college providing secular studies together with traditional talmudic education. It was long the most influential Orthodox institution in the United States, though Orthodoxy was not as centralized as Reform and Conservative Judaism, and many smaller yeshivas existed in cities with big immigrant populations.

In the course of World War I, the eastern European immigrants challenged the long-established German Jewish population for leadership in American Jewish affairs. The Joint Distribution Committee was formed for the relief of eastern European Jewry, caught in the war zone between Russia and the Central Powers (i.e., the main population center of world Jewry in what had formerly been Poland); in this organization, the eastern European representatives sat as equals, though German Jews were the main contributors of funds. The American Zionist movement was organized in order to take over the work of the World Zionist Organization, which was paralyzed for the duration of the war because its headquarters were in Berlin; since the German Jews (except for Supreme Court Justice Louis D. Brandeis, who was chairman) rejected Zionism as compromising their view that Judaism was merely a religion, this gave the overwhelmingly pro-Zionist eastern European Jews of the United States a voice in world Jewish affairs. The eastern European Jews came into their own, particularly in the American Jewish Congress. This organization was an attempt to create an overall structure through which American Jewry could coordinate Jewish policy. In the elections for representatives to the Congress held in the spring of 1918, eastern Europeans came to dominate it and were able to push through a Zionist program.

In the aftermath of World War I, American politics turned toward isolationism, and the "Red Scare" of 1919–21 made foreigners appear sinister. The Jews were particular targets of these attitudes, partly because Jews were indeed prominent among the communists and other left-wing groups. Henry Ford attacked the Jews openly in print as racially inferior and as members of a master plot to control world civilization; he went so far as to republish *Protocols of the Elders of Zion* in his company newspaper. The Ku Klux Klan, which gained wide political power during the early 1920s, added Jews to blacks and Catholics as its targets. Racist government officials produced statistics to demonstrate that Jews, Italians, and Slavs were intellectually and morally inferior to immigrants from northern Europe. The outcome of these attitudes was the Johnson Act of 1924, which restricted all immigration from eastern and southern Europe to a trickle, ending an era in American Jewish history.

During the prosperous 1920s, the children of the immigrants began to enter the white-collar occupations, though most of them entered business, especially the clothing trades and real estate. They were still discriminated against in many professions, such as medicine and dentistry. Despite the popular perception that Jews were engaged in finance, it was virtually impossible for a Jew to own or even be employed by a bank during this period, nor were they employed at the management level of insurance firms. (There were, however, some Jewish investment banking firms.) They were also shut out of law firms and retail chains. When the numbers of Jewish students in the Ivy League universities increased noticeably in the early 1920s, quotas were imposed to reduce their presence at such universities as Harvard, Yale, and Columbia. The small quotas allotted Jews in medical schools forced many to go to Italy to study medicine. But free college education was available on a merit basis in New York, and City College of New York provided thousands of Jews with the education that enabled them to join the professions; thus, the presence of Jews in labor gradually diminished. Jews were also drawn to intellectual and artistic pursuits, such as publishing, entertainment, and motion pictures.

The Great Depression, which began with the stock market crash of 1929, put a strain on Jewish charities. It also caused a worrisome rise in anti-Semitism, which was partly expressed in increased discrimination against Jews in employment. A Catholic priest, Father Charles Coughlin, regularly denounced the Jews to his working-class constituency on his radio program, which Jews found particularly disturbing against the background of the rise of Nazism in Germany. But Jews continued to be successful in business and the professions. The New Deal created a bureaucracy that provided jobs for thousands on the basis of merit, making the U.S. government the major American employer that did not discriminate against Jews. President Franklin D. Roosevelt was the darling of the eastern European Jews also because of his vehement opposition to Nazism and his rejection of anti-Semitism.

The deterioration of the position of the Jews in Germany after 1933 drove some 33,000 German Jews to the United States. Among them were scientists (such as Albert Einstein) and intellectuals; their adjustment was often difficult, especially because the United States itself was experiencing economic hard times. But they were soon wielding great influence on many areas of American intellectual and scientific life. Hitler's anti-Semitism effectively drove Germany's intellectual leadership from Europe to the United States.

The American Diaspora was different from any other Jewish community in world history. We have seen in chapter 2 how the Jews of Babylonia quickly changed from being an exile community (one that was conscious of its foreignness and actively hoped to be restored to its homeland) to a diaspora community (one that had been granted the opportunity to return to the homeland but decided to stay put, at the same time feeling strong kinship with and responsibility for those who did decide to return). Such diaspora communities were generally treated as and felt like foreign bodies within a larger society, corporations linked more closely to other Jewish diaspora communities than to their own non-Jewish countrymen, living more in the remote Jewish past and the yearned-for Jewish future than in the present. The Enlightenment had offered one solution in the form of dissolution of the corporation, and Zionism had offered the opposite solution, reconstitution of the Jewish nation-state. But in the United States, a country founded on the basis of equality for all citizens and composed mostly of recent immigrants, a new type of diaspora emerged. Here, the Jews could be full participants in the larger society while retaining their loyalty to world Jewry and maintaining voluntary institutions for regulating their inner affairs. The immigrants themselves may have been far from becoming fully integrated in this society, but the possibility of full integration for the next generation was easy to imagine, and examples of people who had succeeded, or whose children had succeeded, reinforced the ambition. Thus, the American Diaspora was the first in which it was possible for a Jew to be actively Jewish and yet feel that he was not even a member of a diaspora.

Millions of European Jews had found a home in the United States. They had endured the trauma of uprootedness and dislocation, but they had dramatically improved their own lives. Many had moved in a single lifetime from near-starvation to prosperity and from a world in which they were a hated foreign body to a land in which they were full citizens guaranteed the protection of the law. They could look forward to an even better future. But millions of Jews remained behind in Europe, and in a short time, they would be gone.

The final stretch of the railway tracks leading to Auschwitz. Photo © Sally Soames; image photo-graphed by John Parnell for this book. Courtesy of the Jewish Museum, New York.

NINE

The Holocaust

A thousand years of Jewish history on the European continent ended in mass murder and suffering on a scale almost beyond human imagination between the years 1938 and 1945. The cataclysm permanently changed the shape of world Jewry.

When the Jews of Germany were granted civil rights in the course of the nineteenth century, most of them had gladly accepted German citizenship and cultural identity. The opportunities offered by acculturation were nearly irresistible. Even those who preferred to retain a link to the Jewish past saw the advantages of German culture and the German economic system and responded by adopting the western European style of life and taking German culture as their own. The participation of Jews alongside other Germans in the Franco-Prussian War in 1870–71 was a touchstone of their pride in their German citizenship, and the Iron Crosses won by Jewish soldiers in World War I were to them and their families not just recognition of their courage but evidence of their loyalty to the Fatherland.

But if Jewish attitudes toward the larger society had changed profoundly, the attitudes of that society toward them lagged behind. The

TIMELINE

JEWISH HISTORY		GENERAL HISTORY
	1889	Birth of Adolf Hitler
	1925–27	Hitler's *Mein Kampf* published
	1932	F. D. Roosevelt president of U.S.
Boycott against Jews in Germany	1933	Hitler becomes chancellor
Nuremberg Laws	1935	
Kristallnacht; racial legislation in Italy	1938	Annexation of Austria to Germany; partition of Czechoslovakia
Hungarian Jews lose citizenship; pogroms in Poland	1939	World War II begins with invasion of Poland
French Vichy regime imposes discriminatory laws against Jews; ghettos in Poland	1940	Churchill becomes British prime minister
Jews prohibited from emigrating from Germany; first death camp established in Chelmno	1941	
	1942	Wannsee conference
Mass transports to Auschwitz	1942–44	
Danish Jews smuggled to Sweden; Germany declared free of Jews	1943	German defeat at Stalingrad; Germans defeated in North Africa; Italy surrenders
Extermination of Hungarian Jewry	1944	Normandy landing
Liberation of concentration camps	1945	Germany surrenders
	1946	Nuremberg trials begin

heritage of centuries in which the Jews were viewed with suspicion as an alien body in the midst of a Christian world, centuries in which the clergy was constantly preaching that the Jews had killed the Savior, centuries in which the Jews were seen as the villains responsible for whatever troubles befell—that ancient heritage could not quickly be undone by those who had no special reason for wanting to undo it. When German society came under pressure in the aftermath of World War I, the traditional antipathy of European Christians toward Jews emerged, in a manner and with an intensity completely unanticipated by the German Jews themselves, who had thought that they were reasonably well integrated into German society.

Conditions in Germany after the war favored the rise of extreme nationalist thinking. The defeat and humiliation in the war and the economic crisis brought on by the victorious allies' crushing demand for reparations turned many Germans hostile to the outside world. Furthermore, the political instability and economic crisis of the postwar period led to unrest, and many feared a Communist revolution like the one that had recently overthrown the political system of Russia. In response to these attitudes, a number of extreme nationalist political movements came into being. The National Socialist (commonly shortened to "Nazi") Party, organized and led by Adolf Hitler (1889–1945), was the one that succeeded in becoming a viable nationwide movement.

From the beginnings of Hitler's career, the Jews played a central role in his political thinking. The cause of the German defeat in World War I, he claimed, was not any failure of the German people but the perfidy of the Jews. He also blamed them for the Communist revolution in Russia and claimed that they were working to bring about a similar revolution in Germany. In addition to these political arguments, he propagated a pseudoscientific racial theory, according to which the Germans and the other Nordic peoples belonged to a superior race of humanity known as the Aryans, the master race, distinguished by beauty, strength, and intelligence; other peoples belonged to inferior races and were ranked according to a hierarchy: The Mediterranean peoples below the Aryans, the Slavic peoples below the Mediterranean, and at the bottom, just below the blacks, were the Jews, a genetically criminal race given to corrupting and destroying civilization. Jews, Hitler claimed, had intermarried with Germans in order to dilute Aryan racial superiority; Jews had joined the military as a fifth column, written books to corrupt German intellectual life, become artists in order to pollute Germany with decadent filth, and infiltrated business firms in order to destroy both the firms and the German workingman. Above all, Jews had engineered the economic crisis. But the Germans could not ultimately be defeated, he said, because they were genetically superior to the rest of mankind and genetically predisposed to dominate.

In his early political manifesto, *Mein Kampf* (1925–27), Hitler had written that Germany would recover only if the Jews were destroyed. Thus, from the very beginning, the program of exterminating the Jews was among Hitler's chief goals and one of the reasons for his appeal to masses of Germans. The slogan was "The Jews are our misfortune." There is a very real sense in which Hitler's war, World War II, has been rightly called "The War against the Jews."

The Nazi Party did not come to power by means of a revolution or coup, and Hitler did not "seize power." He won an immense following because of the popularity of his violent message, including its threat to the Jews, and this following was sufficiently large and powerful to make him a player in the democratic political system (generally known as the Weimar Republic) by which Germany was governed between 1919 and 1933. He became chancellor by constitutional means on January 30, 1933, and his control of the government (and therefore, his political program) was duly ratified by 44 percent of the vote in elections held on March 5 of that year.

In the early years of the Nazi regime, the policy of the government was to rid Germany of the Jews by making their lives so difficult that they would simply leave. The importance of this policy to the government can be seen from the fact that it was put into effect soon after the elections, on April 1, 1933, in the form of a national boycott of Jewish businesses and professional offices. On April 7, Jews were expelled from the civil service. On April 11, the legal category "non-Aryan" (defined as someone who had at least one Jewish grandparent) was created to facilitate the isolation of the Jews from the rest of German society, and over time, laws were adopted that applied to members of that category; one by one, the various categories of employment were closed to persons so designated. Eventually, even children were removed from the schools.

The Jews soon became the objects of random violence, arbitrary arrests, and public humiliation at the hands of members of the Nazi militias and government officials. JEWS NOT WANTED signs appeared in businesses, cafés, sports stadiums, and resorts; even park benches were designated for Aryan or non-Aryan occupants. Jewish names on war memorials were effaced, and posters threatening the Jews were seen throughout the country. The culmination of this stage of persecution was the adoption of the Nuremberg Laws of 1935, which stripped Jews of German citizenship. It also prohibited intermarriage and imposed other restrictions and regulations.

In the meantime, the construction of concentration camps had begun. One of the first was built at Dachau in 1933. It was intended for people considered to be politically criminal or dangerous, such as communists, socialists, members of trade unions, Jehovah's Witnesses, and homosexuals, as well as Jews who were considered potentially dangerous, such as writers, journalists, and lawyers. In 1936, the camps were put under the control of the Gestapo (secret police), and the Gestapo was given freedom to detain anyone. New camps were built at Sachsenhausen and Buchenwald. The next year, Jews began being put in concentration camps solely because they were Jewish.

Under these pressures, many Jews did leave Germany, but there was no mass exodus. Not all German Jews had the contacts abroad to permit them to gain entry to another country or the financial resources to allow them to relocate, and most countries (including the United States) had strict limits on immigration. But beyond that, it seemed inconceivable to most Jews that the anti-Jewish policies could last or that a monster like Hitler could long remain in control of a modern, advanced state. Most Jews felt completely German and assumed that their fellow Germans would sooner or later come to their senses and either turn out the Nazi government or force it to change course. They learned, to their dismay, that most Germans were indifferent to the plight of Jews and would not take the risk of opposing government policies, or that they actually approved of government anti-Jewish policies in spite of any personal ties of friendship or long association.

A great irony of the situation was that many of the people who were affected by the anti-Jewish legislation were hardly even Jewish.

204 A Short History of the Jewish People

We have already seen that many German Jews were completely assimilated, having intermarried, converted to Christianity, and given up all ties to the organized Jewish community. Many more, without going to such extremes, had tried to minimize the Jewish element in their lives. But the rigid definition of non-Aryan meant that even the grandchildren of converts to Christianity might be counted as Jewish, no matter if they were hardly even aware of their Jewish origins. Whereas in the Middle Ages, Jews could generally save themselves by conversion, there was no legal escape from the Nuremberg Laws except emigration.

When Germany annexed Austria in March 1938, to the overwhelming enthusiasm of the population of both countries, Austrian Christians spontaneously attacked and abased Austrian Jews. New official measures were also taken against the Jews, as happened again when the Germans invaded western Czechoslovakia later in the year and swallowed up the entire country in 1939. But the incident that truly spelled the end of Jewish existence in Germany occurred on the night of November 9–10, which came to be known as Kristallnacht (Night of Broken Glass). On that night, Jewish businesses and synagogues throughout Germany were damaged or destroyed and Jewish individuals were brutalized in a nationwide pogrom. The government claimed that the event was a spontaneous popular reprisal for the murder of a German government official in Paris by a Jew, but actually, it had been carefully planned and coordinated by government agencies. The government proceeded as if the Jews themselves had caused the damage. The German Jewish community was fined the sum of one billion marks, new anti-Jewish regulations were imposed, Jewish children were expelled from schools, and vast numbers of Jews were interred in concentration camps. At this stage, Jews could still gain release from the camps if they could get a visa permitting them admission to some other country.

After Kristallnacht, Jewish cultural and economic life in Germany simply came to an end. No one now doubted the necessity of flight.

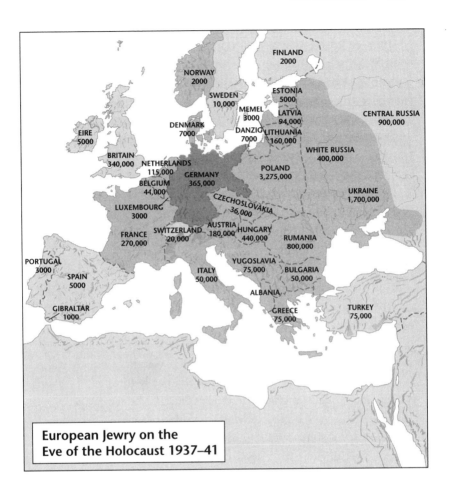

European Jewry on the Eve of the Holocaust 1937–41

Map labels:
FINLAND 2000
NORWAY 2000
SWEDEN 10,000
ESTONIA 5000
MEMEL 3000
LATVIA 94,000
CENTRAL RUSSIA 900,000
DENMARK 7000
DANZIG 7000
LITHUANIA 160,000
EIRE 5000
WHITE RUSSIA 400,000
BRITAIN 340,000
NETHERLANDS 115,000
GERMANY 365,000
POLAND 3,275,000
BELGIUM 44,000
UKRAINE 1,700,000
LUXEMBOURG 3000
CZECHOSLOVAKIA 36,000
FRANCE 270,000
SWITZERLAND 20,000
AUSTRIA 180,000
HUNGARY 440,000
RUMANIA 800,000
PORTUGAL 3000
SPAIN 5000
ITALY 50,000
YUGOSLAVIA 75,000
BULGARIA 50,000
ALBANIA
GIBRALTAR 1000
GREECE 75,000
TURKEY 75,000

Jewish businesses and homes were hastily sold at a fraction of their value, and long lines of visa applicants formed in front of foreign consulates. The government facilitated the process by establishing an emigration center in Vienna, later copied in Prague and Berlin, to accelerate emigration and the appropriation of Jewish property by simplifying bureaucratic procedures. The government hoped to overwhelm the adjacent countries with huge numbers of Jewish immigrants and thereby stimulate anti-Jewish sentiment in them as well.

But few countries were willing to relax immigration restrictions, even now that the plight of the Jews was desperate, and the British, who controlled Palestine, actually chose this moment to reduce the number of Jewish immigrants permitted entrance there (see chapter 10). Horrific situations arose, as ships laden with Jewish refugees, sometimes even with legal immigration papers, were turned back from port after port, only to be sent back to their doom in Europe.

After the outbreak of the war, on September 1, 1939, it became impossible to escape Europe, but the German policy of trying to expel the Jews to adjacent countries continued until late 1941, when emigration was prohibited and the policy toward the Jews of Germany turned to murder.

But in eastern Europe, the systematic murder of Jews had already begun. When Germany invaded Poland on September 1, 1939, Poland was the country with the highest concentration of Jews in the world and was the main center of Jewish religious and cultural life. As the Germans occupied the country, they imposed the anti-Jewish regulations and restrictions that applied within Germany, but they also went far beyond them. Jews were indiscriminately tortured and shot, so that more than a quarter million Jews had died by the end of 1939. The Germans gave high priority to the subjugation and destruction of Polish Jews, sometimes even over military interests. They created ghettos in the cities with good railway connections, such as Lodz, Warsaw, Cracow, and Lublin, and into these ghettos they crowded the Jewish populations of the cities and of thousands of villages; Jews found outside the walls illegally were killed. The Germans required the Jews to wear a yellow six-pointed star to facilitate their identification. They appropriated Jewish property. They forced ghetto dwellers into slave labor, especially at tasks related to the war effort—for example, building roads—and starved and brutalized them.

The ghettos were administered by Jewish councils answerable to the Germans, an arrangement that seemed superficially to continue the old pattern of Jewish semiautonomy, and therefore helped to

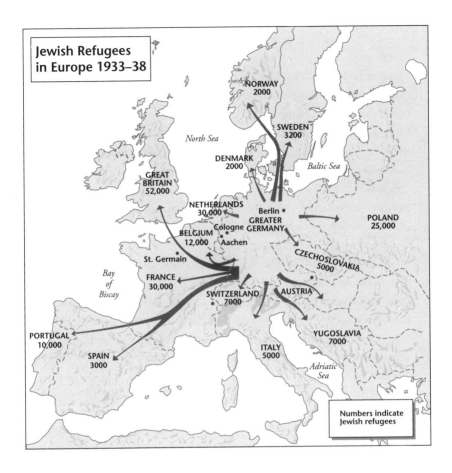

Jewish Refugees in Europe 1933–38

NORWAY 2000

SWEDEN 3200

North Sea

DENMARK 2000

Baltic Sea

GREAT BRITAIN 52,000

NETHERLANDS 30,000

Berlin •

GREATER GERMANY

POLAND 25,000

Cologne •

BELGIUM 12,000

• Aachen

CZECHOSLOVAKIA 5000

St. Germain

Bay of Biscay

FRANCE 30,000

SWITZERLAND 7000

AUSTRIA

PORTUGAL 10,000

SPAIN 3000

ITALY 5000

YUGOSLAVIA 7000

Adriatic Sea

Numbers indicate Jewish refugees

create an illusion of normalcy. But the Germans' ultimate purpose in creating the Jewish councils was to put their own programs into effect, and as the war progressed it became clear that the councils' real purpose was not to provide organizational support for the desperate inhabitants of the ghettos but to satisfy the Germans' demands. As these demands became harsher, the members of these councils faced unbearable dilemmas.

Early in the war, Jews within the ghettos could receive aid from Jewish relief organizations abroad, and the conscripted laborers received rations. The larger ghettos were sometimes quite well organized, with charitable organizations, schools, and medical services functioning as well as possible in the face of the crowding, poverty, disease, and general atmosphere of unreality. Individual Jews sometimes found that they could get special consideration from the German guards in exchange for bribes or collaboration. But the regulations governing ghetto life became continually tighter, and the German demands were continually increased, so that by the end of 1941, when receiving food packages from the outside was prohibited, hunger, disease, and the death rate had risen significantly. With the official food ration set at 1,100 calories a day, whole populations existed in a state of starvation.

With the onset of the war, the function of the concentration camps changed. Formerly, they had been used merely to imprison enemies or suspected enemies of the regime; now they were used to exploit the labor of the prisoners. The camps were also used for group extermination; there was a euthanasia program for killing the insane and the chronically ill and, in the all-women's camp at Ravensbrück, a program for gassing pregnant Jewish women. The number of prisoners thus increased, and new camps were established in Poland: Auschwitz, Treblinka, Majdanek, and Sobibor. Beginning in 1941, several camps added crematoria for disposing of the bodies of prisoners and manned them with prisoners, who were themselves periodically executed to prevent information about the crematoria from being released to the outside world.

When the Germans invaded France in 1940, they expelled non-French Jewish refugees from the occupied part of the country to the part controlled by the collaborationist Vichy government. The Vichy government cooperated in anti-Jewish policies beyond the Nazis' expectations. It banned the Jews from public activities, took away their civil rights, and established concentration camps manned by French personnel, from which non-French Jews were shipped to the East to be killed, but French Jews were protected from deportation.

In occupied France, by contrast, a concentration camp was established at Drancy, near Paris, from which French Jews were shipped to Auschwitz. When the German occupation was extended to most of the south of France late in 1942, Jews crowded into the small zone occupied by Italy. When the Germans invaded Italy in 1943, these Jews were trapped.

In other occupied countries, the degree of cooperation with the German policy toward the Jews varied widely. In Holland, the persecution of the Jews infuriated the public and led to a general strike, which had to be suppressed by the military; Church leaders urged resistance, and many Dutch Christians hid Jews. Nevertheless, most Dutch Jews were transported to concentration camps. Danish Christians, including the king and government officials, protected Danish Jews and managed to save nearly the entire community by ferrying them across the straits to Sweden. Bulgarians also refused to cooperate with the Germans, and the Bulgarian Jews escaped extermination.

Even Italy, which was Germany's ally under a fascist and officially anti-Semitic regime, did not cooperate in the war against the Jews as long as Italy itself remained in the war. It enacted anti-Jewish legislation and duly established concentration camps, but expended little effort in rounding up the Jews, and treatment in the camps was fairly humane. It was only when Italy capitulated to the Allies in September 1943 that fate caught up with Italy's Jews. The Germans occupied the north of the country, where most of the native Jewish population lived, together with many Jewish refugees from France and Yugoslavia. The Germans rounded them up and transported them to the death camps. Even so, many Jews found protectors among their non-Jewish friends. Many institutions of the Catholic Church, such as monasteries, convents, and even the Vatican, subverted the German decrees and hid Jews, but Pope Pius XII never protested the German treatment of the Jews. The failure of the West's most powerful and influential religious leader not to speak out remains a cause of dismay to this very day.

These were the better stories. In other countries, such as Rumania, the German occupation complemented long-standing popular anti-Semitism, resulting in thorough cooperation in the destruction of the Jews. Hungary did not deport its Jews as long as it remained independent, even though it joined the war on the side of Germany; but when, late in the war, the Germans invaded Hungary, the Hungarian police and the local extreme nationalist and anti-Semitic Arrow Cross movement assisted in deporting the Hungarian Jews as well. In Serbia, Croatia, and Greece, the destruction of Jews, who were mostly Sephardic, was almost total. The destruction of Greek Jewry put an end to the Jewish community of Salonika, historically one of the most important centers of Sephardic Jewry (see chapter 6).

When the Germans invaded the Soviet Union in June 1941, they established special mobile killing squads (known as *Einsatzgruppen,* or "action groups"), the purpose of which was to murder Soviet commissars, communists, partisans, Jews, and gypsies in the vast new territories that now came under German control. These squads had complete independence to carry out executions among the civilian population, and they worked in concert with the armed forces. They roamed the eastern European countryside, rounding up the Jewish population of the small towns and machine-gunning them, drowning them, or asphyxiating them with the exhaust of their vehicles. Ukrainian, Polish, Latvian, Lithuanian, Estonian, and Rumanian auxiliaries often participated enthusiastically in these killings. The most notorious action of this type was the one at Babi Yar, near Kiev, on September 29–30, 1941, where Germans and Ukrainians murdered about 33,000 Jews.

Soon after the invasion of the Soviet Union, the Germans made the decision to institute the "final solution of the Jewish problem," the systematic extermination of the entire Jewish population of Europe. Adolf Eichmann was empowered to set the process in motion. Preparations were made to turn Auschwitz into a major death camp. In January 1942, representatives of all the government and military agencies involved assembled at Wannsee, a suburb of Berlin, to clarify the policy and to coordinate the execution of the decision. Considered simply as an operation, it was an immense project, for Europe still contained an estimated 11 million Jews who would have to be moved, housed, killed, and disposed of. The decision to tie down personnel, materials, and transport on such a tremendous scale in order to wage war against a helpless and scattered minority group while fighting a war on several fronts and controlling many hostile occupied territories is a measure of the madness of Germany's obsession with the Jews.

Eichmann chose Poland as the extermination center because that was the main center of Jewish population and because the local population, with its ancient and deeply rooted tradition of anti-Semitism, could be counted on for cooperation. All the Jews of Europe were to be shipped by boxcar to the ghettos of Lodz, Riga, Minsk, and Kovno, and from there they were to be forwarded, together with the local Jewish population, to the concentration camps in Poland. The Jewish councils of the ghettos were responsible for the regular delivery of stipulated quotas of Jews. So brutal were the conditions of the transports themselves that vast numbers died before even reaching the camps. All Jews judged incapable of work were killed on arrival, and the rest were worked to death or killed when they were no longer capable of work.

The administrators of the concentration camps had already been experimenting with mechanized mass killing to replace the less efficient work of the action groups in the Soviet Union. Six concentration camps now became death camps, where the prisoners were gassed with carbon monoxide or prussic acid. In the summer of 1942, a system of gas chambers disguised as showers was introduced; these gas chambers used Zyklon-B, an insecticide manufactured by I. G. Farben. This innovation permitted the gassing of 700 to 800 persons in four to five minutes, while thousands more innocently awaited their turn to be admitted to the "showers." Attendants removed gold teeth, rings, and hair from the bodies before cremation; afterward, the ashes were processed for use as fertilizer and the clothes fumigated for reuse. The gassing of Jews went on until November 1944, though Treblinka and Sobibor had to be abandoned in late 1943 in the face of the advance of Soviet troops.

The labor of the concentration-camp inmates was intended to maintain the industrial production necessary to prosecute the war and supply the home front. Slave labor was put at the disposal of I. G. Farben, Krupp, Thyssen, Flick, and Siemens (all still major German industrial companies), which made up about 40 percent of their work-forces from the camps. Slave labor was very efficient, since the prisoners received little food and virtually no medical care and could simply be worked to death and then replaced with others. The average life span of a slave laborer under these conditions was nine months.

The ghettos raised little resistance to the deportations, even after rumors of their real purpose had filtered back. The Jews, starving and demoralized, were easily controlled. It was mainly the young, especially the Zionist and socialist youth circles, who were responsible for such resistance as occurred. The ghetto leadership did not usually support this course, for it necessarily led to reprisals. The best-known of the uprisings occurred in the Warsaw Ghetto. A Jewish fighting organization had formed there early in 1942 and had managed to smuggle some weapons into the ghetto; it also made contact with the Polish resistance, but could not gain their cooperation. In a skirmish in January 1943, the Jews killed twenty Germans. This event lifted the ghetto's morale and aroused support for more extensive action; it also impressed the Polish resistance, who agreed to sell the Jews arms. The Germans decided to liquidate the ghetto; when they came on April 19, the Jews attacked them so fiercely that the Germans had to burn down the ghetto to quell the uprising. The resistance lasted five weeks. It may have been a hopeless gesture of defiance, but the display of fighting spirit on the part of Warsaw's Jewish youth was an inspiration to Jews elsewhere, and uprisings occurred in other ghettos as well as in some of the death camps.

With the liquidation of the ghettos and villages of eastern Europe in 1942–43, groups of Jews sometimes managed to escape to the woods in order to fight as partisans, either joining Soviet partisan groups or organizing Jewish partisan groups. Conditions were less favorable to them than to the Soviet partisans because such outlaw guerrilla fighters can only survive with the cooperation of the local population, but in eastern Europe the rural population was traditionally hostile to Jews, and even the non-Jewish partisan groups were often unwilling to cooperate with them. Nevertheless, about 20,000 Jews were involved in such operations, sabotaging police stations, killing Nazi guards, blowing up trains, and stopping tanks with hand grenades.

As the war drew to an end and the Soviets advanced through Poland, the concentration camps there had to be dismantled and the prisoners evacuated. This time, no transport was provided. The Jews and other prisoners were simply marched westward toward Germany with no provisions, so that about 250,000 died in the last months of the war in death marches alone. Soviet and American troops who liberated the remaining camps at the war's end were appalled at the condition of the inmates. The postwar period was difficult for most, often involving lengthy sojourns in displaced persons' camps. And many eastern European Jews who found their way back to their old villages were murdered by Polish and Ukrainian townspeople in a series of pogroms that occurred after the war was over, for the devastated population of eastern Europe turned its rage against its traditional scapegoat, the Jews.

Germany continued to wage its war against the Jews nearly until its surrender, despite the cost in resources that it might have used to resist the Allied advance. And although Germany was devastated by the war against the Allies, it was completely victorious in its war against the Jews. When the war was over, there were virtually no Jews left in Germany, and eastern Europe, the center of world Jewry, had been turned into a graveyard, its Jewish institutions shattered, its inhabitants killed or dispersed. Jewish life in Europe had reached a dead end.

The Warsaw Ghetto

When the Germans occupied Warsaw in September 1939, the city had just under 400,000 Jews. In 1940, a wall was built enclosing an area of 840 acres for the ghetto. By mid-November, all Jews were required to live within the walls, which were guarded by German and Polish police on the outside and by a Jewish militia on the inside; no one was permitted to enter or leave the ghetto without a permit. The Germans would reduce the area from time to time by moving the walls, and at one point they divided the ghetto into two separate regions connected by a footbridge. Into the ghetto they crammed an additional 150,000 Jewish refugees from the region around Warsaw, until the density reached thirteen persons to a room, and homeless people dying of exposure, hunger, and disease crowded the streets.

Within the walls, the Jews were governed, as in other ghettos, by a Jewish Council (*Judenrat*), which was responsible for such social services as could be maintained under the circumstances, as well as for implementing German demands. The Warsaw Ghetto was headed, under impossible circumstances, by an engineer named Adam Czerniakow, an intelligent, conscientious administrator. Czerniakow kept an extensive diary, one of several that survived the war and from which much of our information about the ghetto derives. Czerniakow did what he could to ameliorate the conditions of life in the ghetto and to balance the needs of the various groups competing for scarce resources. When the Germans demanded that he cooperate with them in organizing deportations to concentration camps, he committed suicide (July 23, 1942).

In spite of all hardships, the ghetto managed to function as a city, after a fashion. Illegal workshops and a system for smuggling raw materials in and the products out permitted a subsistence economy. (Illegal imports of food were actually responsible for keeping the ghetto inmates alive, since the legally permitted daily allotment of food amounted to no more than 1,100 calories per person.) Soup kitchens dispensed food and served as cover for illegal secular, religious, and trade schools; technical, medical, and scientific training was available. Though the synagogues were closed and public worship was prohibited, services were held and talmudic academies functioned in secret. Even cafés and cabaret-type entertainment could sometimes be found in operation. And underground organizations produced illegal periodicals in Hebrew, Yiddish, and Polish.

It was these underground organizations that led the resistance efforts, culminating in the famous uprising. The first wave of mass deportations, beginning in July 1942, induced these organizations—quite diverse in their political commitments and, in some cases, even hostile to one another—to coordinate their activities by creating the Jewish Fighting Organization (ZOB). This body included most of the organizations, some of which were able to obtain arms from Polish underground organizations or the black market. The ZOB established secret workshops to manufacture grenades and bombs and constructed a network of bunkers and underground channels for communication. The second wave of deportations, beginning in January 1943, touched off four days of street fighting, the first such case in occupied Poland. The Germans responded by imposing a round-the-clock curfew. Life in the ghetto now ground to a halt; the *Judenrat* was paralyzed and social institutions stopped functioning. But the ZOB, headed by Mordecai Anielewicz, continued to prepare for armed resistance when the deportations would resume.

When the Germans returned, on April 19, 1943, they met with such intense resistance that they had to retreat. The commander was replaced, and the attack resumed. Now encountering determined resistance, the Germans responded by burning the ghetto down. Though the population of the ghetto had been decimated, underground fighting continued until May 8, when the ZOB headquarters on Mila Street fell and Anielewicz was killed. Some armed resistance continued until June; some fighters who were able to escape formed a partisan unit named for Anielewicz. On May 16, the Germans celebrated the liquidation of the ghetto by blowing up the Great Synagogue on Tlomacka Street.

Parade in Israel in the 1940s. Photo © David Rubinger/Corbis. Used by permission.

TEN

Zionism and the Origins of the State of Israel

The nationalist movements of nineteenth-century Europe brought about the unification of Italy and of Germany and resulted in the creation of independent states in the Balkans and eastern Europe at the expense of the Ottoman and the Austro-Hungarian Empires. European Jews were still seeking a solution to the continuing problems of their status as a barely tolerated foreign body in eastern Europe and continued anti-Semitism even in western Europe, where they had achieved full citizenship and civil rights. The movements of national resurgence offered the Jews a potential model. Perhaps what had worked for the Serbs, the Bulgarians, and the Rumanians would work for them.

The declining Ottoman Empire, regarded by all nations as the "sick man of Europe," had already lost some of its territories to nationalist movements. Many Jews began to conceive the solution to the Jewish problem in terms of restoration to a normal existence as a national entity.

The natural location for a Jewish state was the Land of Israel, given the Jews' devotion of nearly two millennia to the idea of a

TIMELINE

JEWISH HISTORY		GENERAL HISTORY
Moses Hess publishes *Rome and Jerusalem*	1862	
Petah Tikva founded	1878	
Eliezer Ben-Yehuda arrives in Palestine; pogroms in southern Russia	1881	
Pinsker publishes *Autoemancipation*; Bilu organized; Rishon le-Zion founded	1882	
Herzl publishes *The Jewish State*	1896	
First Zionist Congress	1897	
Second Aliya	1902	
Death of Herzl	1904	
Tel Aviv founded	1909	
	1914–18	World War I
	1917	Russian Revolution
British capture Jerusalem	1917	
Third Aliya	1919–23	
British mandate begins; Arabs riot in Jerusalem	1920	
Herbert Samuel high commissioner	1920–25	
Weizmann president of Twelfth Zionist Congress	1921	
Fourth Aliya	1924–32	
Churchill White Paper	1922	
Hebrew University opened	1925	
Arabs riot in Jerusalem; massacres in Hebron and Safed	1929	
Irgun founded	1931	
Fifth Aliya	1933	Hitler becomes chancellor of Germany
Arab riots	1936	
Peel Commission proposes partition of Palestine	1937	
MacDonald White Paper	1939	
	1939–45	World War II
Death of Jabotinsky	1940	
Palmah organized	1941	
Revisionists strike at British; Jewish Brigade formed	1944	
Intensification of illegal immigration and struggle against British	1945	End of World War II
Revisionists blow up King David Hotel	1946	
U.N. votes to partition Palestine	1947	

return to that territory. Palestine already had a substantial Jewish population, consisting of descendants of the Sephardic refugees from Spain, descendants of more recent immigrants from the Middle Eastern countries, and descendants of various European religious movements who had settled in Palestine during the eighteenth and early nineteenth centuries. The pre-Zionist Jewish population had grown to the point that in 1860, Jews began to build new quarters outside the walls of Jerusalem, the neighborhoods that today make up the city's downtown. Although life still followed traditional religious and economic patterns, there was some interest in establishing agricultural settlements, especially after the Alliance Israélite Universelle founded an agricultural school in 1870.

The first clear articulation of the hope for a Jewish state was Moses Hess's *Rome and Jerusalem*, which appeared in Germany in 1862; the idea was taken up in eastern Europe by Leon Pinsker in *Autoemancipation* (1882) and by writers in the Hebrew press such as Eliezer Ben-Yehuda (who is discussed below). But it was the Russian pogroms of 1881 (see chapter 8) that precipitated the emergence of the nationalist Jewish organizations known collectively as the *Hibbat zion* (Love of Zion) movement. The movement originated among Jews of eastern Europe, where most Jews had despaired of integration into general society and where the Jewish education and traditional life, and therefore national cohesiveness, were very strong. The first of these organizations that actually emigrated to Palestine as a group was the Bilu movement (its name is an acronym of the biblical exhortation "House of Jacob, go, let us go").

Western European Jews, who were, on the whole, committed to the emancipation ideal of integration with non-Jewish society and less thoroughly steeped in Jewish traditions, were either cool to Jewish nationalism or actively hostile to it, except perhaps as a solution for their eastern European brethren. Nevertheless, it was an assimilated Hungarian Jew who turned the Zionist idea into an international movement. Theodor Herzl (1860–1904) was an unlikely person to take such an initiative. He was a writer and journalist in Vienna with little knowledge of Judaism and an admirer of France as a land of progress and enlightened ideas. As the Paris correspondent for a Viennese newspaper, he was so shocked by the French anti-Semitism uncovered by the Dreyfus Affair that he devoted the rest of his life to seeking a global solution for the Jewish problem. In his book *The Jewish State* (1896), he argued forcefully for the establishment of a Jewish state, and in a novel, *Old-New Land* (1902), he spoke prophetically about the social and technological achievements of which such a state would be capable. Though he found little support among Western Jews, he was acclaimed by the Jews of eastern Europe.

In 1897, Herzl organized the First Zionist Congress in Switzerland, which culminated in a resolution stating, "Zionism aspires to the securing of a national home for the Jewish people in Palestine, guaranteed by public law." Failing to obtain the sanction of the Ottoman sultan to establish the Jewish state in Palestine, Herzl entered into negotiations with Britain to permit a Jewish settlement in Uganda. This plan demonstrated how distant Herzl was from the sensibilities of the eastern European Jewish masses, and their angry reaction temporarily weakened his leadership. But Britain ultimately withdrew from the negotiations, and Herzl reverted to the plan of creating the Jewish state in Palestine, where the Jewish people had originated and which had for so long been the object of their yearning.

Meanwhile, the Bilu immigrants had joined the various Jewish populations that had been present since the Ottoman conquest in the fifteenth century. Their intention was to establish agricultural colonies as the basis of future Jewish settlement and as the main step toward the return of all Jews to Palestine. Full of idealism, but lacking the necessary practical skills, they would certainly have foundered had it not been for extensive financial support by Baron Edmond de Rothschild.

Parallel to the rise of Jewish nationalism was the revival of Hebrew as a spoken language, the outstanding collective cultural achievement of the Jewish people in modern times. Hebrew had ceased to be spoken during the first century C.E., but it was in wide use as a written language throughout Jewish history. Unlike the case of Latin in Christendom, a knowledge of Hebrew had not been restricted to the clergy or a wealthy elite. Judaism had early adapted to the lack of normal national institutions by making the lifelong study of the Bible and the rabbinic tradition in the original languages a religious duty incumbent upon all Jews. Lengthy and complex prayers in Hebrew were recited daily not by clergy alone but by all adult men. Schooling for most Jews began with the study of Hebrew and entailed memorizing extensive Hebrew texts. Thus, in traditional communities, even the relatively unlearned had retained since antiquity an extensive passive knowledge of the language. It was the near-universal knowledge of Hebrew in eastern Europe that had made it possible in the late eighteenth century for the Jewish "enlighteners" to use it as a vehicle for educating the eastern European masses in such modern subjects as mathematics, science, and geography, and we have seen that by the mid-nineteenth century, Hebrew was being used for both poetry and fiction.

Herzl, as a man of modern Europe, had assumed that the language of the Jewish state would be German or Russian, but given the role of language in the rise of the various nationalist movements of the age, the more traditionally educated eastern European Jewish intellectuals and activists turned naturally to Hebrew. The catalyst of the Hebrew movement was Eliezer Ben-Yehuda (1858–1922), who devoted his life to the restoration of the Jewish people to their historic land and language. In 1881, he moved to Palestine and began his campaign for the revival of Hebrew by announcing to his wife that from that moment on, he would communicate with her only in that language. He adopted the Sephardic pronunciation, which was widely used in Palestine and which remains the basis of spoken Hebrew today.

Although Hebrew had not been spoken in everyday life for centuries, it was a natural link between the mostly Sephardic population

Revival of Hebrew

The most remarkable collective achievement of the Jewish people in modern times, perhaps even more remarkable than the establishment of the State of Israel itself, has been the revival of Hebrew. No other language has ever been revived after a long period in which it had ceased to be spoken.

In the late nineteenth century, Hebrew had strong appeal to the idealistic young Zionists of eastern Europe, who saw the language as an essential part of the national identity they were striving to re-create. They also used Hebrew to help them enforce a sharp break with the Yiddish-based culture of the eastern European shtetl. The revival of Hebrew seemed to them a natural concomitant to the attempt to remake the Jews as a people of workers and tillers of the soil in their original homeland. It also suited the conception of Palestine as a homeland for the Jews of all Diaspora communities; Hebrew may have been only a literary language, but it was the only language all Jews had in common. This fact had practical application in nineteenth-century Jerusalem, where Arabic-, Yiddish-, and Ladino-speaking Jews living side by side often used Hebrew, their common literary language, for oral communication.

In the late nineteenth century, several different traditions for pronouncing Hebrew existed, partly going back to antiquity, and partly resulting from the influence of the Jews' spoken languages on their Hebrew. The pronunciation of Hebrew common among Arabic-speaking Jews (inaccurately known as the Sephardic pronunciation) prevailed in the early stages of the revival because of the large population of Middle Eastern Jews in Jerusalem. But the Ashkenazic immigrants who began arriving in waves early in the twentieth century were unable to master some of the sounds that came easily to Jews who were accustomed to speaking Arabic. As a result, the so-called Sephardic pronunciation that has become standard Hebrew is actually a synthesis of Ashkenazic, Sephardic, and Middle Eastern features.

The greatest problem in reviving Hebrew was to find vocabulary words for everyday needs and for modern conceptions that had no parallel in the familiar ancient texts. The Hebrew Language Committee, formed in 1890 to deal with such problems and which was succeeded by the Hebrew Language Academy in 1953, scoured talmudic and medieval Hebrew literature in search of words for plants, tools, items of clothing and furniture, and other vocabulary items. They also coined new words. This process was facilitated by the structure of the language itself. Like those of other Semitic languages, Hebrew words are usually constructed out of three-consonant roots. Vowels, prefixes, and suffixes modify these roots according to fairly regular patterns. When a word is needed for some new item that did not exist in ancient times, an ancient root can often be found that can be used to build a new word, using one of these standard patterns.

Thus, a word for railroad train was crafted out of the ancient root *r-k-b*, which is found in words that include the idea of riding. The Bible has the verb *rakhav* (to ride) and the nouns *rekhev* and *merkava* (chariot); the Talmud has the verb *hirkiv* (to graft); and modern Hebrew now has *rakevet*. In some cases, Hebrew speakers have simply adopted foreign words, such as *akademya* for academy and *universita* for university. Sometimes such words have been replaced by newly coined Hebrew words: thus, *informatsya*, which was commonly heard until the 1960s, has given way to the new word *meda*, which was coined from the ordinary Hebrew root meaning "to know" and which fits much more naturally into the familiar patterns of Hebrew nouns. Sometimes verbs can be appropriated from foreign languages by imposing Hebrew verb patterns on them; thus, *tilfen* (to telephone) and *gilven* (to galvanize) have a naturally Hebrew "feel," despite their deriving from foreign roots. The Academy continues to debate and rule on questions of spelling, pronunciation, grammar, and vocabulary and issues dictionaries from time to time to provide linguistic guidance in specialized areas.

of Palestine and the increasing numbers of Ashkenazim who began to arrive with early Zionist settlers, for it was the language of a tradition shared by a people of disparate vernaculars. Ben-Yehuda introduced Hebrew as the language of some of the instruction in the Alliance school in Jerusalem and published newspapers and periodicals in Hebrew, dealing with Jewish and general topics, coining Hebrew words as needed. He spent years compiling a massive historical dictionary of Hebrew—the publication of which was completed after his death—in seventeen volumes, which, though in some respects outdated, remains the most comprehensive dictionary of the language. He also founded and chaired the Hebrew Language Committee, the forerunner of the present-day Hebrew Language Academy, the arbiter of linguistic usage for the State of Israel. In a development without parallel in world history, Ben-Yehuda's efforts bore fruit, and Hebrew was accepted, in the face of considerable debate and dissension, as the language of the nascent Jewish homeland.

A second wave of immigration, lasting ten years, was precipitated by the Kishinev pogrom in Russia in 1903 and the failure of the 1905 Russian revolution. These immigrants were mostly idealistic pioneers devoted to socialism and the use of Hebrew as the everyday language of the Jews. Their spokesman was A. D. Gordon, who, though not a socialist, promoted the idea that the Jewish people could only regenerate themselves through the beneficial power of labor and by returning to nature. They developed the characteristic agricultural institutions of Israel: the collective settlement (kibbutz) and the cooperative settlement (moshav). Out of their ideological disputes emerged the political parties that would later unite in the Mapai party, forerunner of the present-day Labor party. From their numbers came the leadership of the Palestinian Jewish community during the period of the British mandate (after World War I) and of the State of Israel (after 1948): men such as David Ben-Gurion, first prime minister of Israel, and Yizhak Ben-Zvi, Israel's second president. The year 1909 saw the founding of Tel Aviv, the first all-Jewish city in Palestine and today the metropolis of Israel.

The increase of Jewish population and the expansion of Jewish agricultural settlements caused a corresponding intensification of opposition by local Arabs; this opposition increased after the Turkish revolution in 1908, which led to the establishment of an organized Arab nationalist movement. Security became a problem for the Jewish settlements.

During World War I, Turkey joined the Central Powers in fighting Britain. Fearing sedition on the part of both Arab and Jewish nationalists, the Turkish governor of Palestine, Jamal Pasha, carried out extensive arrests and banished many of the Jewish settlers. The discovery of a Jewish espionage outfit working for the British was used as a pretext for the persecution of Jewish settlements, even those who opposed such activity. When the British general Edmund Allenby entered Jerusalem in December 1917, the Jews welcomed him as a liberator.

Throughout the war, Arab and Jewish leaders had been working to obtain British support for their national aspirations at the expense of Turkey. The Hashemites, a powerful family in Arabia headed by the emir Hussein, carried out acts of sabotage against Turkey (coordinated with the British by T. E. Lawrence—Lawrence of Arabia) in support of the British war effort; in return, they were promised Arab independence after the war and a kingdom under Hashemite rule. The Jews organized the Jewish legion to fight on behalf of the British, and the Zionist leadership did its best to persuade the British government to recognize the rights of the Jewish people in Palestine after the liberation of the country, to permit free immigration, and to recognize the legal status of Zionist institutions there. Particularly effective in this work was Chaim Weizmann, a chemist who made a major contribution to the war effort by discovering a process to synthesize acetone. These efforts culminated in 1917 with the formal declaration by British foreign secretary Lord Balfour: "The British government view with favour the establishment in Palestine of a national home for the Jewish people, and will use their best endeavours to facilitate the achievement of this object." Coming only a month before

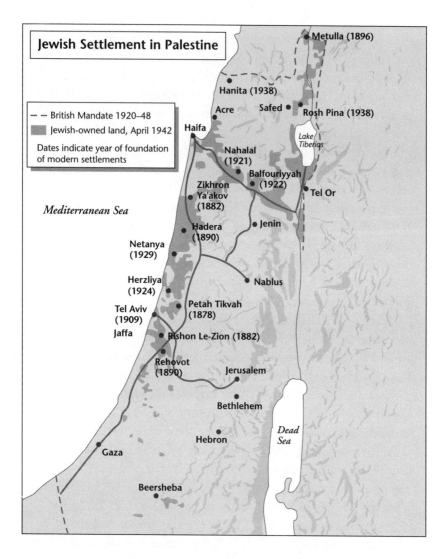

Jewish Settlement in Palestine

Metulla (1896)

Hanita (1938)

Acre   Safed •   Rosh Pina (1938)

– – British Mandate 1920–48

Jewish-owned land, April 1942

Dates indicate year of foundation
of modern settlements

Haifa

Lake
Tiberias

Nahalal
(1921)

Balfouriyyah
(1922)

Zikhron
Ya'akov
(1882)

Tel Or

Mediterranean Sea

Hadera
(1890)

• Jenin

Netanya
(1929)

Herzliya
(1924)

• Nablus

Tel Aviv
(1909)

Petah Tikvah
(1878)

Jaffa

Rishon Le-Zion (1882)

Rehovot
(1890)

Jerusalem

Bethlehem

*Dead
Sea*

Hebron

Gaza

Beersheba

Allenby's liberation of Jerusalem, the Balfour Declaration was greeted
with wild joy by Jews worldwide. But the conflict between the British
commitment to the Jews and the British commitment to the
Hashemites poisoned the Middle East for decades to come.

After the war, Britain received a mandate for Palestine, including both banks of the Jordan, from the newly formed League of Nations. The mandate's purpose was to implement the Balfour Declaration, while guaranteeing the rights of other groups in the territory. The mandatory administration established the Jewish Agency, which was to cooperate with the British administration in creating the Jewish national home by encouraging Jewish immigration and settlement. Working closely with the World Zionist Organization (which was headed by Weizmann), the Jewish Agency became a kind of Jewish quasi-government under British control. Throughout the mandatory period, the agency was dominated by Labor Zionists.

But in the postwar settlement, the Hashemite demand for an independent Arab kingdom had been ignored. Seeking to partially satisfy the Hashemites, the British divided Palestine, creating the emirate of Transjordan and bestowing it upon the Hashemite emir Abdallah, whose brother Faisal the British had already made king of Iraq. But the Arab nationalists demanded the annulment of the Balfour Declaration and rioted in 1921. Even earlier, during the long period of negotiations prior to the official granting of the mandate, there had been Arab attacks on Jewish settlements and the British had briefly stopped Jewish immigration. Jewish battalions were formed to counter the attacks, but the British authorities would not permit them to operate, so they were disbanded. This experience showed the Jewish leadership that it would be necessary to create an independent but clandestine military force, the Haganah. It led the British to redefine their commitment to the Zionists, reducing the territory that they had promised the Jews and promising the Arabs to limit Jewish immigration. The British soon retreated from this attempt to revise the Balfour Declaration, but this sequence of events established a pattern for British policy during the entire mandatory period as Arab objections to the Jewish presence in western Palestine grew ever stronger, exacerbated by the appointment of an extreme Arab nationalist, Amin al-Husseini, as mufti (Muslim religious authority) of Jerusalem.

The postwar period saw a third wave of Jewish immigration, consisting mostly of Labor Zionist *halutsim* (pioneers) from Poland who threw themselves into agricultural and manual labor, draining swamps, establishing collective settlements, and fostering the growth of Hebrew language and culture. A fourth wave of immigration, beginning in 1925, was nonideological, consisting of refugees from Polish anti-Semitism. This period saw the establishment of the Jewish institutions of Palestine, such as the Haganah (Defense Organization), the Histadrut (General Federation of Hebrew Workers), and the Hebrew University. The decade also saw the growth of a right-wing movement, the Revisionists, headed by Vladimir Jabotinsky, in opposition to the Labor Zionist parties. Tension between the Revisionists, under Jabotinsky, and Labor, which was increasingly dominated by David Ben-Gurion, became severe in the 1930s. One outcome was the secession of Revisionists from the Haganah and the creation of an independent Revisionist military force, the Irgun.

Arab opposition to the Jewish presence intensified. There were many grounds for this opposition. The leading families who owned the land on which the impoverished Arab *fellahin* (small farmers) lived were fearful of any change in the status quo; they particularly feared that European political institutions being imported by Western Jews streaming to Palestine would give the fellahin ideas of representative government. To the average Arab of Palestine, the Jewish immigrants appeared to be not members of an ancient Middle Eastern people attempting to reestablish their national identity in their historical homeland but rather, another invasion of Western colonizers. From an Islamic point of view, the growing presence of Jews altered the religious complexion of the region, and the Jews' goal of attaining sovereignty offended the Islamic view of the properly subservient role of *dhimmis*. Finally, the Arabs, who had been for four centuries under the thumb of the Ottomans and were now under the control of the British, were developing their own nationalist aspirations. Serious riots, incited by the mufti's inflammatory propaganda in 1929, led to murderous attacks in Jerusalem, Safed, and especially Hebron. In an effort to appease the Arabs, the British briefly halted Jewish immigration.

But the persecutions of Jews in Europe during the 1930s resulted in increased immigration to Palestine and therefore in increased tension between Jews and Arabs. These tensions were exacerbated by the growing confrontation between Britain and France on the one hand, and Germany and Italy on the other. As mentioned in chapter 6, the Arab nationalists saw Germany as their natural ally against the hated British and French colonial regimes, while the official anti-Semitic policies of the German Nazi government gave lavish expression to Arab resentment of the Jewish presence in Palestine. With the threat of another European war in the air, Britain was anxious to placate the Arabs so as not to jeopardize its control of Palestine, with its important harbor of Haifa and its proximity to the Suez Canal. These considerations increased the Arabs' leverage with the British and reduced that of the Jews.

Under the leadership of the mufti, the Arab Higher Committee was formed in 1936, and, with Axis support, began a propaganda campaign that resulted in a series of Arab assaults on Jewish settlements. The British stood aside at first, but when the Arabs began attacking British garrisons, they allowed the Haganah to go openly into action and even provided an officer for its training. The violence lasted until 1939, but meanwhile, the British decided to revise their policy toward Palestine. The Peel Commission, empowered by the government to study the problems of the Palestine mandate, concluded that the national aspirations of Jews and Arabs were irreconcilable and that the territory should again be partitioned. The new plan was for a Jewish state that would comprise the coastal strip, Galilee, and Jezreel Valley; an Arab state comprising the central hill country and the Negev; and a British enclave including Jerusalem, Jaffa, and Nazareth. The Jews were divided as to whether to support the plan, Labor mostly being in favor and the Revisionists being strongly opposed; the Arabs rejected it completely. A recurrence of Arab violence in 1937, followed by the refusal of the Arabs even to participate in a conference on partition at which Zionist leaders were present, convinced the British that the plan could not be implemented. Accordingly, in 1939 the British issued the infamous White Paper, severely restricting Jewish immigration to Palestine and, in effect, rescinding the Balfour Declaration. This betrayal had a devastating effect on the Jewish settlement in Palestine, but it did not gain its purpose of preventing the Arabs from supporting the Axis powers when the war began later in the year and threw the entire Palestine issue into the background.

World War II put the Palestinian Jews in a difficult political position. Although Britain had clearly become their antagonist, the Jews had to work with it for the defeat of the Germans, whose victory would put an end to Jewish history altogether. As in World War I, the Jews also hoped that by actively cooperating with Britain they would earn credit with it after the war. Large numbers of Palestinian Jews fought for Britain; the Jewish Brigade was formed in 1944 and flew a yellow Star of David on its flag. Nevertheless, once the German forces in Libya were defeated in 1942, relations between the Jews and the British government again deteriorated; the British imposed restrictions on Jews' obtaining arms and turned back ships carrying Jewish refugees from Europe to Palestine. Several of these ships sank, with the loss of hundreds of lives.

The plight of tens of thousands of Jewish refugees in European displaced persons' camps at the war's end convinced everyone but the British and the Arabs of the need to open Palestine to the free immigration of Jews. But the geopolitical considerations that had led Britain to favor the Arabs before the war remained in effect, except that, with the beginning of the cold war, the Soviet Union replaced Germany as Britain's antagonist and the Arabs' patron. As ramshackle boats laden with refugees arrived from Europe, they were sent back by the British or intercepted on the high seas. The Revisionists declared war on the mandatory government and embarked on a program of sabotage; an even more extreme group, the Stern gang, fought the British by political assassination. Thousands of Jews were arrested in June 1946, and Jewish arms were confiscated; in retaliation, the Irgun blew up the King David Hotel in Jerusalem, where many government agencies maintained their offices.

The Jewish Agency and the other official Jewish institutions of Palestine repudiated such extremism on moral and tactical grounds and because the independent actions of the Revisionists threatened their own authority; they at first cooperated with the British in bringing about arrests, with the result that relations between the Jewish Right and Left broke down. The British authorities responded to the violence with mass arrests and by establishing detention camps in Cyprus for the illegal immigrants, who had only recently been released from the German death camps. Some ships did manage, with the help of the Haganah, to slip through the British blockade; there were a few dramatic confrontations, of which the most notable was the battle between the bedraggled refugees and the British military on board the *Exodus*. The predictable result of the British intransigence was to intensify the opposition even of Jewish moderates to the British mandate and to draw the Right and the Left together again. The Palestinian leadership was now unified in its opposition to British policy, and in effect, a state of warfare came into being between Britain and the Palestinian Jews.

Exasperated by its inability to reconcile the competing interests of Jews and Arabs, Britain abandoned the attempt and referred the problem to the United Nations. On November 29, 1947, the General Assembly voted to repartition Palestine into two sovereign states; the Jewish state would consist of the eastern Galilee, the coastal plain, and the Negev; Jerusalem would be internationalized; the rest would become the Arab state. The motion was supported by the United States and, unexpectedly, the Soviet Union. The League of Arab

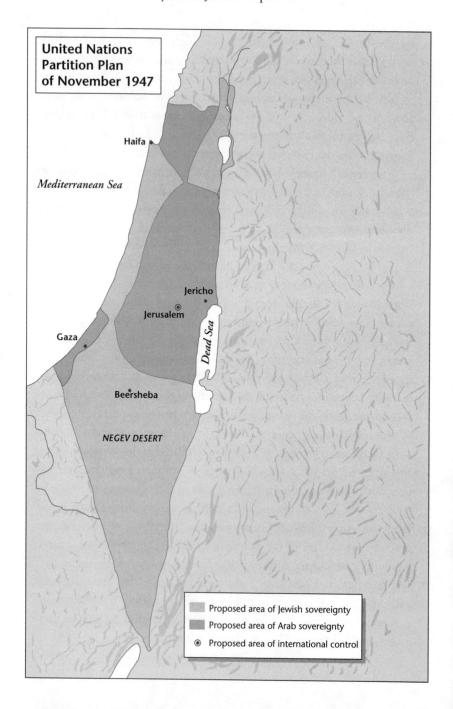

**United Nations
Partition Plan
of November 1947**

Haifa

Mediterranean Sea

Jericho

Jerusalem

Dead Sea

Gaza

Beersheba

NEGEV DESERT

Proposed area of Jewish sovereignty

Proposed area of Arab sovereignty

⊙ Proposed area of international control

States, which had been established in Cairo in 1945 and which took responsibility for the affairs of the Palestinian Arabs, announced that it would resist partition by force. Britain announced that it would not cooperate in implementing the plan. Thus, the implementation of the partition plan was left to the Jews of Palestine and world Jewry. The date for the end of the British mandate was set for Friday, May 14, 1948. On that very day, in Tel Aviv, David Ben-Gurion, as head of the Jewish Agency, proclaimed the establishment of a Jewish state in Palestine, to be known as the State of Israel.

But the Israeli War of Independence had already begun.

A baseball game at Camp Massad, a Hebrew-speaking summer camp in Pennsylvania, in the 1950s. Behind the umpire is a list of baseball terms with their Hebrew equivalents for ready reference in the course of play. Photo © Rivka and Shlomo Shulsinger. Courtesy of the National Museum of American Jewish History, Philadelphia.

ELEVEN

The Jewish People after 1948

Israel

Immediately after the U.N. voted to partition Palestine and create both a Jewish state and an Arab state, on November 29, 1947, Arab irregulars from the surrounding countries began pouring into Palestine and attacking Jewish settlements. Although the British refused to intervene and continued to disarm Jewish forces, the Jews managed to maintain control of most of the parts of the country in which they had settlements. When Israel declared its independence, on May 14, 1948, and the last British troops left, the armies of Jordan, Iraq, Syria, Lebanon, and Egypt, with the support of Saudi Arabia and Yemen, launched large-scale military attacks on Israel.

The odds of an Israeli victory seemed poor, given the size and geographical advantages of the seven Arab nations converging upon it. But by the armistice, in March 1949, Israel was in control of the Galilee, the coastal strip, the Negev, and the road to Jerusalem, as well as the western part of the city—more territory than the partition plan would have allowed. Jordan had occupied the hill country west of the

TIMELINE

Jewish History		General History
Israel declares independence; Arab states attack	1948	
First Knesset opens with Ben-Gurion as prime minister; cease-fire agreements with Arab states	1949	
Yemenite Jews flown to Israel	1949–50	
Iraqi Jews flown to Israel	1950–51	
Weizmann dies; reparations agreement with Germany	1952	Revolution in Egypt puts Gamal Abdel Nasser in power
	1953	Death of Joseph Stalin
Moshe Sharett prime minister	1954–55	
Mass emigration from Morocco	1954–55	
Sinai campaign	1956	
Eichmann brought to Israel	1960	
	1962	Algeria gains independence
	1963	John F. Kennedy assassinated
	1964	PLO founded
	1965	U.S. offensive in Vietnam
Six-Day War; unification of Jerusalem	1967	Hungarian Revolution
War of Attrition begins; Golda Meir prime minister	1969	
Israeli athletes killed at Munich Olympics	1972	
Yom Kippur War	1973	
Likud replaces Labor as dominant political power; Begin becomes prime minister; Sadat comes to Jerusalem	1977	
Camp David agreement	1978	
	1981	Sadat assassinated
Lebanon War	1982	
Begin resigns; Shamir prime minister	1983	
Beginning of Intifada	1987	
	1988	King Hussein renounces claim to West Bank; Palestinians declare state
Madrid conference	1991	Collapse of Soviet Union
Labor returns to power; Rabin prime minister	1992	
Oslo accord; signing of document of intent with PLO	1993	Palestinian Authority created
Peace treaty with Jordan	1994	
Assassination of Rabin; Peres prime minister	1995	
Likud party wins election; Netanyahu prime minister	1996	First elections held by Palestinian Authority

Jordan River (now known as the West Bank, and originally intended for the Palestinian Arab state) and the eastern half of Jerusalem (which was to have been internationalized), including the Old City, the part within the Ottoman walls.

Many Arab civilians living in the regions now under Israeli control fled on the demand of either Arab or Israeli forces, or simply fearing the violence of the war. At least one atrocity was committed, in the village of Deir Yassin, where Israeli forces massacred civilians, causing further waves of refugee flight. Arab leaders assured the refugees that the Arab countries would regroup, return to the battle, and restore them to the land of their origin; the refugees were not absorbed into the other Arab countries, but were placed in camps, which turned into permanent abodes of poverty and despair, and where generations of refugees and their descendants nursed their hatred for Israel.

Meanwhile, Israel had begun the process of state-building. General elections were held in January 1949, establishing the parliament (known as the Knesset) and the first government, with David Ben-Gurion as prime minister and Chaim Weizmann as president. Jerusalem became Israel's capital, in view of its ancient and historical role in Jewish history, though some nations—including the United States—refused to recognize it.

Refugees now flooded the country as Jews from Middle Eastern and North African countries, fearing the hostility of their native countries because of their association with the Jewish state, fled to Israel, as did the remainder of the European refugees from World War II. The Knesset enacted the Law of Return, which entitled Jewish immigrants to immediate, automatic citizenship. The manpower was badly needed, but the resulting population explosion confronted the young state with enormous economic and social difficulties, especially given the cultural and technological disparities of the countries from which the immigrants were arriving.

While Israel was absorbing more immigrants per capita than any country in the world, it was simultaneously coping with continuing political tensions. The Arab nations never concluded peace after the War of Independence. Jordan and Egypt continued the struggle by fostering gangs of guerrillas, called *fedayeen,* who carried out ambushes against small targets within Israel. The Arab states not only boycotted Israel itself, but also boycotted companies that did business with Israel and shipping companies that called at Israeli ports. Israel was prohibited from using Arab air space, and travelers who had been to Israel or who held Israeli visas were not allowed into Arab countries. Egypt closed the Suez Canal to Israel, and blocked access to Israel's southern port of Eilat. Jordan barred Jews from Jerusalem's holy sites (most of which were in the part Jordan had occupied) and systematically desecrated them. The Arab nations not only refused to recognize the state, but refused even to mention it; for decades, Israel's usual designation in the Arabic press was "the Zionist entity."

During the cold war, the Middle East became one of several zones of contention between the United States and the Soviet Union, which made the Arab world its sphere of influence by supplying it with arms and which had particularly close ties with Syria and Egypt. Egypt was headed by Gamal Abdel Nasser, a pan-Arabist with an aggressive vision of Arab unity and expansion. With Soviet encouragement, Egypt seized control of the Suez Canal and stepped up fedayeen raids against Israel. On October 29, 1956, the British and the French conspired with Israel to attack Egypt. Israeli forces captured the Sinai and decimated the Egyptian army within a week; then, on the pretext of separating the Egyptians and the Israelis, Britain and France entered the region and recaptured the canal. In the face of international outrage against Britain, France, and Israel, Israel abandoned the Sinai, receiving in return the United Nations' guarantee for the security of the Israeli-Egyptian border and relief from the Egyptian blockade of Eilat (though Israel could not gain the use of the Suez Canal). But given the U.N.'s position between the Soviet Union and the United

States during the cold war, these guarantees had little force, and Israel remained subject to constant attacks.

Israel enjoyed about a decade of relative tranquillity in which it could turn its attention to economic and social development and to absorbing its immigrants, who continued to stream in from the Arab world, communist countries, South America, Australia, and South Africa. In 1959, Israel formalized its relationship with West Germany, which agreed to invest millions of dollars into Israel's economy as reparations for its treatment of the Jews during World War II. Ben-Gurion accepted reparations in the face of intense controversy, for many who had suffered from the persecution were opposed to any reconciliation. These funds were a great boost to Israel's new economy.

In 1960, Israel again confronted the Holocaust when Adolf Eichmann (the Nazi official largely responsible for organizing the extermination of European Jewry) was captured in Argentina by Israel's security service. Eichmann's trial in Jerusalem was used as an opportunity to educate the world about Germany's atrocities against the Jewish people and to remind the Jews just how vital it was for them to have a state of their own. Eichmann was hanged in 1962 for crimes against humanity, the only crime punishable by death under Israeli law.

The Soviet Union continued to cultivate the Arab countries, especially Syria and Egypt. When tensions between Israel and Syria mounted in 1967, President Nasser, encouraged by the Soviet Union, attempted to use this situation as the occasion to settle accounts with Israel. Egypt and Syria accused Israel of mobilizing for attack on its northern borders. Nasser massed troops in the Sinai, expelled the U.N. Emergency Force, and blocked the shipping route to Eilat. Certain of an Egyptian victory, King Hussein of Jordan put his army under Egyptian command, as did several other Arab states.

Faced with these preparations for war and bloodthirsty proclamations by Egypt, Iraq, and the Palestine Liberation Organization (see later) of their intention of seizing Israel and slaughtering its Jewish population, Israel carried out a preemptive strike on June 5, 1967. Within three hours, it destroyed Egypt's entire air force, and went on to capture the Gaza Strip and the entire Sinai in just three days. When Jordan attacked Jerusalem, Israel's army responded by taking the Old City, East Jerusalem, and the entire West Bank. In response to the continuing barrage from Syria, Israel seized the strategic Golan Heights, long a chief staging area from which Syria shelled Israel's low-lying northern settlements. Israel immediately annexed East Jerusalem and occupied the West Bank, the Golan Heights, and the Gaza Strip. Six days had elapsed.

The country was euphoric at its decisive triumph over all who had challenged its right of survival and at having recovered what was left of Jerusalem's holy sites. Israel was sure that the captured territories had provided it with bargaining chips that it would be able to trade for recognition and a final settlement of the hostilities that had begun in 1947. But the Arab countries not only still refused to accept Israel's existence, but also demanded that it return to the borders of the 1947 partition plan (which the Arabs themselves had rejected at the time), and they would not agree to sign peace treaties, even ones based on those borders. Intermittent fighting between Egypt and Israel continued until 1972, a period known as the "War of Attrition." More ominously, Israel was now an occupying force ruling a territory containing 1.25 million Arabs, an explosive situation that would later come to plague it. But in the euphoria of the moment, few were sufficiently prescient to foresee that.

Israel's wars had so far been waged against neighboring countries, each of which had been fighting for itself or nominally on behalf of Arab nationalism; none of these countries represented the interests of the Arabs actually living in Palestine or of their relatives crowded in the refugee camps. With the conquest of East Jerusalem and the West Bank, Palestinian nationalism (as opposed to Arab nationalism) began to emerge as an active force in the region. An umbrella of Palestinian Arab organizations known as the Palestine Liberation

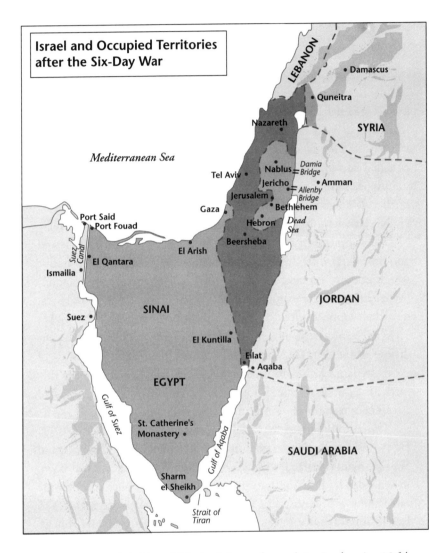

Israel and Occupied Territories after the Six-Day War

Organization (PLO), which had been formed in Jordan in 1964, adopted a charter in 1968 calling for the liberation of the Palestinian Arabs from Israeli domination, the restoration of Palestinian dignity, the destruction of Israel, and the establishment of a homeland for Palestinian Arabs on its territory.

The most active of these organizations was Fatah, headed by Yasir Arafat, who became president of the PLO after the 1967 war. The PLO coordinated organized terrorism within Israel as well as outside the Middle East, arranging for the highjacking of airplanes and the bombing of Jewish facilities throughout the world. The PLO was ousted from Jordan as a destabilizing element in a bloody purge by King Hussein, and found a new base in Lebanon, from which it planned and executed continuous hijackings, kidnappings, and killings. The most notorious example was the murder of Israeli Olympic athletes in their hotel in Munich at the Olympic games in 1972.

Nevertheless, Israel thrived after 1967 in a period of seemingly boundless optimism and economic growth. Soviet immigration and good relations with the European community boosted the economy, which was also propelled by mass tourism. But the relative tranquillity encouraged laxness in the military establishment. Egypt and Syria saw their opportunity to regain the Suez Canal and the Golan Heights, respectively, by a surprise attack that would reverse the conditions of the Six-Day War of 1967. Israeli intelligence was aware of the Egyptian and Syrian mobilization, but failed to evaluate it correctly; the public was not informed of the buildup, and there was no Israeli countermobilization until the very day of the attack.

The date chosen for the attack was Yom Kippur, October 6, 1973. Israel was caught unprepared on the one religious holiday observed even by many secular Jews, and the soldiers had to be tracked down in synagogues. The simultaneous attack on Israel's north and on the Sinai came with devastating force, posing the most serious threat to Israel's survival since 1948. Yet despite its disadvantage, and though forced back on both fronts, Israel held on. The Soviet Union began massive airlifts of supplies to support Egypt and Syria, and the United States responded with a military airlift in support of Israel. Israel quickly recovered, broke through the Syrian front, and began heading in the direction of Damascus. In the Sinai, Israel crossed the Suez Canal and advanced twenty-five miles into Egypt before a cease-fire was called by agreement between the United States and the Soviet Union. Despite far smaller forces in men and matériel, Israel had again demonstrated its military superiority, but there was no joy in its victory.

The surprise attack had a lasting and traumatic impact on Israeli society. Some of its most distinguished leaders had lost the public's confidence. The people's trust in their state's defensive capabilities was damaged, and resentment over the perpetual elusiveness of a real peace treaty festered. Increased PLO terrorism and attacks on northern towns exacerbated this sentiment. In one of the most dramatic of such events, PLO terrorists hijacked an Air France flight and diverted it to Entebbe, Uganda. In a daring and hastily improvised raid, an Israeli commando unit under the leadership of Yonatan Netanyahu (the brother of Benjamin Netanyahu, who would later become prime minister) stormed the airfield and flew the hostages to Israel. Netanyahu, who was killed in the raid, quickly became a national hero and martyr.

Other problems beset Israel in this period: a sharp decline in international support, culminating in the 1975 resolution of the United Nations General Assembly declaring Zionism a form of racism; economic difficulties; a decline in immigration; increased resentment by immigrants from the Arab and other Middle Eastern countries over their feeling of being excluded by the Ashkenazi domination of Israeli political and cultural life; anger over corruption in the Labor party; and above all, the recognition that all the hardships Israel had undergone had not led to normalization of relations with its neighbors. The discontent resulted in a political revolution in the 1977 elections, in which the Likud party—a descendant of the old Revisionist party, which until now had always been in the opposition—came to power for the first time. The Likud was headed by Menachem Begin, a former leader of the Irgun.

In November 1977, Egyptian president Anwar Sadat stunned the world by visiting Israel and addressing the Knesset; the peace talks with Egypt that opened shortly thereafter were encouraged by President Jimmy Carter of the United States, who helped the two sides to break their impasse by organizing the Camp David conference in 1978. Israel agreed to return the entire Sinai to Egypt in exchange for full recognition and the normalization of relations between the two states. The entente thus reached by Begin and Sadat was favored by Egypt's difficult economic condition, developments in the cold war, the personality of the Egyptian leader, and the persistence of Jimmy Carter.

Begin was able to win support within Israel for the necessary concessions to Egypt precisely because of his well-established reputation as a hard-liner. But both leaders took risks in carrying out these negotiations, particularly Sadat, who alienated the entire Arab world in the process; in 1981, he was assassinated by a Muslim fanatic while he reviewed a military parade. A kind of "cold peace" has evolved over the years between Israel and Egypt, which has held, despite vicissitudes.

The following year, Begin embarked on Israel's first military campaign that was not a response to an immediate threat to the state's existence. Against the background of extremely complex relations between many parties with an interest in Lebanon—involving the PLO, Syria, Lebanese Christians, and Lebanese Muslims—Begin and his defense minister, General Ariel Sharon, decided to end the attacks by the PLO on northern Israeli settlements by driving the guerrillas out of their bases in southern Lebanon. This objective was achieved quickly and a security zone established in southern Lebanon, but Sharon pressed on until Israeli forces reached and besieged the PLO forces in Beirut itself. Public opinion inside and outside Israel was outraged when Sharon permitted Lebanese Christians to raid the Palestinian refugee camps of Sabra and Shatila, which were under Israeli guard, and massacre the inhabitants.

The Lebanon War did succeed in destroying the infrastructure of the PLO in Lebanon and resulted in its being exiled to Tunisia, but the war strengthened Syria's position in Lebanon, cost Israel support in the international community, and aroused considerable anger within Israel itself, as Israelis realized that their troops were suffering and inflicting heavy casualties for very little political return. Israel did not manage to extract itself from Lebanon until 1985, under a different prime minister. The failure of the Lebanon War broke Begin's spirit and ended his long political career; when his wife died 1983, he resigned.

Guerrilla operations against Israel from the north changed character in the 1980s with the rise of the Hezbollah, an Iran-backed Islamic fundamentalist movement, which set off a new wave of terrorism. But it was the Palestinian masses who came to dominate the scene beginning in 1987, when a spontaneous riot in the Gaza Strip spread throughout the occupied territories in a general protest against Israeli rule. Far away, in Tunisia, the PLO managed to take control of the uprising, known in Arabic as the Intifada, and organized a "day of solidarity" a few weeks later, in which Arab citizens of Israel demonstrated in sympathy. There followed a long period of organized strikes, demonstrations, and civil protest against the occupation in the West Bank and the Gaza Strip. Despite harsh Israeli reprisals, the violence was continuous. The Intifada came to be symbolized by the grim specter of children and teenagers throwing rocks at Israeli troops, themselves not much older, who were caught between the instinct to retaliate and the horror of shooting at children.

Years of unrest followed, with Palestinian violence being punished by curfews, demolition of terrorists' homes, lengthy closings of West Bank schools and universities, and extensive jailings, all of which increased the violence. In 1988, King Hussein of Jordan officially relinquished Jordanian claims to the West Bank, and later that year, Arafat announced that he was ready to accept the existence of Israel and a Palestinian state; but no amount of pressure on Israel to enter into discussions with the Palestinians availed against the rigid stance of Prime Minister Yitzhak Shamir, who not only refused to acknowledge the PLO, but also greatly exacerbated the tension by actively encouraging Jewish settlement in the occupied territories.

In 1991, in the aftermath of the Gulf War and the collapse of the Soviet Union, President Bush of the United States made intense efforts to set up negotiations between Israel and the Arab nations. The meetings that were held in Madrid and later in Washington were a breakthrough for Israeli and Arab representatives, who faced each other for the first time, but Israel would only deal with Arab governments and continued to refuse to acknowledge the PLO as a negotiating partner.

When a Labor government headed by Yitzhak Rabin took office in 1992, the possibility for a breakthrough appeared. As the Intifada had grown more devastating to both sides, Israeli society became ever more polarized between those who were convinced that peace lay in recognizing some kind of Palestinian autonomy in the West Bank and Gaza and those who were equally convinced that such a course was either suicidal or contrary to God's will, or both. Rabin, a hero of the War of Independence and the Six-Day War, a former hard-line general with a well-established reputation for concern over Israel's security, concluded that the harm caused by the Intifada was worse for Israeli life than the benefits of control over the territories. Partly thanks to initiatives by Foreign Minister Shimon Peres, he came to accept the principle of dialogue with the PLO. While American-sponsored negotiations laggardly proceeded in Washington, another set of secret negotiations took place in Oslo in 1992 and 1993. The result was the joint Declaration of Principles, signed in an emotional ceremony on the White House lawn on September 13, 1993, in which Israel for the first time recognized the PLO as the spokesman of the Palestinian people. This agreement mapped out a phased process of Israeli retreat from the territories and gradual assumption of control by the Palestinians as an entity called the "Palestinian Authority"; the vexed problem of the status of Jerusalem and other details were left for later negotiation. The image of President Bill Clinton, Rabin, and Arafat shaking hands, in a scene reminiscent of the historic handshake between Begin, Sadat, and Carter in 1978, seemed like the opening of a new era.

The agreement created a wave of optimism in Israel and the Middle East. Jordan, which had long been quietly eager for normalization, signed a peace treaty with Israel, and some other Arab states began to thaw in their relations with Israel. The prospect of peace also encouraged foreign investment in the region. Nevertheless, many felt betrayed by the agreement. Many Palestinians were angry at an agreement that granted them not statehood but a phased-in autonomy for an undefined Palestinian entity. Some were dissatisfied with the leadership of Yasir Arafat. Islamic fundamentalists, particularly the members of the extremist Hamas organization, rejected the legitimacy of any Jewish state, and therefore of the Palestinian Authority, which exists by virtue of having accepted it. Many Israelis could not bring themselves to accept the new respectability of a former terrorist organization that was founded with the avowed purpose of destroying the Jewish state and killing its Jewish population. And a large number of Orthodox Jews could not live with the idea of losing sovereignty over any part of the Holy Land. Continuing extremist violence impeded the momentum toward a final settlement.

Hope for a final settlement was exploded on November 4, 1995, when Yitzhak Rabin was assassinated by a Jewish fanatic at the close of a massive peace demonstration in Tel Aviv. Rabin was the one public figure with the authority to command the support of the public for the peace process. Although his successor, Shimon Peres, was equally committed to an accommodation with the Palestinians, he was not able to retain public support for the process in the face of continuing terrorist attacks. A series of suicide bombings by Palestinians in February and March 1996 brought down the Labor government, and by a narrow margin, a Likud government was elected. The new prime minister, Benjamin Netanyahu, campaigned on the slogan of "peace with security," but he delayed implementing

important parts of the Oslo agreements and systematically strengthened the position of the Orthodox Jewish settlers in the occupied territories and East Jerusalem.

The apparently downward spiral of relations between Israel and
the Palestinians has by now taken a habitual form. Young Palestinians
recruited and trained by Hamas carry out suicide attacks or other
kinds of sabotage resulting in deaths of Israelis. Israeli leaders blame
the Palestinian Authority for not deterring these activities, as agreed
in the Oslo accords, and block access to Israeli territory for longer or
shorter periods to residents of the occupied territories. This does
result in a reduction of terrorist activity, but it also creates severe economic hardship for the Palestinians and intensifies their rage against
Israel. Palestinian anger is also directed at the PLO, resulting in gains
by the extremist fundamentalist movement Hamas.

The continued support by the Likud government for Orthodox
settlers in the West Bank and new building projects for Jews in East
Jerusalem are a constant provocation to the Palestinians. There have
also been atrocities by Orthodox Jews against Muslims; most notable
was the incident in Hebron in 1994, when an Orthodox Jewish set-
tler murdered twenty-nine Arabs praying at the Tomb of the
Patriarchs. Each incident strengthens the hand of the other side's
hard-liners.

Fifty years after the establishment of Israel and 101 years after the
First Zionist Congress, Israel exists as a strong, modern, democratic,
and prosperous country. The doubts that it could be established at all,
or that it would long survive, which lasted until 1967, have been completely refuted. It is now the quality of Israel's future that is uncertain.
Israel's relations with the Palestinians, far from nearing a resolution,
seem to be settling into a chronic and intractable state of violence, like
the situation of Britain with Ireland or of Spain with the Basques. The
polarization of secular and religious Israelis threatens to undermine
the Zionist conception of Israel as a modern, democratic state where
Jews of all stripes can live in harmony. But the foundation is strong.

The Diaspora

By the time of Israel's independence, the distribution of world Jewry had radically changed. In Europe, the only major Jewish communities that remained intact were those of England and Switzerland; on the Continent, the Jews had ceased to be a significant presence, millions having been murdered and millions more having fled. In the Middle East, most Jewish communities were rapidly liquidating themselves. Israel, though growing, was still rather small, its population growth inhibited first by the exclusionary British immigration policy and, later, by the country's insecurity and poor economic conditions. The Jewish communities of the Western Hemisphere were now dominant. The mass emigration from eastern Europe beginning in the 1880s had created important Jewish communities in Latin America (especially in Argentina and Mexico) and in Canada, and these communities were now augmented by war refugees. But the Jewish community of the United States was the main center of Jewish population.

It was precisely in the most open of these Western countries, the United States, that the Jews were faced most clearly with the great problem of modernity: how to keep Jewish identity alive in a society where individual lives were shaped less by communities than by individual ambition, where acceptance by non-Jews was easy to achieve for anyone who was willing to adopt the common American culture, and where materialism and commercialism overwhelmed most other value systems. We have seen how modernity began to fray the cohesiveness of the Jewish community and weaken the sense of Jewish identity among western European Jewry in the nineteenth century, but the problem was more acute in the United States because both America's Jews and its Gentiles were less bound by tradition. Social disdain for Jews existed in the United States, especially in the highest and lowest echelons of society, but Jews were protected by the same laws that protected the Irish and the Italians (whose great immigrations overlapped that of the Jews), and anti-Semitism did not have anything like the virulence it had had in European countries where the medieval tradition was never completely lost. The great question was not how long the Jews would be tolerated in the United States, but how long Jewish identity and Jewish culture could be maintained.

By the end of World War II, the second generation of American Jews had come of age, and traditional ideas and behavior came to be associated more and more with the elderly. Jewish neighborhoods in the cities declined as Americans moved to the suburbs; immigrant synagogues, Yiddish newspapers, and Yiddish theaters dwindled and closed, and Jewish identity lost its centrality in the lives of most Jews. Even anti-Semitism faded, as third- and fourth-generation American Jews grew up with non-Jews, went to school with them, lived side by side with them, increasingly married them, and came to be indistinguishable from other white Americans. Occasional incidents of synagogue desecration were shocking because they were so out of character for the United States, which had emerged from the war confirmed in and proud of its commitment to guarantee the freedoms of minorities. Life for Jews in the United States was so easy that it seemed as if they might merge with the rest of the population and disappear.

The establishment of the State of Israel was an enormous source of pride. American Jewry supported Israel generously, financially and politically; both kinds of support were indispensable for Israel's survival. But few American Jews went so far as to immigrate to Israel. Many Jews in apartheid South Africa and unstable Argentina either moved to Israel or were involved in immigration-oriented Zionist activities, but American Jews had no incentive to leave the United States. It was only the rare idealist who would consider exchanging the postwar prosperity of the United States for the material hardship and the insecurity of the newborn state. Zionism in the United States meant merely supporting Israel, to the despair of Israelis, for whom Zionism meant risk and hardship endured in hope of a better future. As Israeli culture developed and found its own style and way of life, and as American Jews became more Americanized, these two most important Jewish communities became socially more and more unfamiliar to each other. This development was not so apparent in the early years of the state, when few American Jews visited Israel and when few Israelis reached the United States. But even when it became hard to ignore, it did not diminish American Jewry's passionate support of Israel.

Through the 1960s, American Jews experienced being Jewish through affiliation with a synagogue, mostly Conservative or Reform, and through financial contributions to the network of Jewish charities and to Israel. Affiliation with a synagogue did not imply a high degree of religious observance; most congregation members were motivated more by group loyalty and ethnic cohesion than by religion. For most Jews, being Jewish meant associating mostly with Jews, observing some of the rites of the Jewish New Year and Passover holidays, and life-cycle events such as circumcisions, weddings, bar mitzvahs (which were increasingly extended to girls and, in that case, called bat mitzvahs), funerals, and *yahrzeit* (the annual commemorations of parents' deaths). Rare was the second-generation American Jew who was deeply familiar or truly comfortable with the ritual aspect of these observances. Millions of Jewish children attended Hebrew-school classes operated by their synagogues two or three afternoons a week, but few among these millions mastered even the most basic synagogue skills or home rituals in such programs.

Yet large numbers of Jews did affiliate with the Jewish community through synagogues, Jewish community centers, and a complex network of organizations that raised funds for Jewish educational and charitable causes as well as for Israel. Most cities have a federation of Jewish charities for joint fund-raising and allocation of funds, and these are united in the Council of Jewish Federations and Welfare Funds, which has become one of the main decision-making bodies for American Jewry. Another influential organization is the Conference of the Presidents of Major American Jewish Organizations, which sometimes serves as a spokesman for American Jewry.

But contrary to what is often assumed by non-Jews, there is no single body that speaks for all American Jews.

When the United States' middle-class youth rebelled against the authority of the adult generation, in the 1960s, many Jewish young people turned actively against all Jewish behavior and traditional values, viewing their parents' vestigial Jewish religious observances—with some justification—as just another case of the empty conformism with which they reproached American society in general. There was also a political aspect to this rebellion. The generation that revolted against the Vietnam War interpreted Israel's wars for survival as militarism and Israel's existence as colonialism; Israel, which had given pride to American Jews and had been admired by liberal intellectuals through the mid-sixties, came to be tarred with the same brush as was being wielded on the United States "military-industrial complex." The New Left that emerged from this period, unlike the Old, was distinctly pro-Arab and anti-Zionist, and it had many Jewish intellectuals among its adherents. By the time the "flower children" came to be of an age to raise their own families, in the 1970s and 1980s, Jewish identity had very little concrete meaning for most of them.

At the same time, two developments held some small promise for a Jewish revival. Among the many thousands of Jews swept up by the youth culture were a tiny number whose Jewish education had been more intensive than was usual in the American middle class. This tiny group consisted mostly of young people who had attended educational Jewish summer camps in the late 1950s and early 1960s. Small groups of Jewish youths emerged in Boston and New York who synthesized the style and some of the ideology of the youth culture with Jewish, especially Hasidic, traditions. Quite in the spirit of the youth culture, they denounced the Jewish establishment institutions, especially the large, impersonal suburban synagogues. And, emerging just after the Six-Day War left Israel in occupation of the West Bank, Gaza, and the Sinai, they also denounced the older generation's unquestioning support of Israeli foreign policy. Unlike the indifferent masses of Jewish youth, these groups were well informed about and deeply engaged in Jewish affairs and eager to wrest leadership away from an establishment that they saw as less moral and less committed than themselves.

Predictably, the Jewish establishment excoriated these youths for breaking with the community's tradition of trying to present a united front to the outside world, particularly when they organized demonstrations opposing Israel's occupation of Arab territories. Some of the rebels eventually themselves joined the establishment as rabbis, educators, and functionaries of Jewish organizations. They have introduced an original element into American Jewish education and religious life that was not evident before—a greater emphasis on spiritual values, an eagerness to mine the byways of the Jewish tradition in quest of resources that might make for a more varied and engaging Jewish life, a taste for the exotic in the Jewish tradition, and a readiness to improvise. They had a small but significant effect on synagogue life by encouraging the formation of *havurot*, fellowships either within large congregations or independent of them, providing those who desire it with a more intense but non-Orthodox Jewish community life and a more experimental synagogue service. They were also influential in the movement to admit women into the Jewish clergy, which bore fruit in 1972 with the ordination of the first woman rabbi, Sally Priesand, by Hebrew Union College. By 1989, both the Reform and Conservative seminaries were training women as rabbis and cantors.

The other development was the unexpected revival of orthodoxy. Among the refugees at the end of World War II were the remnants of Hasidic groups originating in eastern Europe, some of whom had spent the war years in the Far East, others of whom had survived the concentration camps. Joining the small Hasidic groups already present in Brooklyn, these immigrants developed into a large and prosperous community. For a long time, they seemed to be merely exotic vestiges of a lost world. Then in the 1970s, the Lubavitch Hasidim, one of the groups already established in Brooklyn before the war, burst into public consciousness with a dynamic international campaign to win over world Jewry for religious orthodoxy, especially in the form advocated by the Lubavitch.

The Lubavitch campaign, under the leadership of Menahem Mendel Schneerson, was organized with great sophistication and dedication, unexpectedly making full use of contemporary advertising techniques and technology in propagating a religious style that most American Jews thought merely outlandish. Lubavitch missionaries were dispatched to every major population center in the United States and to most Jewish population centers worldwide, where they made contact with Jews far removed from tradition and attempted to win them over to performing simple ritual observances like lighting candles on Friday nights. Young Lubavitch emissaries accosted Jewish-looking passersby from "mitzvah-mobiles"—vans parked in downtown streets or near college campuses in major American cities blaring traditional Jewish music—trying to wheedle them into performing religious rituals. The Jewish establishment, which was pouring millions of dollars into trying to solve the problem of reviving Jewish education for the masses of American Jewry, looked on in amazement at the success and influence of the obscurantist rabbi from Brooklyn. The actual numbers of Jews retrieved from assimilation and brought into the Lubavitch fold was not great. But the mere presence of the Lubavitcher Rebbe, as he was called, in advertisements and on television, and of his emissaries on street corners raised consciousness and lent vitality to religious orthodoxy. In the 1980s, the Lubavitch campaign took the form of attempting to unite world Jewry in religious observances in preparation for the imminent coming of the Messiah. The rumor took hold that Schneerson himself was the Messiah, though Schneerson, who died in 1994, never personally made this claim.

Lubavitch was not the only evidence of an Orthodox revival. As public consensus on all issues of behavior and morality collapsed in the 1970s and 1980s, many Americans, both Christian and Jewish, have sought the security of traditional religion. This trend may be part of the explanation for the success of Lubavitch, and it certainly explains why many Jews, especially in the New York area, have been drawn to a kind of "normal" or "modern" orthodoxy. Such *baale teshuva* (repentants) are generally persons who grew up in ordinary suburban middle-class acculturated homes but turned to strict religious observance. Unlike the Hasidim, they are full participants in the American middle class, becoming doctors, lawyers, businessmen, accountants, academics, stockbrokers, journalists, and so on. They dress like ordinary middle-class people and participate in the consumer culture typical of American life, but they strictly observe religious traditions and endeavor to acquire a sound traditional Jewish education and to provide the same for their children by sending them to Orthodox day schools, rather than to public schools.. Large law firms that before World War II had excluded Jews or limited their numbers now have partners who wear traditional head-coverings at meetings at work. This trend has been supported by a general tendency in American society of the 1980s and 1990s to encourage ethnic differentiation, as opposed to the decades immediately following the war, which had encouraged the acculturation of America's minorities.

The numbers of these young "modern Orthodox" are small within the context of the United States. Some of them, finding Israel a more congenial environment for leading a totally Jewish life, emigrated there. In Israel, they tend to identify with the political Right, supporting the hard-liners in negotiations with the Arabs; many have even settled in the occupied territories, seeing themselves as a new generation of pioneers with the mission of saving "Jewish" territory from falling into non-Jewish hands.

At present, American Jewry seems to be polarizing in a way analogous but not identical to the polarization in Israel. Large numbers of American Jews still belong to the Reform and Conservative synagogues. The Conservative movement has intensified its educational programs by developing a network of day schools, in the realization that the couple of hours a week of afternoon Hebrew school, traditional since the immigration period, had failed to produce a Jewish community knowledgeable about its own history and traditions and had failed to stem assimilation. But the numbers of Jews affiliated with the liberal movements are declining; there has been a corresponding decline in contributions to the network of voluntary Jewish organizations that defines the American Jewish community. Support for Israel is still strong, but there is an overall diminution of the role played by Jewish identity in the lives of ordinary Jews. Yet, while declining in numbers, the Reform and Conservative movements are both becoming more traditional, and Orthodoxy is growing significantly in wealth and political power, abetted by the general trend in the United States favoring the differentiation of minorities. It is conceivable that in a century's time, America's Jewry will consist of a small number of very traditionally observant Jews.

Other Diaspora Communities

Although the American Jewish community is the largest Diaspora community, there are a number of important Jewish communities besides that of the United States; in fact, it is safe to say that there are Jews in every developed country. In the Western Hemisphere, Canada and Argentina are preeminent, in their numbers and in the strength of their Jewish institutions, both religious and secular. Mexico also has an important Jewish community. In the southern part of the Eastern Hemisphere, the important communities are South Africa and Australia.

Fifty years after World War II, Jewish life is slowly reviving in Europe. The communities of England and Switzerland were, of course, not directly touched by the war. On the Continent, despite the annihilation of the old communities of Alsace-Lorraine, the French Jewish community is the largest, its numbers having been replenished by immigrants from Algeria, Tunisia, and Morocco. This immigration has resulted in anti-Semitic outbreaks from time to time, though the Muslim immigrants from these same countries bear the brunt of French xenophobia. Although Jews had quietly been entering Spain for several decades before the war, a community was permitted to organize in 1968, under the Franco dictatorship; today, there are active communities in Madrid and Barcelona and in several cities of the south.

Surprisingly, a small but well-organized Jewish community has emerged in Germany, made up of Jews who returned after the war, Jews who have come in pursuit of business from the United States or Israel, and Jews from the Soviet Union in search of a better life. After reunification in 1990, the German government invited Russian Jews to settle in Germany and has made earnest efforts to protect these small renascent Jewish communities from anti-Semitism, which is still very much in evidence (though it is now the Turkish immigrants who bear the brunt of German xenophobia). In Poland, which a century ago was the most important center of Jewish life worldwide, there is no longer any significant Jewish population, but there are small organized communities in the Czech Republic and Hungary.

The Soviet Union had as many as 3 million Jews at the end of the war. Despite the cultural decline of the Jewish community described in the preceding chapter, they enjoyed reasonable conditions until 1948, when a period of oppression set in. In 1952, the most important Yiddish authors were executed. The persecution culminated in the "Doctors' Plot," when dictator Joseph Stalin arrested Jewish doctors of Moscow and charged them with medical assassinations; they were spared only by Stalin's death in 1953. For a long time after Stalin's death, Jewish institutions remained closed, severe restrictions were placed on Jewish religious behavior, and Jews' access to universities and sensitive positions was strictly limited. In the 1950s and 1960s, small numbers of Jews were permitted to leave the Soviet Union for Israel under the principle of reuniting families.

Estimated Jewish Population, 1994*

Country	Total Population	Jewish Population
United States	263,200,000	5,675,000
Israel	5,471,000	4,441,100
France	58,100,000	530,000
Russia	147,000,000	375,000
Canada	29,600,000	360,000
United Kingdom	58,600,000	294,000
Other countries of former USSR (Belarus, Estonia, Latvia, Lithuania, Moldova, Ukraine)	74,300,000	282,000
Argentina	34,600,000	208,000
Brazil	157,800,000	100,000
South Africa	43,500,000	96,000
Australia	18,000,000	92,000
Germany	81,700,000	55,000
Hungary	10,200,000	54,500
Former Central Asian Islamic Republics of USSR (Kazakhstan, Kyrgyzstan, Tajikistan, Turkmenistan, Uzbekistan)	54,300,000	44,900
Mexico	93,700,000	40,800
Belgium	10,200,000	31,800
Italy	57,700,000	30,000
Netherlands	15,500,000	26,500
Uruguay	3,200,000	23,600
Venezuela	21,800,000	20,000
Turkey	61,400,000	19,400
Switzerland	7,000,000	18,000
Azerbaijan	7,300,000	15,000
Chile	14,300,000	15,000
Sweden	8,900,000	15,000

*Statistics based on those in the *American Jewish Year Book 1996*, ed. by David Singer (New York: American Jewish Committee, 1997). The accuracy of the figures varies from country to country, as explained in that work.

Israel's victory in the Six-Day War was a defeat for the Soviet Union's pro-Arab foreign policy and was followed by a virulent anti-Israel campaign by the Soviet government. At the same time, the victory infused Soviet Jews with immense pride and resulted in a noticeable increase in the numbers of applications for emigration to

Country	Total Population	Jewish Population
Rumania	22,700,000	14,500
Iran	61,300,000	14,000
Georgia	5,400,000	12,000
Spain	39,100,000	12,000
Austria	8,100,000	8,000
Denmark	5,200,000	6,400
Morocco	29,200,000	6,400
Colombia	37,700,000	5,000
Panama	2,600,000	5,000
Greece	10,500,000	4,500
New Zealand	3,500,000	4,500
India	930,600,000	4,400
Slovakia	5,400,000	3,800
Countries of former Yugoslavia (Bosnia-Herzegovina, Croatia, Slovenia, Serbia, Montenegro)	20,800,000	3,500
Poland	38,600,000	3,500
Peru	24,000,000	2,900
Costa Rica	3,300,000	2,500
Czech Republic	10,400,000	2,200
Tunisia	8,900,000	1,700
Bulgaria	8,500,000	1,600
Puerto Rico	3,700,000	1,500
Hong Kong	6,000,000	1,000
Japan	125,200,000	1,000
Zimbabwe	11,300,000	1,000
Cuba	11,200,000	700
Ethiopia	56,000,000	500
Egypt	61,900,000	200
Iraq	20,600,000	100

Israel. Obtaining an exit visa was difficult, often involving years of waiting, loss of employment, and harassment by the police. During this period, various foreign Jewish organizations set up underground educational operations in the Soviet Union and smuggled in prayer books and ritual objects in an attempt to keep Soviet Jews involved in Jewish life. Israel encouraged this emigration as a means of building up its own population, and the American Jewish community campaigned intensively to pressure the Soviet Union to relax its prohibition of emigration for Jews. In 1971, many Jews began receiving exit visas; most preferred to go to the United States, but a significant number of them settled in Israel. Greater numbers were permitted to leave after 1971. Under Mikhail Gorbachev, the emigration restrictions became more relaxed, especially after 1989, and with the collapse of the Soviet Union in 1991, the emigration became a deluge. Most of these Jews have gone to Israel, where they are so numerous as to have redefined the demographic makeup of the country. A political party has been created specifically to represent their interests; it is headed by Natan Sharansky, a Soviet Jew who spent years in Siberian prisons because of his activism on behalf of Jewish emigration.

Afterword:
The Outlook for the Jews

In many ways, the Jewish condition in the present is better than it has been at any time since antiquity. The problem of exile, which has defined Jewish history and determined the character of Judaism for centuries, has been resolved. In fact, the Jewish problem has found not one, but two, solutions.

There is now a Jewish state. It is again possible for a Jew to redefine his Jewish identity in terms of citizenship. As an Israeli, a Jew can speak the national language, celebrate the national festivals, and live amid the physical remains of the remote Jewish past among fellow citizens of similar historical background. He does not need to cling to any traditional set of beliefs or behavior, any more than an Italian does to be considered Italian. For such Jews, religion takes its place as one among many aspects of the national culture; one can observe Jewish religious practices if he chooses to, or he can drop them, as most Israelis have done, without compromising his Jewishness.

Life in Israel is not yet fully normal because of the unresolved problem of Israel's relations with the Palestinian population of the region and the hostility of most of the Arab states, but Israel is not the frontier it was a generation ago. It has prospered economically and has shown extraordinary intellectual vitality, particularly in the fields of science, technology, and literature. Israel's most productive people are in demand in the larger world; many leave, but they are continually being replaced by the children of new immigrants and by new generations of equally qualified successors. Thus, Israel has become a world resource, with an influence out of all proportion to its size. Modern Hebrew has become the language of a world-class literature; Hebrew books are widely available in the United States and Europe in translation, attracting more interest among non-Jews than among Diaspora Jews, reflecting the fact that Jewish literature no longer is limited to internal Jewish problems, but has become part of the world at large.

For Diaspora Jews, it is easier and more acceptable to be a Jewish citizen of a non-Jewish state today than it has ever been in the entire course of Jewish history. Western democracies, especially the United States, guarantee civil rights to all citizens, whatever their religion. Anti-Semitism may not have been eliminated on the highest and the lowest rungs of society and public officials do not always protect the rights of minorities in accordance with the best official principles, but in the Western democracies, Jews are full citizens with full civil rights. In many countries, they are well organized and prosperous. Where they have chosen to preserve their traditions and communal structure, they have had little difficulty doing so. The United States has strong Jewish institutions; the field of Jewish studies has found a place in the secular universities; and Jews sometimes learn, to their astonishment, that internal Jewish affairs arouse considerable sympathetic interest among non-Jews.

Diaspora Jewry's great problem is the ease with which Jews leave the community now that they have the freedom to do so. Judaism in the United States has always tended to define itself more as a religion than as a national identity. As religion receded in importance in American society during much of the twentieth century, synagogues emptied out, and the majority of American Jews had little left of their traditions but a few food preferences and their family names. But the recent resurgence of religion and the renewed prestige of ethnicity in the United States in general have been paralleled by a resurgence of religion among Jews. No one can say where this development will lead. Fifty years ago, it was agreed that orthodoxy could not survive modernity. Today it is thriving, not because masses of Jews are joining Orthodox synagogues, but because small numbers have become extremely devoted and are raising large families that are well educated in Jewish traditions. Even if most Jews assimilate, a core of people will remain who are passionately attached to the Jewish heritage while living a life not too different in its externals from that of their non-Jewish neighbors.

Not very long ago—in the lifetime of the author of this book— European Jewry was in ashes and there was no place in the world where the refugees were entitled to take shelter; American Jewry, for all its numbers and prosperity, seemed ripe for assimilation, and Jewish identity had little to offer but nostalgia for a dead Old World. Today, there is a culturally and intellectually productive national home, one can be actively engaged in Jewish life and be a full citizen of any civilized country, and there are any number of ways to be Jewish: culturally, religiously, intellectually, or organizationally. Both Israel and the Diaspora face challenges, but there has never been a better time to be part of Jewish history.

Bibliography

General

Baron, Salo W. *A Social and Religious History of the Jews.* Second edition, 18 vols. Philadelphia: Columbia University Press and the Jewish Publication Society, 1952–83.

Ben Sasson, H. H., ed. *A History of the Jewish People.* London: Weidenfeld and Nicolson, 1976.

Ben Sasson, H. H., and S. Ettinger, eds. *Jewish Society through the Ages.* London: Vallentine, Mitchell, 1971.

Encyclopaedia Judaica. 16 vols. and supplements. Jerusalem: Keter Publishing House, c. 1972.

Finkelstein, Louis. *The Jews: Their History, Culture, and Religion.* Fourth edition. New York: Schocken Books, 1970.

Gribetz, Judah, et al. *Timetables of Jewish History.* New York: Simon and Schuster, 1993.

Hallo, William W., et al., eds. *Heritage, Civilization and the Jews.* New York: Praeger, 1984.

Schwartz, Leo. *Great Ages and Ideas of the Jewish People.* New York: Random House, 1956.

Yerushalmi, Yosef Hayim. *Zakhor: Jewish History and Jewish Memory.* Seattle: University of Washington Press, 1982.

Chapter One: Israelite Origins and Kingdom

Aharoni, Yohanan, and Michael Avi-Yona. *The Macmillan Bible Atlas.* New York: Macmillan, 1977.

Bright, John. *A History of Israel.* Second edition. Philadelphia: Westminster Press, 1972.

Shanks, Hershel. *Ancient Israel.* Englewood Cliffs, N.J.: Biblical Archaeology Society, 1988.

Chapter Two: Judea and the Origins of the Diaspora

Bickerman, Elias J. *From Ezra to the Last of the Maccabees.* New York: Schocken Books, 1962.

Cohen, Shaye J. D. *From the Maccabees to the Mishnah.* Philadelphia: Westminster Press, 1987. Also for chap. 3.

Modrzejewsky, J. Mélèze. *The Jews of Egypt from Ramses II to Emperor Hadrian.* Philadelphia and Jerusalem: Jewish Publication Society, 1995. Also for chap. 3.

Schäfer, Peter. *The History of the Jews of Antiquity: From Alexander the Great to the Arab Conquest.* Luxembourg: Harwood Academic Press, 1995.

———. *Judeophobia: Attitudes toward the Jews in the Ancient World.* Cambridge, Mass.: Harvard University Press, 1997.

Schürer, Emil. *The History of the Jewish People in the Age of Jesus Christ.* Rev. and ed. G. Vermes and F. Millar. 4 vols. Edinburgh: T & T Clark, 1973–87. Also for chap. 3.

Tcherikover, Victor. *Hellenistic Civilization and the Jews.* Philadelphia: Jewish Publication Society, 1959.

Vermes, Geza. *Dead Sea Scrolls.* Third edition. London: Penguin, 1987.

Chapter Three: Roman Palestine and Sassanid Babylonia

Avi-Yonah, Michael. *The Jews of Palestine.* New York: Schocken Books, 1976.

Cohen, Shaye J. D., and S. Frerichs, eds. *Diasporas in Antiquity*. Atlanta: Scholars Press, 1993.

Levine, Lee I. *The Synagogue in Late Antiquity*. Philadelphia: American Schools of Oriental Research, 1987.

Neusner, Jacob. *There We Sat Down*. Nashville, Tenn.: Abingdon Press, 1971.

Simon, Marcel. *Verus Israel: A Study of the Relations between Christians and Jews in the Roman Empire (135–425)*, trans. H. McKeating. Oxford: Oxford University Press, 1986.

Chapter Four: The Jews in the Islamic World

Ashtor, Eliahu. *The Jews of Moslem Spain*. 2 vols. Philadelphia: Jewish Publication Society, 1992.

Cohen, Mark R. *Under Crescent & Cross: The Jews in the Middle Ages*. Princeton, N.J.: Princeton University Press, 1994.

Gerber, Jane S. *The Jews of Spain*. New York: Free Press, 1992. Also for chaps. 5 and 6.

Goitein, S. D. *Jews and Arabs: Their Contacts through the Ages*. New York: Schocken, 1974.

Hirschberg, H. Z. *History of the Jews in North Africa*. 2 vols. Leiden: Brill, 1974–80.

Lewis, Bernard. *The Jews of Islam*. Princeton, N.J.: Princeton University Press, 1984.

Stillman, Norman. *The Jews of Arab Lands*. Philadelphia: Jewish Publication Society, 1979.

Chapter Five: The Jews of Medieval Christian Europe

Baer, Yitzhak. *A History of the Jews in Christian Spain*. Trans. Louis Scheffman et al. 2 vols. Philadelphia: Jewish Publication Society, 1961–66.

Berger, David. *The Jewish-Christian Debate in the High Middle Ages*. Philadelphia: Jewish Publication Society, 1979.

Marcus, Jacob R. *The Jew in the Medieval World*. New York: Meridian Books, 1960.

Parkes, J. *The Conflict of the Church and the Synagogue*. Second edition. New York: Hermon Press, 1974.

———. *The Jew in the Medieval Community.* Second edition. New York: Hermon Press, 1976.

Stow, Kenneth. *Alienated Minority: The Jews of Medieval Latin Europe.* Cambridge, Mass.: Harvard University Press, 1994.

Chapter Six: The Jews in the Ottoman Empire and the Middle East

BenBassa, E., and Aron Rodrique. *The Jews of the Balkans: The Judeo-Spanish Community, Fifteenth to Twentieth Centuries.* Oxford: Blackwell Publishers, 1995.

Chouraqui, André N. *Between East and West: A History of the Jews in North Africa.* Philadelphia: Jewish Publication Society, 1968.

Hirschberg, H. Z. *History of the Jews in North Africa.* 2 vols. Leiden: Brill, 1974–80.

Lewis, Bernard. *The Jews of Islam.* Princeton, N.J.: Princeton University Press, 1984.

Roth, Cecil. *The House of Nasi: Doña Gracia.* Philadelphia: Jewish Publication Society of America, 1948.

———. *The House of Nasi: The Duke of Naxos.* Philadelphia: Jewish Publication Society of America, 1948.

Stillman, Norman. *The Jews of Arab Lands in Modern Times.* Philadelphia: Jewish Publication Society, 1968.

Chapter Seven: The Jews of Western Europe

Bonfil, Robert. *Jewish Life in Renaissance Italy.* Trans. Anthony Oldcorn. Berkeley and Los Angeles: University of California Press, 1994.

Israel, Jonathan. *European Jewry in the Age of Mercantilism, 1550–1750.* Oxford: Oxford University Press, 1985.

Katz, Jacob. *Tradition and Crisis: Jewish Society at the End of the Middle Ages.* New York: New York University Press, 1993.

Mendez-Flohr, Paul, and Jehuda Reinharz. *The Jew in the Modern World: A Documentary History.* New York: Oxford University Press, 1980.

Meyer, Michael. *The Origins of the Modern Jew.* Detroit: Wayne State University Press, 1967.

Netanyahu, Benzion. *The Origins of the Inquisition in Fifteenth-Century Spain.* New York: Random House, 1995.

Roth, Cecil. *A History of the Marranos.* Fourth edition. New York: Hermon Press, 1974.

Sachar, Howard M. *The Course of Modern Jewish History.* Cleveland: World Publishing Co., 1958. Also for the following chapters.

Weinryb, B. D. *The Jews of Poland.* Philadelphia: Jewish Publication Society, 1973.

Chapter Eight: The Jews of Eastern Europe and the United States

Baron, Salo W. *The Russian Jew under Tsars and Soviets.* Second edition. New York: Schocken, 1987.

Gitelman, Zvi. *A Century of Ambivalence: The Jews of Russia and the Soviet Union, 1881 to the Present.* New York: Schocken Books, 1988. Also for chap. 11.

Hertzberg, Arthur. *The Jews in America.* New York: Simon and Schuster, 1989.

Karp, Abraham J. *Haven and Home: A History of the Jews in America.* New York: Schocken, 1985.

Marcus, Jacob R. *The Jew in the American World: A Source Book.* Detroit: Wayne State University Press, 1996.

Chapter Nine: The Holocaust

Bauer, Yehuda. *The Holocaust in Historical Perspective.* Seattle: University of Washington Press, 1978.

Dawidowicz, Lucy S. *The War Against the Jews.* Second edition. Ardmore, Pa.: Seth Press, 1986.

Gilbert, Martin. *The Macmillan Atlas of the Holocaust.* New York: Macmillan, 1982.

Hilberg, Raul. *The Destruction of the European Jews.* 3 vols. New York and London: Holmes & Meier, 1985.

Chapter Ten: Zionism and the Origins of the State of Israel

Hertzberg, Arthur, ed. *The Zionist Idea.* Garden City, N.Y.: Doubleday, 1959.

Laquer, W. *A History of Zionism.* New York: Schocken, 1989.

Near, Henry. *The Kibbutz Movement: Origins and Growth, 1909–39.* Auckland, New Zealand: Oxford University Press, 1992.

Pawel, Ernst. *The Labyrinth of Exile: A Life of Theodor Herzl.* New York: Farrar, Straus, and Giroux, 1989.

Sachar, Howard M. *A History of Israel from the Rise of Zionism to Our Time.* New York: Alfred A. Knopf, 1979.

Chapter Eleven: The Jewish People after 1948

American Jewish Year Book. Published annually by the American Jewish Committee and the Jewish Publication Society.

Heilman, Sam. *Portrait of American Jews: The Last Half of the Twentieth Century.* Seattle: University of Washington Press, 1995.

Sachar, Howard M. *Diaspora: An Inquiry into the Contemporary Jewish World.* New York: Harper and Row, 1985.

———. *A History of Israel, Vol. II: From the Aftermath of the Yom Kippur War.* New York and Oxford: Oxford University Press, 1987.

Sklare, Marshall. *American Jews: A Reader.* New York: Behrman House, 1983.

Wasserstein, Bernard. *Vanishing Diaspora: The Jews in Europe since 1945.* Cambridge, Mass.: Harvard University Press, 1996.

Wertheimer, Jack. *A People Divided: Judaism in Contemporary America.* New York: Basic Books, 1993.

Index

Page numbers in *italics* refer to maps or captions.

274   Index